T0382648

# Network Origins of the Global Economy

The upheavals of recent decades show us that traditional models of understanding processes of social and economic change are failing to capture real-world risk and volatility. This has resulted in flawed policy that seeks to capture change in terms of the rise or decline of regimes or regions. In order to comprehend current events, understand future risks, and decide how to prepare for them, we need to consider economies and social orders as open, complex networks. This highly original work uses the tools of network analysis to understand great transitions in history, particularly those concerning economic development and globalization. Hilton L. Root shifts attention away from particular agents – whether individuals, groups, nations, or policy interventions – and toward their dynamic interactions. Applying insights from complexity science to often overlooked variables across European and Chinese history, he explores the implications of China's unique trajectory and ascendency, as a competitor and counterexample to the West.

HILTON L. ROOT teaches international economics and political economy at George Mason University in the Schar School of Public Policy and Government. He co-directs Mason's Computational Public Policy Lab. His academic career has included faculty positions at Stanford University, University of Pennsylvania, the California Institute of Technology, the University of International Business and Economics (Beijing), and King's College London. He advises the US Department of the Treasury, the Asian Development Bank, and the UNDP, and has authored more than 200 publications, including ten books.

# Network Origins
# of the Global Economy

East vs. West in a Complex Systems
Perspective

HILTON L. ROOT

*George Mason University*

**CAMBRIDGE**
UNIVERSITY PRESS

# CAMBRIDGE
## UNIVERSITY PRESS

University Printing House, Cambridge CB2 8BS, United Kingdom

One Liberty Plaza, 20th Floor, New York, NY 10006, USA

477 Williamstown Road, Port Melbourne, VIC 3207, Australia

314–321, 3rd Floor, Plot 3, Splendor Forum, Jasola District Centre, New Delhi – 110025, India

79 Anson Road, #06–04/06, Singapore 079906

Cambridge University Press is part of the University of Cambridge.

It furthers the University's mission by disseminating knowledge in the pursuit of education, learning, and research at the highest international levels of excellence.

www.cambridge.org
Information on this title: www.cambridge.org/9781108488990
DOI: 10.1017/9781108773607

First published 2020

Printed in the United Kingdom by TJ International Ltd. Padstow Cornwall

*A catalogue record for this publication is available from the British Library.*

*Library of Congress Cataloging-in-Publication Data*
Names: Root, Hilton L., author.
Title: Network origins of the global economy : East vs. West in a complex systems perspective / Hilton L. Root, George Mason University, Virginia.
Description: Cambridge, United Kingdom ; New York, NY : Cambridge University Press, 2020. | Includes index.
Identifiers: LCCN 2019033289 (print) | LCCN 2019033290 (ebook) | ISBN 9781108488990 (hardback) | ISBN 9781108773607 (epub)
Subjects: LCSH: Economic history. | Economic policy. | Complexity (Philosophy)
Classification: LCC HC21 .R66 2020 (print) | LCC HC21 (ebook) | DDC 330.01/ 1–dc23
LC record available at https://lccn.loc.gov/2019033289
LC ebook record available at https://lccn.loc.gov/2019033290

ISBN 978-1-108-48899-0 Hardback

*Dedicated to my young sons, Benjamin Waverly and George Prescott.*

*Today I read you bedtime stories. One day, I hope, you'll take as much pleasure in your father's work.*

# Contents

# Figures

# Tables

# Contributors

**W. Brian Arthur** is External Professor at the Santa Fe Institute, and Visiting Researcher in the Systems Sciences Lab at Palo Alto Research Center.

**Liu Baocheng** is Professor at the University of International Business and Economics, Beijing, China.

**Kevin Comer** is Simulation Modeling Engineer at Mitre Corporation and holds a PhD in Computational Social Science from George Mason University.

**Jack Goldstone** is Virginia E. and John T. Hazel, Jr. Chair Professor of Public Policy at the Schar School of Policy and Government, George Mason University.

**Cameron Harwick** is Assistant Professor at the College of Brockport, State University of New York, and holds a PhD in Economics from George Mason University.

**David Masad** holds a PhD in Computational Social Science from George Mason University.

**Qing Tian** is Senior Associate at the Computational Public Policy Lab, George Mason University and holds a PhD from University of Michigan.

# Preface

W. Brian Arthur, Santa Fe Institute

How does an economic system's basic architecture – the way it is put together, the way it is connected – affect its long-term stability, its openness to change, and its efficiency? These are the questions this book asks, with a particular historical emphasis on China and the West. The questions are especially relevant at this time. China has been rising in the world, and the West, at least in relative terms, has been diminishing, and there is every prospect this will continue. As China expands in power and modernizes, can we expect it simply to replicate the West? If not, how will China function globally in the future? If we take the view that old, deeply embedded structures affect how cultures behave, then what are these structures and how do they determine the way these two different systems function? These questions of course are not exactly new. What *is* new is that Hilton Root brings a new perspective to their study: complexity. On a more general level, he brings this new perspective into political economics itself.

Let me give some background on complexity as it applies to economics. Economics before 1870 or so concerned itself with two great problems. One was *allocation* within the economy: how quantities of goods and services and their prices are determined within and across markets or between trading countries. The other was *formation* within the economy: how an economy emerges and changes structurally over time. In the years since 1870 and the development of neoclassical economics, the allocation problem became mathematized and could be treated rigorously, to the degree that in the twentieth century allocation came to constitute "economic theory" itself. The formation problem was not easily mathematized and was left to political economists, who largely restricted themselves to case studies and qualitative rumination. Questions of formation thus faded from the central core of economic theory, and economics had little to say about adaptation, adjustment, innovation, the formation of institutions, and structural change itself. In particular it had little to say about how economies and their supporting institutional structures arose in the first place, and how they changed over time.

That has now changed. A new approach – complexity economics – provides a rigorous way to look at questions of how systems form. Where the standard framework sees behavior in the economy as in an equilibrium steady state, with agents in the economy facing well-defined problems and using perfect deductive reasoning, the complexity framework sees the economy as always in process, always changing, with agents trying to make sense of the situations they face, using whatever reasoning they have at hand, and together creating outcomes they must react to anew. The resulting economy is not a well-ordered machine, but a complex, evolving system that is imperfect and perpetually constructing itself anew. Complexity economics gives us a world closer to that of political economy than to neoclassical theory, a world that is organic, evolutionary, and historically contingent.

Hilton Root's book applies complexity thinking to the question of how economies have evolved over time. He thinks in terms of how systems form and how the opportunities of the past lock in the possibilities of the present, how the way systems are structured determines their resilience, or promotes innovation, or enhances communication between their parts. The view is more organic than mechanistic. It lies in how the elements or substructures are connected and function together and how this determines overall system behavior.

In particular, Root uses the idea of networks to inquire into the differences between the historical evolution of Europe and that of China. Europe had a set of organizational connections with a few major hubs and linkages between these, in other words a small-world network. It operated with a loosely connected set of multiple kingships. China had a single central hub, with radial links going out from an imperial center progressively to intermediate, lower, and still lower levels. Information and command could flow quickly. Europe's system, Root shows, was less efficient in many ways than the Chinese one; but it was more resilient and could absorb changes without its basic structure being damaged. It absorbed the Reformation and many wars, with much hardship but with little effect on its basic organization: networks and institutions reorganized quickly. China's system was more stable and dynasties lasted for generations, but when the central hub was deposed, collapse could cascade downward and the entire system could fall into chaos. The frequent result was long periods of war.

Root is careful to point out that more than two levels in an economy are important, not just the micro (individual agents) and the macro (the overall outcome) as in standard theory. He brings in a hierarchy of levels, from emperor or king, to feudal lords or senior administrators, to lesser leaders, to families, businesses, and finally individuals themselves. All these are connected and mediated by institutions – legal systems, fealty systems, trading arrangements, administrative arrangements, and trading frameworks – that constantly change and adapt to the new possibilities they together create. In complexity language, he concerns himself not just with a simple system of elements and the patterns they create, but with the emergence of hierarchies of structures that mediate individual behavior and constrain what the higher levels in the system hold sway over. This emphasis on the meso-level runs throughout, and gives the arguments realism and power. It allows for real history, and cannot be captured easily within the standard agent/outcome framework.

Chapter 2 offers an excellent introduction to the complexity approach and how it can handle issues such as resilience, adaptability, and innovation; and Chapter 11 is an excellent summary of the book's findings. In between are chapters devoted variously to how stability is created in contrasting network topologies, how Western liberalism arose, and how Europe's network structure showed itself as particularly favorable to the rise of technology and science. These are followed by chapters that deal with the recent rise of China, globalization, and the question of global stability. All of these are analyzed within the context of networks, the institutional rules that govern these, and the shifting allegiances and changes they undergo. Chapter 5 presents a beautiful account of how, in the Middle Ages, Germanic custom and Roman law became combined and provided a foundation for liberal democracy, future innovation, long-distance trade, and constraints on the arbitrary power of rulers. Encouraged by a legal system that was not dominated by central power interests, cascades of change could ripple through the system. Such possibilities were not as easily attainable under the Confucian and legalistic system of China. A hub-and-spoke system cannot tolerate radical change without the legitimacy of the higher nodes being challenged, and so these suppress not only change, but the idea of change. Change in centralized systems happens slowly and almost imperceptibly as its constituent parts adapt and alter to conform to their slowly changing environment, but tinkering at the margins may not be sufficient to address internal stresses that can lead to collapse and chaos.

I find Root's analysis insightful and original. What strikes me as I read it is that the architecture of structure determines so much of a system's outcome. Parts of the structure, of course, change continually, but the overall topology persists and so the distant past creates the future. And the lessons are broad. As I read about China, I can't help comparing it with another ancient, centrally networked institution, the Catholic Church.

On a more general level, Root brings a new, nonequilibrium perspective into political economics. I believe this book may well initiate a new genre of studies that apply complexity theorizing to political economy.

# Overview

In recent years a number of authors have begun to rethink the grand narrative of political and economic history by which we have come to understand the march of progress.[1] The topic has attracted attention in part because of heightened fears since 2001 of global instability and a diminished confidence in the solutions of the past. Two sources of uncertainty have amplified. One concerns the direction of change, i.e., the potential arrest of a global advance toward liberal democracy. The other concerns whether global change processes are best depicted as an equilibrium phenomenon.

A principal source of global uncertainty is the rise of the East and its divergence from the norms of the West in governance and economic organization. To offer a fresh perspective on its spread, we have engaged insights from political economy, complex systems, and computational social science, especially network science. Our review covers a number of questions that are fundamental to the stability of historical regimes. What, for example, did the barbarian sack of Rome and the collapse of political order have to do with the development of the West's modern legal tradition? Or the industrialization of the continent with the persistence and then eventual demise of Europe's interconnected monarchies? Why was the revolutionary impact of the rising bourgeoisie never sufficient to overturn the social structure of the Old Regime – why did it require the arrival of US troops to bring about the demise of monarchy on European soil, something the French Revolution of the eighteenth century failed to achieve? What links the contempt of China's imperial bureaucracy for merchants to the formation of a state capitalist regime and the global ascendency of the People's Republic? Will China's ascendency harm free-market innovation? What do all these and other great transitions in social organization share?

The chapters that follow will trace the lineages of the global economy to the network topographies of the premodern regimes of Europe and China. In fact, when we examine the great transitions in history, i.e., those that have fashioned the fundamental institutions for economic growth, it is important to consider that an "economy" is a network of networks. These networked systems are all processing "information" and feedback loops from other networks with which they interact; and being open to a wide range of "information," they are subject to constant reassemblage. The risk for extreme events tends to amplify as systems become more interconnected; and the probability of surviving such events depends as well on properties of the network.

Network science already has wide currency among economists who employ it to understand structural network properties, epidemics, innovation systems, discovery, social reputation, influence and trust, and information spreading, especially in social media, rumors, financial, trade, and supply chain networks. Employing often overlooked observables, such as the rules governing dynastic succession, the relationships between custom and formal law, and the receptivity of rulers to disruptive innovation, this book applies network science to a subfield of economics: the political economy of institutions that examines the effect of institutions on economic performance over time. Its purpose is to help researchers develop new conceptual frameworks, tools, and ideas to more fully capture the social and economic world – to move beyond neoclassical economics and beyond institutional structures into the origins and behaviors of the network structures themselves.

A COMPLEX SYSTEMS APPROACH TO GLOBAL HISTORY

Scholarship on the political economy of institutions, and economic history more generally, has been transformed by Douglass North's efforts in tracing the sources of the West's dynamism to institutions that incentivize economic performance over time. He describes institutional change as a smooth, gradual "evolutionary process" essentially of human design. But he also identifies an important source of change that is not of human design (North 1991). Institutions, he reports, exhibit path dependence, meaning that if those from which they evolved had appeared in some different order, they would be different as well. They also evolve through the effects of increasing returns. Think of computers or software platforms that improve with use and adaptation, leading to further adaptation. These two phenomena, path dependence and increasing returns, both of which constrain the further possibilities that are built from the originating sets, are not of human device or intent; they are neither purposeful nor anticipated, and the combinations they produce do not always progress by the steady accumulation of small changes. The resulting work of transformation need not be a version of an earlier object; abrupt and radical novelties can spring forth. The transmission of an idea or a technology or a new form of organization often occurs explosively – consider the Protestant Reformation, the French Revolution, the Arab Spring, the printing press, the steam engine, jet propulsion, computers, the Internet, and genetic engineering.

North also acknowledges that a complete explanation of economic performance cannot be attributed to institutions alone but must consider the effects of political organizations (1991). The interactions of political and economic variables contribute fundamentally to changes in economic history, an insight that is taken further by Daron Acemoğlu and James A. Robinson (2006). They try to capture that relationship between politics and institutional change in a general equilibrium framework.[2] This approach advances the notion that political change is an equilibrium-induced process. However, it does not fully account for the bottom-up processes that are critical to long-term economic growth. North knew better. He understood the relationship between the polity and the economy to be inherently complex, and that increasing returns make multiple subsequent combinations possible. Network science can help to augment North's framework on institutional change by demonstrating how networks can evolve from the bottom to the top level as a consequence of local rules being applied without a "central controller."

Nevertheless, research on long-term patterns of change in historical regimes has become dependent upon the concept of equilibrium. But what the general equilibrium framework misses is that change processes do not all occur on the same timescale, and that when a major change in a system's global properties arises, sometimes suddenly, from small local-level variations, the agent interactions can produce emergent outcomes, but even when brief patterns of change and long patterns of stability are observed in social systems, this need not denote equilibrium. With multiple variables interacting in an environment that is open to continuous feedback, efforts to distinguish what is exogenous from what is endogenous can be futile. Knowledge, practices, and norms fluctuate continually; negotiation and contestation are constant. Minor local events or modifications in the controlling variables can engender forceful movements for change.

Historical regimes are multiscale systems; change at one level may have effects at lower or higher levels that are neither proportional nor consistent with the size of the input. Change can arise episodically. With many degrees of freedom, no two systems are governed by the same internal dynamics. A virtually unlimited range of dynamical processes is possible. A complex systems approach is ideal for investigating change in the structure of historical regimes, comprised as they are of many connected networks of interacting components.

In this book we compare the characteristics of the long-lived European and Chinese regimes, considering that each is a connected system in which a path exists from any node to any other in the network, and that their respective structures, or topologies, affect innovation, adaptability, and robustness. By identifying key differences in their network topologies, we can observe how both path dependence and increasing returns accrue to initial institutional formations, influencing subsequent political and economic organization. Theoretical models of each society are developed, based on historical/sociological knowledge. The contemporary chapters (7–10) employ data collected by several international organizations to compare investments, coalitions, alignments, and decision making in international relations. Social network analytics are employed throughout to explore the dynamics of regime formation and dissolution through time.

When comparing China with the West, qualitative differences in the structural (spatial) organization of the networks continue to influence behavior in ways that reveal the arc of time. Western nations retain the institutional forms that limit centralization. The European Union (EU) draws on the principle of subsidiarity, its own form of polycentricism, to balance and monitor competing interests while harnessing the synergies of interjurisdictional competition. The different units have autonomy and speak with different voices but they are not isolated; they are linked vertically via a network of large hubs with many connections. Distributed authority also characterizes the political organization of the US system, based on checks and balances across regions and across institutions. In both the EU and the United States, a distributed network of competing jurisdictions is connected via a network of hubs, and this allows the diffusion of innovations from anywhere within the system to spread rapidly. Without disabling the existing networks, connectivity expands, permitting a constantly shifting relationship among the principle hubs in a system that rarely succumbs to disintegration.

Modern China, too, exhibits continuity in its organizational structure, here from the Confucian model utilized by imperial dynasties. Compared with the highly skewed concentration of linkages among the primary nodes in Europe, China's connectivity is constrained to reduce redundancy in rule making, and replication in rule enforcement. In the Chinese model the nodes are connected to a very few other nodes, and all ultimately through just one central node, not from any node to any other. The higher-order decision-making units of government form a series of interlocking ministries organized to speak with one voice; the ideal is to enable decision making to cohere into a harmonious whole. As a network with a central hub that stands above the state itself, the Chinese Communist Party (CCP) has designed a nexus of market-enabling institutions that link finance, investment, rule enforcement, and market access, affording a level of central control that far exceeds the concentration of power of China's prior regimes. The design, which harnesses the competitive synergies of a global marketplace while allowing society to operate as an integrated whole, is a great innovation of contemporary institution building, and may enable China to gain economic parity with the West. Yet a weakness persists similar to that which caused the disintegration of prior regimes: the spread of lateral connectivity and corruption that can evade centralized rule enforcement. The regime is vulnerable to collapse if the legitimacy of the CCP, its central organizing mechanism, is eroded. Not surprisingly, the party has made anti corruption and "social credit" a major theme over successive decades.

Network science applied to social change processes brings to light the varying characteristics of stability and resilience that shape the feasible sets of institutional possibilities and influence the divergent economic trajectories of the two systems. It allows us to delve into the building blocks of North's framework for economic change: learning effects, knowledge transfers, and the adaptive capacity for innovation. We get a better sense of how the social dynamics inside societies are bound up with international relations, and with international regimes more generally, and how the internal logic of national developments reflects the social dynamics of wider-world historical trends. With better tools to chart the topology of the interdependent webs of interactions that link the economy and the polity, we can evaluate the impacts of increasing returns, path dependence, and sensitivity to initial conditions on regime transitions. All are self-reinforcing properties of the network structure, and trying to understand their dynamics will unfold a new era of comparative economic analysis, with connectivity becoming pivotal to the analysis of change.

Finally, there is a policy concern: How can the interactions of the two systems, that of China and the West, be governed? Will there be an innate tendency for the two systems to disengage and break apart, or will they collide and be a source of permanent global conflict? Can a unified global governance system be designed that is equally applicable to both – will a polycentric balancing of overlapping jurisdictions ensure stability without hegemonic control? Such questions about global order are the prevailing theme in both policy and academic discussions of global governance and will, for the foreseeable future, determine the patterns of formation, continuity, and change in the economy within and across regimes, and globally.

A harsh debate divides the community of economists between equilibrium-based theories and those considering the complexity, heterogeneity, and connectivity that contribute to the dynamical aspects of economic exchanges. This volume seeks to explore what lies beyond this debate and to persuade those willing and eager to undertake novel researches into *terra incognita* that there may be opportunities in the direction set out before them.

OUTLINE

This volume is divided into three distinct parts. The first advances theory that connects political economy with other sciences, especially with the study of complex systems and complex networks (Vega-Redondo 2007). Chapter 1 identifies five important historical transitions in the creation of global order. Chapter 2 summarizes a range of structural network properties that are applicable to the analysis of political economics; some are given more weight than others in the chapters that follow, especially the consequences of small-world versus star-shaped network formation (a juxtaposition that reappears in Chapters 4, 6, 7, 8, and 11). Chapter 3 takes a slight detour and surveys cognitive network science and political economy. Each of these first three chapters connects economic history with complexity and the study of human behavior. In this first part, key concepts include the coexistence and complementarities of order and disorder, and of closed systems within an open universe; the irreversibility of time and therefore of evolution; and the networked interdependence of different levels of social order.

Chapters 4–6 trace how network topology — not any dichotomy of state and society — molds the relationships among agents that in turn give rise to societies and hold sway over their trajectories. This part examines the historical regimes of China and Europe, and the hypernetwork structures that influence how information is spread, which in turn circumscribes the behaviors of different groups that make up each system. It offers analysis of three critical transitions in the creation of stability in historical networks during the past thousand years: political succession, the formation of legal traditions, and the diffusion of technology. Each of these transitions is both the backdrop for, and driver of, massive transformations in economic order as well. Chapter 4 probes the first, the resilience that European society derived from the creation of rule-based principles of dynastic succession. By lengthening the periods of stability, these rules encouraged long-term economic growth. In contrast with China, Europe's solution to the problem of dynastic succession was a system of competing royal houses. While many vied for regional domination, none obtained a monopoly on power. China established laws for dynastic succession, too, and a unified monarchy governed the realm as an integrated whole.

In Chapter 5, the law plays a central role in the transition from large- to small-world connectivity. We examine the Western legal tradition as a network of social interactions, and trace its role in a second major transition, one that encompassed the tectonic breakaway of twelfth-century medieval society from the hold of Germanic custom through the amalgamation of those customs with Roman law. The structure of the legal tradition influenced dynamic behavior in long-term historical change processes and resulted in the creation of contract law, ensuring that trade would become less dependent on kinship. It played an important role in the growth dynamics of the European economy and laid the foundations for a third great transition in economic productivity, the industrialization of Europe, which is addressed in Chapter 6. Europe's unique network structure accelerated receptivity to applications of science and technology that had potentially disruptive implications for social order – yet, surprisingly, that network still comprised the relations among royal families, who were sponsors and consumers of the innovations. Europe's monarchs recognized the political benefit of engaging with the merchant classes and the newly formed literati of the Enlightenment. These great transitions in social order endowed Western society with a set of core institutional characteristics that distinguish it from China into the present, where it encounters a new set of risks.

The final part, Chapters 7–11, moves to the present day and considers global instability, identifying two transitions that are occurring simultaneously. Chapters 7 and 8 examine the rise of China and its creation of a market economy with unique structural characteristics. China has the potential to become the central node of a giant cluster of networks, forming linkages with other, smaller nodes across the global economy. If this occurs, the information that travels on the newly formed network cluster will test existing notions of economic morality and policy. China's transition thus is consistent with one primary rule observed in the previous three major historical transitions: topology determines how ideas and behavior spread on a network.

In Chapters 9 and 10, globalization becomes the larger theme, as does the question of whether it is bringing us into a new macro order in which networks of communities interact without a hegemon. Chapter 9 documents the shift in global networks since the end of the Cold War, showcasing methods to represent how network structures change over time. We measure changes in the density and centrality of various interstate networks since the Cold War and calculate the transformative effects on global relations caused by the relative declines of Russia and the United States. A considerable increase in lateral interactions is observable in the interstate system of trade, diplomacy, arms transfers, and technology. Traditional "communities of nations" are breaking down, and a network structure is taking shape in which there will be no "central" position of power. Hegemonic efforts to redesign the world and drive global progress miss an important insight: that globalization – and the dense interconnectivity and heightened competition it fosters – inherently weakens hierarchical control structures while fostering an environment of many powerful forces struggling for influence. The densification of global networks increases the risk that instability can come from almost anywhere and propagate widely. Accounts of historical change in terms of the rise or decline of particular regimes or regions, for example, a declining West being overtaken by a rising East, are insufficient to capture the essential change dynamics that are occurring globally.

What will this entail for the West and the architecture of globalization that it has attempted to put into place? What will competition between East and West mean for the diffusion of the Western liberal tradition? How will the sheer magnitude and influence of China's economy, built as it is upon different foundational notions of social and economic order, affect governance standards worldwide? Even more generally, how will the rise of China challenge us to think in new ways about what disposes people to respond to markets?

In Chapter 10, we explore why, in a world of ever-increasing interdependence, we should not expect a return to a definite equilibrium. The chapter raises another question: Can there be stability without a hegemonic option? Cycles of hegemony in which domination by one absolute leader is replaced by another are likely to end with the dispersion of power and the eclipse of the United States. The networks of global interdependence will be structured in significantly different ways. As the problems of different countries, and of formerly separate sectors of the global economy, continue to lace into one another, new forms of risk will develop that are not readily discernable or even amenable to top-down solutions. Chapter 11 concludes this study of complex networks and their applications to global political economy, concentrating on how structural network properties contribute to the resilience and adaptiveness of long-lived historical regimes.

In the years ahead, scholars engaged in applying network analytics to historical problems are likely to raise new topics for inquiry as they discover novel ways to interpret issues of longstanding concern that a more traditional institutional or game-theoretic bargaining model would not detect. A world examined for its complexity presents an opportunity to reduce the distance between the hard sciences and economics. Tools such as network theory, widely used in the analytics of complexity, can help researchers to understand the abrupt bursts to which the economy is prone, and to characterize changes in structure or alterations in the flow of information that take the form of cascades of new behaviors. In the hard sciences, researchers strive for progress amid elemental unknowables – the origins of the universe, for example, its structure and expanding fabric, and the organisms that populate it. We in the social sciences can take lessons from this more modest approach to identifying the causal effects in instances of complex phenomena.

This endeavor aims to link continuity and change in historical regimes with the flow of "information" in the processes of social transformation. The progress of human society cannot be divided into binary antagonisms, such as the opposition of state and society, markets and states, or networks vs. hierarchies. Our pursuit is informed by considering that historical regimes of long duration are of a universal class whose structures comprise many differing patterns of intersections but share one fundamental property: they are giant webs of communication in which, at some fundamental level, every node is processing "information" from the other nodes that comprise the system.

## NOTES

1. Aoki (2001); Hall and Soskice (eds., 2001); North, Wallis, and Weingast (2009); Morris (2010); Hodgson and Knudsen (2010); Hausmann et al. (2011); Fukuyama (2011; 2014); and van Bavel (2016). In one way or another, each of these studies takes up ideas found in Hayek (1973, 1976, 1979).
2. Acemoğlu and Robinson establish an equilibrium framework in which political transitions, such as widening the franchise, result from bargaining among elites and non-elites for the resources needed to rule the polity, avoid revolt, and ensure stability (2006).

# Acknowledgments

A worldwide network contributed to this endeavor. It includes contributors, students, colleagues, and institutions. Let me begin by thanking Qing Tian, Baocheng Liu, Kevin Comer, David Masad, Jack Goldstone, and Cameron Harwick. All could have channeled their extraordinary talents into doing something different but chose to share their time and energy.

I am grateful to have worked with Kanishka Balasuriya, Mary Boardman, Snigdha Dewal, Ammar Malik, Joseph Shaheen, and Aris Tranditis, who are beginning their journey to the frontiers of knowledge.

Colleagues from an assortment of disciplines joined the conversation: Kenneth Arrow, Jeff Johnson, Paul Ormerod, Heidi Smith, Henrik Jensen, Kenneth Comer, Nadeem ul Haque, Shaun Hargreaves-Heap, John Meadowcroft, Mark Pennington, John Wallis, Nancy Wei, and Dingxin Zhao.

At my home institution, George Mason University, I am grateful to have enjoyed the collegiality of Paul Dragos Aligica, Robert Axtell, Tyler Cowen, Jack Goldstone, James Olds, Noel Johnson, Eduardo López, Mark Koyama, César Martinelli, and John Nye. Zoltan Acs reviewed the manuscript at every stage and commented in provocative and constructive ways.

Working with Philip Good and the editorial team at Cambridge has been a pleasure. I also want to acknowledge the editors and anonymous reviewers of early versions of Chapters 3 and 4, which appeared in the *Journal of Institutional Economics* and the *Cambridge Review of International Affairs*. Remarkable editing has been provided by Dinah McNichols at all stages of manuscript preparation.

Institutions, despite their inherent imperfections, were indispensable: King's College London hosted me as a senior research professor for a year, during which the ideas started to germinate and concepts to form. The Economics Department at Ibero-American University in Mexico City, the Max Weber Program of the European University Institute in Florence, and Beijing's University of International Business and Economics, all hosted events to discuss the work in progress. George Mason University's Institute for Humane Studies sponsored a manuscript workshop. I am grateful to all and cannot thank each sufficiently.

# PART I  Political Economy and Complex Systems

# I  Great Transitions in Economic History

In the second half of the twentieth century, in the wake of World War II, social scientists began to tweak development models they had built based on the economic trajectory of the West.[1] Their hope was to use these models as guides for policy and forecasting, and to make economic growth and institution building seem manageable and understandable worldwide. There was every reason for optimism: from the late fifties, those models were close approximations to Western reality.

The United States and its European and Asian allies were enjoying stable economic growth. There was no depression on the horizon and no war between global powers (who were waging the Cold War by proxies, far removed); and advances in technology were bringing about higher wages, social mobility, better health and quality of life. Small wonder then that social scientists looked to apply their models of international development through bilateral and multilateral assistance. They held that the processes of change, often referred to as modernization, would produce rising incomes, improved health, economic openness and cooperation, and greater pluralism and tolerance. The culmination, the end of history as it were, would be a broad convergence of the world's nations, operating with free markets and limited government, into the most productive and desirable mode of social order.

Although some people claim the world changed on 9/11, the terror attacks in 2001 merely brought into sharp focus the fact that the world is far less stable and predictable than previously thought. Since then we've seen terrorism spike across Europe, Asia, the Middle East, and the Americas. Civil wars, drug cartel wars, trade wars, military aggression, ethnic cleansing, and other human-made catastrophes have brought about massive flows of refugees and internally displaced populations. The global economic crisis of 2007–2009 was the worst since the Great Depression. A black market in enriched uranium and other nuclear materials has evolved from the breakup of the Soviet Union. More telling has been the retreat from democracy in the developing world, and the rising populist hostility to notions of free trade and globalization, reflected among voters of the world's leading economies.

The upheaval of the first two decades of the twenty-first century has shocked social scientists, in great part because they continue to update their development models, still hoping to portray a world of converging ideals. But their models are failing in the real world to predict important patterns in the development of the global economy. In truth, they worked best for closed systems near or at equilibrium. The convergence that modernization was expected to produce worldwide was predicated on the belief that the global system in which it would occur was also edging toward some state of equilibrium.

It is now clear that the equilibria of liberal political and economic convergence is not inevitable. Prosperity appears alongside nationalism and intolerance. It coexists with religious violence. It can be found coincident with nuclear proliferation and heightened risk of war. It thrives in authoritarian states as readily as in full-fledged democracies. Meanwhile, convergence seems to float just out of reach, over some ever-shifting horizon. What becomes clear as well is this: global societies are not part of a single, overarching, convergent social order that can be fine-tuned and managed with equilibrium models. Instead, global societies are, as they have always been, parts of open, adaptive, complex systems. Not only are their dynamics less predictable than we are comfortable acknowledging, but they are subject to large cyclic swings and cascades of change.

Here is the great disconnect: contemporary social thought in the West uses the ideas of "globalism," "world order," "modernization," and "models of development" as if these were synonymous, reflecting a continuum in which one instantiates the other. Yet once we start to recognize that global society is a complex adaptive system, we must begin to consider the dynamics to which such systems are prone, dynamics that can, on account of their own internal stresses, veer into conditions of criticality. This also raises a question upon which this book rests: Is change best conceived in terms of mechanical or organic processes?

The complex systems approach has greatly expanded our understanding of the natural, self-organizing processes of change. It utilizes a number of concepts, including imitation, herding, self-organized criticality, and positive feedback, which are captured by network analysis. In addition, and most important, is the realization that a system's behavior depends on its network structure. This helps us understand how behavior can vary greatly from system to system. If researchers don't account for network patterns of interactions, they will overlook such variables as how information, ideas, and technology spread; how relationships with peers, friends, neighbors, and acquaintances influence our decisions; behavioral shifts; and the role of explosive percolation (Jackson 2014). The chapters that follow apply complex systems thinking to help us understand great transitions in economic history, particularly the divergence of China and the West, through network models. They explore how China has attained global leadership and why the West is struggling to maintain its own global influence. They address future risks and explain why we must prepare for them.

Throughout history, those living in the midst of each great transition were rarely aware of its breadth or import, and this is also true today, meaning that wholesale shifts are not apparent from a personal, or microscopic, perspective. Yet because we can apply to past shifts the concepts of complex adaptive systems, we are better able to observe their dynamics and draw inferences about the future.

This study of five great transitions in economic history attempts to apply the science of complex networks to historical economic development, with a particular focus on network topology (structure) and its contribution to the differing trajectories of Asian and European societies. Will the technology wars of the future be won by China or by the West? This question is often asked, although it cannot be answered. Yet Chapters 4–6 demonstrate how network science applied to history can help us to identify crucial variables and to think about patterns that might otherwise be overlooked.

## I.I   NETWORKS IN ECONOMIC TRANSITIONS

A key concern is how network dynamics determine the type of stability displayed by each system. The first great transition, addressed in Chapter 4, is the gradual formation and sudden demise of dynastic lordship as the pivot of social organization. Solving the problem of leadership succession was critical to the economic progress of both Europe and China, and a significant contributor to the accumulation and transmission of social and technological capital over a wide geographic area. This transformation, characterized by the emergence of clear rules for dynastic succession, emerged in stages, with its onset varying from region to region.

Despite their fundamentally different origins, the monarchical systems in Western Europe, Russia, and China endured for a thousand years before they abruptly declined in the same decade of the twentieth century. To understand the resilience that ensured the duration of dynastic lordship, we delve into the endlessly rewoven relationships between the macro and the micro as part of a coevolutionary dynamic, in which macro- and microsystems each operate under their own sets of laws and cannot be simultaneously determined. Being able to define one does not necessarily allow us to define the other. It is widely acknowledged among scientists who study complex systems that many systems exhibit identical large-scale behaviors, although their microscopic descriptions can diverge significantly.

The second great transition, addressed in Chapter 5, comes from the formation of Western law through the confluence of Germanic custom and the Roman codified system of laws. Western law offered adaptive mechanisms to ensure obligations and protections, and made it possible for communities to channel cooperation and resolve conflicts in parallel with their societies' growing economic complexities.

The evolution of law parallels Brian Arthur's description of technology: that every new development of technology opens up opportunities for new uses, new supporting technologies, or new ways to organize, distribute, maintain, or enhance its performance (2009). Just as each novel element creates opportunity niches for supporting technologies, as new laws or rulings are brought in, new opportunities appear for further combinations. Social relations adjust to the new legal protocols and change accordingly. Thus the Western legal tradition can be described as self-creating.

The legal system, in fact, predated the European tradition of nation states and aided in their formation. In this role, as a subculture and integral partner of the continent's cultural, economic, and political elites, it enabled a synthesis of Germanic customs, Roman law, and canon law.[2] Like the Church itself, the legal system operated as a hub in the wider network assemblage. It gained increasing density over time and in parallel with key developmental processes that contributed to the unique character of European civilization.

As the legal platform grew in importance, its use by various parties also grew. The legal tradition took hold between 1050 and 1150, at a time when Europe was a mosaic of hundreds of different political structures. During this period, the character of Europe was being shaped by a number of factors, including the First and Second Crusades in Spain;[3] the conflicting ambitions of the princely nobility and the bishops; the spread of commerce and competition within the urban centers; the power structures of rural lordship; and the *Herrenfrage* and restructuring of the gender system.[4] The law was partner to a social process, the rise of an independent merchant class; to an economic process, the rise of both towns and private enterprises; and to a political process, the rise of the monarchical state. The feudal lords turned to the law to obtain constraints on royal prerogatives and to contain royal discretion. Merchants turned to lawyers for contract law and risk mitigation, and to ensure their towns remained free of the grasp of the feudal lords. Monarchs turned to Roman law precepts so as not to be bound by law and custom, and to obtain absolute rights and power, like the *dominus* over his estate. This included gaining permanent powers of taxation and jurisdiction over the peasantry. They were resisted by advocates of popular sovereignty, who used the same language of *dominium* (ownership) to assert popular resistance to the monarch's unlawful actions. Eventually, even peasant communities resorted to the legal system to gain liberation from feudal exactions.

Law played a crucial role in all of these episodes, and in each, the status of the law in society mattered as much as its actual content. An important feature of the Western network architecture is that it could grow organically by the addition of new "nodes." This capability enabled the law to acquire the status of an interdependent "hub" within a small-world system in which it had multiple connections with other principal hubs, such as networks of royal families, aristocratic land owners, and the elites of the principal trading centers. As a hub that served a much wider set of interests than those of political leadership, the Western legal tradition permeated and perpetuated the small-world properties of the system.

Yet while this adaptive process of blending legal theory and local context continues to animate the Western legal tradition, it is the notion that law transcends politics and holds the lawmakers and the state itself accountable that most contributed to the unleashing of Western Europe's economic potential. Together, the creation of rules for orderly succession and the binding of elites to law are foundational to the rapid growth of the Western economies, and are among the main reasons for their distinctive pattern of development. Europe's legal tradition developed the unique capacity to commit the monarch and other elites to a system of legal limits on their power, and this in turn molded the West's journey to wealth. At each stage of its enlarged use, we see increasing returns at work.

Crucial to the formation of Western firms, markets, and economic institutions was the linkage of economic and political freedom: the freedom to create or join enterprises, acquire and maintain goods for profit or sale, determine the activity or sector in which to operate, and test or ignore different ideas. As well, assets are taxed at predetermined rates and protected from outright confiscation. Each linkage represents a grant of freedom from political and religious authority, contributing to a third great transition.

We can observe this linkage of enterprise and freedom in trends from the 1670s that led to this third great transition, the industrialization of the means of production that began in earnest in the late eighteenth century (Mokyr 2017). The Industrial Revolution, addressed in Chapter 6, is frequently understood simply as an expansion in the means of production. Nevertheless, there was also an ideational backdrop, in the formation of a cultural ethos that encouraged scientific and technological innovation. Administrative trends also surfaced, in the formation of nation states; and sociological trends helped to form a Europe-wide civil society. After almost two millennia of mediocre growth and gradual technological change, industrialization stimulated the pace of urbanization and greatly augmented overall wealth. That dramatic shift in productive capacity is linked to the network structure of Europe that allowed new hubs to form in an orderly manner without causing the demise of the network's underlying structure, as was to occur in China.

The dynamics of this great economic transition were hardly linear. Indeed, the transition showed all the behavioral characteristics of a phenomenon found in complex systems. Called *self-organized criticality*, it can be understood as a two-part process. The first stage, self-organization, refers to the development of structures and patterns without the direct influence of an external agent; examples can be seen in the flocking of birds, the synchronicity of fireflies, the coordination of bees, the formation of an embryo. The second stage, called a *phase transition*, occurs when the system crosses a critical point at which its dynamics change abruptly and irreversibly. Again in the natural world, we find examples: the stresses caused by the movement of tectonic plates build up over thousands of years but are released in just a few moments during an earthquake. Self-organized criticality can involve a phase transition during which something extraordinary occurs: the components that normally interact indirectly suddenly all transition together, and the transition spans the entire system, with all members of the system influencing one another.[5] Indeed, during the late eighteenth century, criticality affected the European economy as a system-wide cultural phenomenon whose many interacting parts and currents abruptly coalesced to create an environment that valued and competed for innovation.

Western firms matured in an environment where ideas were protected, interweaving innovation with freedom and making it the essential driver of growth. This environment nurtured diversity in product development and in firm organization. During the nineteenth century, as the links between science and industry became more systematic, much of the West's industrial research capacity was privately funded. Leaders in private enterprise had basic decision-making power over the innovation process, making firms the basic units for organizing innovation. Government innovations were generally limited to military applications, public health, or the food supply. With this freedom came accountability. Markets determined winners and losers, rewarding innovation according to an innovator's ability to recoup an investment until it could be improved upon by someone else. Innovators depended on legally sanctioned priority over imitators or successors, making patent laws and an efficient legal system essential. Investment in innovation became the cause of capital formation, rather than its consequence. Even political control over science, art, literature, music, and education relaxed. In other words, freedom in the economic sphere was coupled with other mutually reinforcing freedoms with the legal system reaching all facets of life, including the rise of labor unions to protect workers.

## 1.2 A COMPLEXITY TRANSITION THAT MAY RESHAPE THE WORLD

The fourth transition (the topic of Chapters 7–8) has been by far the shortest, spanning just a few decades, and is not yet complete. This is

China's trajectory from a planned socialist economy to essentially a market-driven economy, enabling its dramatic rise as a global power and competitor to the West. Considering the speed and effectiveness of China's policy reforms, which fostered market relations where none existed, its transition is without parallel in economic history. In the late seventies, Chinese policymakers turned to market economics as part of their struggle to obtain positional advantage within the international system. Contemporary China has learned from, and seeks to avoid, the mistakes of the Soviet Union. It seeks to build a globally competitive economy and to master digital technologies while bolstering central rule. Its leaders turned to markets, hoping that China could gain enough agility to carve its own future, based on indigenous social capacity and traditional values and notions of order, rather than having to conform to a future dictated by Western institutions. Accordingly, China is also taking a different approach, by de-emphasizing the role of private initiative in how firms and markets are organized.

China has grown even more ambitious, offering its model and development loans to other nations, and its success poses a challenge to the linkage between innovation and freedom. In numerous public declarations, Chairman Xi Jinping has announced that the innovation mechanism of the free-market system could be replaced on the basis of the CCP's proven track record in stimulating economic growth by providing domestic stability, international security, and public goods, such as education, public health, transport, and water, along with standardized market procedures. Indeed, China's agriculture, commerce, and manufacturing make it as capable as Western rivals of meeting the demands of the modern age.

Can the CCP take China's radical economic experiment to the world stage, and continue to maintain control? Will a rising China create and invoke institutional rules and arrangements that conflict with attempts by Western nations to shape the overall normative environment of the world in ways designed to protect their own security? Will China be able to reposition itself as a global rule maker and establish a new model of development for the benefit of the whole of global society? Much of the potential for global stability hinges on whether China's rise will bring with it domination of global resource flows and information, along with a network of coalitions that prompts conflict with the West, or even global conflict.

Looking beyond the looming East–West conflict and whether China's global impact will trigger a coevolutionary change across the system of international relations, another transition (Chapters 9 and 10) is surfacing: a multipolar world is emerging that is vulnerable to unexpected shocks from any corner. China's transition is taking place while the entire network structure of international relations is becoming more locally coupled, with increasingly dense connectivity in trade, diplomacy, weapons, and finance. This then is the fifth transition. It is also only beginning to unfold and may deliver a momentous transformative effect on the global economy. It is being shaped by the relative decline of Russia and the United States, and by the economic success of China, India, Germany, and Japan – and it is making the strategies and institutions for global stability of the Cold War's bipolar world increasingly irrelevant.

During the Cold War era, countries aligned in one network, such as trade, tended to share other networks, such as diplomatic or military cooperation. In the years since, however, countries can be found in partnership networks, such as China's extensive role in Latin American and African economies, that would have been inconceivable a generation or two ago. It is in the context of this increase in the density of lateral interactions and the resulting complex interdependence that the global rise of China will play out. Of importance, the increasing density of global interactions in trade, in diplomacy, and in arms transfers heightens the risk that instability can come from almost anywhere in the system.

Volatility caused by increasing global connectivity will demand new ways of approaching problems. The danger is that nationalist sentiment, whether it causes a drifting apart or alternatively places some countries on a collision course, will preclude the cooperation needed to resolve the deeper problems of globalization faced by all nations. The vulnerability of the economy to global connectivities that defy nationalist remedies is the subject of Chapter 10.

It is not news that contemporary processes of global change call for new theoretical and methodological approaches. Global studies programs and curriculums have spread from the university to the high school level, but traditional social science disciplines, even when combined within a multidisciplinary curriculum, provide unsatisfying analyses of global-scale processes and impacts. The towering accomplishments of the greatest economic thinking on risk and uncertainty of the past century leave an incomplete framework for understanding the challenges of the epoch we are entering (Root 2018).

To understand great transitions, we must shift our attention away from the microscopic levels of particular agents, whether individuals, groups, nations, or policy interventions, and toward their dynamic interactions. This is not a repudiation of traditional economic approaches; rather, it is an effort to deal with issues of large-scale social change that those traditional approaches have often neglected. The great advances in economic theory have generally been associated with the application of equilibrium models used in mechanical physics. Our approach is to adapt models from statistical physics, which applies to systems with many degrees of freedom.

This effort is to seek in foundational science the theories, analytics, and methods to grasp human and societal behaviors, and to place the political economy of global development on a new footing of complex adaptive systems. We hope to provide a perspective that sheds insight on five important historical transitions that one cannot gain from standard economic assumptions and institutionalist approaches to development. This new foundation will enable scholars and policymakers to better understand the past, to identify the change cycles of far longer duration than previously considered, and to engage with the interconnected, multidimensional risks and uncertainty we face today.

NOTES

1. By the West, we are referring here, as elsewhere, to the high-income Organisation for Economic Co-operation and Development (OECD) countries of Western Europe, the United States, Australia, New Zealand, Canada, and Japan. By the end of the nineteenth century, the West's share of global GDP exceeded 50 percent, and by the late 1960s the share peaked at more than 60 percent (Bolt and van Zanden 2013; Maddison 2001). Japan belongs in the group economically, although its political antecedents diverge.

2. Roman law can be traced to the sixth century BCE, when the Twelve Tables were promulgated.

3. The *Reconquista* of the Iberian Peninsula spanned approximately 780 years between the Islamic conquest of Hispania in 711 and the fall in 1492 of Granada, Iberia's last Islamic state, to the expanding Christian kingdoms.

4. *Herrenfrage* is a modern term coined to describe the restructuring of the gender system in the eleventh and twelfth centuries to exclude women from institutions and professions of the celibate clergy. See McNamara (1994).

5. Bak, Tang, and Wiesenfeld (1987) introduced the idea of self-organized criticality as a general characteristic of complex systems.

# 2 Growth, Form, and Self-Organization in the Economy

## 2.1 THE ECONOMY HAS THE GLOBAL PROPERTIES OF A COMPLEX SYSTEM

In the study of economies as multilevel systems, change at one level alters the options for change at another. Even as the individual agents that populate the system arrange themselves into networks they are also continually adapting, acquiring new characteristics as they adjust their behaviors to new sets of rules and to the anticipated reactions of nearby agents. And these ongoing individual adaptations are taking place at every level of a system. The analytical challenge in such constantly shifting environments, explained Friedrich Hayek in his 1974 Nobel acceptance speech, is to understand an economy as an "organized complexity." Although the term "complex systems" wasn't yet well established, Hayek recognized structures of "essential complexity" whose characteristics depend "not only on the properties of the individual elements of which they are composed, and the relative frequency with which they occur, but also on the manner in which the individual elements are connected with each other."

Why does one network structure offer greater latitude than another for change within tradition? How do fundamental transformations – revolutions, for example – occur relatively rapidly, and often at several levels of social organization at once? These are questions to explore as we examine the adaptive capacity of agents to *self-organize* into networks to help ensure greater compatibility with their changing environments. Self-organization occurs throughout nature, in flocks of birds and schools of fish and in the creation of honeycombs and crystals. How these behaviors unfold depends on the relationships between self-organization at the agent level and the structure their self-organization creates at the system level.

## Institutions and Equilibrium in Political Economy Analysis

In the wake of the general equilibrium revolution in economics that began in the nineteenth century and crested in the twentieth, theorists put aside questions of decision making among heterogeneous agents and how economies form and change structurally over time. Topics once central to political economy – innovation, structural change, collective action, and history – were shelved from theoretical inquiry and receded into obscurity. The conversion of economics to an equilibrium science concentrated attention instead on questions of resource allocation, i.e., employment, consumption, distribution, production, and prices. However, the tools and the data that have proved useful to describe the economy's allocative functions are not well suited for describing the formation of its structure. The scholars who continued, both intuitively and empirically, to explore the great drama that connects the irrevocable past with the uncertain future, rarely did so within the mainstream of economics.

Continuing interest in the distribution of power and wealth has kept political economy current within the realm of the political and social sciences. But within economics itself, the study of history went in the direction of mechanistic simplification, inquiring about problems that could be solved in purely technical terms. The great debate between John Maynard Keynes and Hayek on the relationship of the state and the market did not become the frame in which contemporary political economy evolved. Topics such as legitimacy, essential to political economy, disappeared from economic analysis. The moral drama that informs history and sociology was eclipsed by the idea that experts could fine-tune the market into a positive-sum equilibrium. Political economy itself, which had occupied a central place in economic analysis, receded. The elimination of imbalances so as to attain equilibria became the key analytical device to explain change and shape policy.

That sidelining of political economy analysis began to find a remedy in the works of scholars such as Daron Acemoğlu, Avner Greif, Douglass North, James Robinson, John Wallis, and Barry Weingast, among others, who apply the established behavioral assumptions of game theory and the core, simplifying assumptions of microeconomics to study agent behavior and the role of institutions in economic growth. They model agents who mostly interact indirectly through the market collectively as homogenous, rational actors, fully able to construe the risk and rewards of their actions.

One idea has come to occupy a central place in the study of institutions: that the system has an innate tendency to converge to a steady, or equilibrium, state. Today the political economy of institutions enjoys a central position in the study of large-scale political, economic, and social change; and with the concept of *institutions as equilibria*, it joins the very mainstream of economic analysis, where a "model" usually implies a search for equilibrium, a point of balance, a condition of rest, a state of the system toward which the model depicts convergence over time.[1] An economy is assumed to be either at equilibrium (or one of its equilibrium positions) or moving, and probably moving rapidly, toward an equilibrium.[2] That position presumes three basic properties: the consistent behavior of the agents; stability, which is the outcome of some dynamic process; and the lack of incentives for agents to change their behavior or coalitional structure once an equilibrium is attained.

Pointing to the shifting consensus in favor of this approach, institutional economists Avner Greif and Christopher Kingston (2011, 14) remark that "a growing body of recent research on institutions places a theory of motivation at the center of the analysis, and thereby endogenizes the 'enforcement of the rules.' ... This perspective focuses on how interactions among purposeful agents create the structure that gives each of them the motivation to act in a manner perpetuating this structure." Inter-level connectivity is not an issue because macro factors are aggregates of micro variables.

The concept of *institutions as equilibria* does enable us to see how individuals, acting in self-interested ways and according to environmental constraints, create, evolve, and enforce rules (*institutions as rules*) to transact business and engage productively. Over time, as rules become formalized, and as penalties are prescribed to punish deviations, these interactions lead to an overall social equilibrium in which it becomes in everyone's self-interest to adhere to the institutional setups (the rules of the game). The result, according to this approach, is an agent-level equilibrium that translates to an overall systemic equilibrium formalized as an institutional setup, or pact, such as the laws enacted by Parliament or Congress, contract enforcement procedures to conduct trade, and electoral systems. From this overall equilibrium, derived from agent-level interactions, we are said to be able to observe a system-level stability.[3]

However, when the examination of a complex historical phenomenon uses the mechanics of equilibrium analytics at the agent level, this does not reveal how policy selection and agent dynamics correlate to the change processes at the network or macro levels. For example, in accounts of endogenous institutional change, threats of revolution or coups d'état are identified as the micro-level mechanisms yielding macro-level change.[4] But revolutionary challenges are unlikely to be durable unless they penetrate the macro environment. The network linkages between multiple system levels are critical to whether enduring institutions will form after a cleavage or shock. In a study of bourgeois revolutions, historical sociologist Neil Davidson reports that uprisings are capable of being nullified "by a mixture of external pressure and internal subversion as long as they remain isolated in a world where different and hostile systems prevail" (2012, 575).[5] Revolutionary outcomes in individual states are unlikely to be secure until they reach a point of systemic irreversibility. Thus efforts in Europe to establish a republic, for example, by the Dutch in the late sixteenth century, and later by revolutionary France in the eighteenth century, were short lived and suffered numerous reversals after incurring the strong opposition of neighboring monarchs.[6] Republics couldn't survive without changes in the *macro* structure of power in Europe. The irreversibility of individual revolutionary movements depends on the international environment.

Napoleon grasped this idea, which is why he invaded Russia and risked losing most of his army in 1812. He understood, in the language of his day, that the command structure of Europe resided in its network of royal families, and that they functioned as hubs, with connections to subordinate members across the entire continent. Napoleon believed that the only way to disseminate the fundamental values of the French Revolution was to destroy the hubs of the old structure and to create a new structure, establishing himself as the central hub. His fear was that even if a few hubs of the old distributed system remained, they could restore the deleted hubs, putting the revolution in jeopardy. (And had Napoleon succeeded, he would likely have established a network governed, as we shall see, like China's.)[7]

Napoleon was proved correct by the events that followed his defeat. A reactionary Russia under Czar Nicholas I became the gendarme of nineteenth-century Europe, eventually helping the Austrians defeat the Hungarian uprising in 1848. The czar's own empire was predominantly Slavic, but he identified his interests with the fortunes of Emperor Ferdinand, a fellow monarch, the leader of the Austro-Hungarian Empire, and not with the people he ruled. The failure of Europe's 1848 revolutions, more generally, illustrates how revolutionary pacts in particular states are unlikely to survive unless they can alter the network structure's macro logic.

The restoration of political economy analysis to the fold of the larger discipline has stimulated a wealth of new research, but this book calls into question whether the continued use of rational actor assumptions and the repurposing of the same equilibrium models are the only ways to revive it (Foley 1994; Smith and Foley 2008). For example, in standard equilibrium analysis of consumer risk, responses to gradually changing conditions can be observed in linear sequences, with representative agents (i.e., consumers, households) responding to continuous, linear trends. The assumption is that change cycles typically result from the slow accumulation of modifications. But agent strategies designed to smooth out susceptibility to risk over the course of a lifetime can neither anticipate nor eliminate macro-economic shocks that affect all asset categories.

That a general equilibrium approach leaves important questions in economics unanswered was made apparent by Brian Arthur's (2014) studies of increasing returns to agglomeration economies clustered in geographical locations, namely that looking at systems dynamically, there could be typically more than one equilibrium and the solution was indeterminate. Small random events can steer the system some-times into one equilibrium, sometimes into another.

Equilibrium analysis of risk is limited by its failure to predict certain large-scale changes and thresholds, or the actions of agents affected by them. As such, it cannot offer useful depictions of the great transitions that arise from time to time and do much of the work of enabling social change.[8] Radical shifts need not require an externally administered shock but can arise from the system's internally gener-ated dynamics. In fact, regime shifts from one stable state to another occur with great regularity, as an ordered regime is driven to disorder because of unforeseen changes in agent behavior.[9] The agents react to the patterns they create, causing changes in the shared macro envir-onment that in turn trigger new waves of adaptations and responses.[10] An economy forms and changes endlessly as agents introduce new elements that are constructed out of existing ones. These changes occur with sufficient regularity in the economy that it is de facto in a state of non equilibrium.

## 2.2   CHANGE PROCESSES IN COMPLEX SYSTEMS

If the evolution of complex systems in nature were described in simi-lar terms of linear accumulations of change, then scientists who study those systems would similarly base their analysis of change on equili-brium mechanics. In fact, they do not. The presumption of equili-brium isn't helpful for understanding how agents constantly assess and reassess their actions in response to the increasingly complex behaviors of others, and how in doing so, they create and transform the environment they share.

A complex systems approach endeavors to understand the emergence of institutions and regimes (patterns and behaviors) in terms of the interactions between different self-organizing agents and networks at the micro level, as they interact with the larger, interconnected macro system. As the agents adapt their behaviors to the successive models of others, their adaptations change the decision rules of still more agents. Even when the rules of an incumbent regime remain active, complexity can amplify and intensify due to the system's internal dynamics – and when regime shifts occur, the culprit is not necessarily an externally administered shock.[11]

By comparison, equilibrium is a beautiful but superficial account of the dynamical properties of complex systems. But the information necessary to describe the internal dynamics prior to a phase transition – the intricate and dynamic webs of interactions that lead to the critical event? That information is lost.[12]

The observation that there were brief patterns of change and long patterns of stability does not mean there is an equilibrium. Long-lived historical regimes are artifacts of complex emergence in which collectively agreed upon knowledge and practices fluctuate continually through constant negotiation and contestation. We want to better understand the variations in connectivity or fluctuations in feedback within existing relationships before a threshold transpires and the system enters a critical phase, and then to understand how it behaves during a critical event – and why either system growth or breakdown occurs afterward.[13] *Resilience* is one such system-level property that we want to understand. Microbiologist David Chandler (2014) and ecologist Crawford Stanley Holling (1973) argue that *stability* is another, and illustrate that there are trade-offs between stability and resilience, although these trade-offs may not even be knowable by the agents, as they often involve epochs that exceed the lives of individual agents.

"Resilience determines the persistence of relationships within a system," writes Holling, "and is a measure of the ability of these systems to absorb changes in state variables, driving variables, and parameters, and still persist"(1973, 17). Resilience can be defined as a gauge of the maximum perturbation that a regime can withstand, and its capacity, afterward, to make adaptations that foster the next wave of transition. C. S. Holling et al. (1995) refine the definition of resilience further, pointing to (a) the degree of the disturbance that can be absorbed before a change in state occurs, and (b) the rate of recovery after a perturbation.[14]

The challenge for both physical and biological sciences is to understand systems when they behave abnormally and when the variables deviate from equilibria – and this is comparable to the great policy challenges of contemporary economics. Fortunately, a parallel scholarly endeavor spanning the natural sciences is helpful here and offers insight into the properties of complex adaptive systems. Of the global properties that an economic system shares with other complex systems, we concentrate on five.

(1) An economic system is hierarchical, in the sense that it exhibits an order of many subsystems. As a nested hierarchy, it is constructed of other simple or complex systems. The critical analytical work is to determine where, meaning at what level, a system is embedded in a wider system, and how its integration creates boundaries and constraints.

(2) It has a macro structure that is distinct from the micro levels. Macro refers to system properties that are global as distinct from micro-level behaviors. The macro is not necessarily an aggregate of what happens microscopically within the same system.

(3) It is an "open" system. The fitness or functionality of the components cannot be separated from their environment; in an open system, internal and external components are not readily separated from each other. Openness separates real, living systems from laboratory experiments or models. In the laboratory, one can design experiments whose variables are controlled and operate independently of other variables. In the real world of complex systems, we cannot control what trespasses into our experiment.

(4) It is a complex system made up of networks, and networks of networks. Change occurring within and between these networks ultimately affects the behavior of the system.[15]

(5) It evolves episodically, and exhibits phase transition dynamics. The larger the system and the more connected its components, the greater the chance that some extreme event can reframe the interactions of all the agents.

To provide an appropriate framework for understanding how an economy's structures form and change over time, it is essential to understand it as a system whose individual agents change their behaviors as the system they inhabit evolves, and that their adaptations cause changes in the system as well. If we look more closely at those five shared properties of economic systems, it will be easier to understand how they function as complex adaptive systems.

(1) *A complex system is hierarchical, in the sense that it exhibits an order of many subsystems. As a nested hierarchy, it is constructed of other simple or complex systems. The critical analytical work is to determine at what level a system is embedded in a wider system, and how its integration creates boundaries and constraints.*

The definition of *hierarchy* in complex systems research differs from its usage among social scientists. Complexity scientists use the term to explain how complex systems are composed of interrelated subsystems. "By hierarchy," explains Herbert Simon, "I do not mean a structure of power, although that may be present, but a boxes-within -boxes arrangement of subsystems" (2000, 8). Although they contain heterogeneity, hierarchies are interconnected, meaning they are *decomposable* into other hierarchical levels, or subunits, down to the lowest level of the most elementary subunit.

A system with a large number of interacting parts can be described at various levels of detail, or *scale* (such as a family unit, an extended family, a community, a village, a city, and a nation; or a lichen, a forest, a regional ecology, and a planetary system). At each scale, or level, in the system, patterns that are unique will have unique causes and consequences, and the rules of interaction may vary. Individual agents apply rules differently at different scales of a hierarchical ordering. Even if the rules do not change, they can be applied differently when agents join groups or when the group interacts with other groups (Simon 2000).

Nevertheless, while using Simon's boxes-within-boxes metaphor, we must remember that the different levels of hierarchy are all connected via feedback loops that process information both upward and downward, inward and outward. To study the dynamics at one level while dismissing as irrelevant the dynamics on different scales is misleading. Volatility may arise, for instance, when subsystems of the larger system cross paths and respond in unexpected ways. In a financial system, for example, interconnectivity can allow a serious problem in one part of the system, such as the bond, equity, or insurance market, to spill over to the rest of the financial system, either by causing problems of serious counterparty risk or by triggering a cascade of credit defaults when one insolvent institution is suddenly forced to liquidate its financial asset portfolio, thereby causing credit markets to dry up.

Furthermore, the more microscopic our description, the *less* helpful it becomes for predicting a general character. "The most detailed, but often least useful, level is the microscopic level, where the time-dependent state of each component is specified," report physicists Paolo Sibani and Henrik Jeldtoft Jensen (2013, 14). "A useful *thermodynamic* or *macroscopic* description only requires a handful of variables. . . . These do not reflect properties of individual molecules or system components, but rather describe collective, i.e., statistical, properties of the system as a whole. They become useful as gradually larger systems are considered, and for this reason are often called *emergent* properties" (14–15).[16] A developed modern economy is a type of emergence: it is a condition of a social collective not found in its individual elements, much the way a single person kicking a ball cannot play a game of soccer – the game emerges from the parts and their interactions. Large systems and large-scale change within those systems do most of the work in economic history, and thus we are most interested in them.

(2) *A complex system has a macro structure that is distinct from the micro levels. Macro refers to a network's global properties as compared to its micro-level dynamics. The macro is not necessarily an aggregate of what happens microscopically within the same system. An understanding of top-down influences is needed to fully grasp lower-level behaviors.*

Natural scientists have long warned against the penchant to seek some fundamental law from which to reconstruct the entire system. "Broken symmetry" exists in the hierarchical structures of nature, announced P. W. Anderson in his now-famous *Journal of Science* article "More Is Different." He explains that nature's "original symmetry is no longer evident" as systems grow progressively bigger, and that "the whole becomes not only more than but very different from the sum of its parts" (Anderson 1972, 395). Thus, in complex systems, "the ability to reduce everything to simple fundamental laws does not imply the ability to start from these laws and reconstruct the universe." Instead, each level must be identified and characterized through an inductive process, usually requiring specific analytical tools.

What Anderson meant by "more is different" is that the properties of the whole are not observable in the microscopic details of the system's parts. As shown in Robert Axtell's work with large-scale agent computing, the dynamics and characteristics of a system's macro properties are different from those of its components and are not reducible to agent-level variables that can be manipulated into a linear aggregation. This idea will enable us to delve into the relationship of revolution and tradition in which constituent parts are altered while the system's basic identity is maintained, which legal scholar Harold J. Berman argues (1983, 19) is the most distinctive characteristic underlying the formation of the Western legal tradition:

The history of the West has been marked by recurrent periods of violent upheaval, in which the preexisting system of political, legal, economic, religious, cultural, and other social relations, institutions, beliefs, values, and goals has been overthrown and replaced by a new one. There is by no means a perfect symmetry in these periods of great historical change; yet there are certain patterns or regularities. Each has marked

> a fundamental change,
> a rapid change,
> a violent change,
> a lasting change,
> in the social system as a whole.

Each has sought legitimacy

> in a fundamental law,
> a remote past,
> an apocalyptic future.

Each took more than one generation to establish roots.

Each eventually produced

> a new system of law,
> which embodied some of the major purposes of the revolution,
> and which changed the Western legal tradition,
> but which ultimately remained within that tradition.

The secularization of Church canon law is an example of Berman's point of social upheaval seeking legitimacy in a prior tradition. As we will see in Chapter 5, changes to canon law that began in the fifth century eventually, over the course of many centuries, influenced the secular law of all European states. Yet all the great national revolutions in European history – among them the English Civil War, the French Revolution, the Bolshevik Revolution, and the Spanish Civil War – were directed against the established Church. The great anti-clerical rebellions like the Reformation and the Enlightenment were uniquely Western phenomena. Groundwork for the Reformation was set in several countries at once, by John Wycliffe (1320–1384) in

England and Jan Hus (1369–1445) in Bohemia, and via active reform movements in almost every other country, before finally breaking out nearly a century later in 1517 with revolutionary impact in Germany. The Enlightenment became the foundation of the American, French, and English reforms, enabling industrialization to blossom across all of the countries of Western Europe and North America. The International Communist Movement that transformed Russia was formed of elements that arose in Germany and appeared in the Paris commune of 1870.

Berman observes that revolutionary changes in European history shared two related traits: first, that national revolutions had an international character; and, second, that their preconditions appeared in more than one country at once, thus initiating changes in the macro system. The great revolutions of Copernicus, Newton, and Einstein in science mirror the evolution of Western law and run in parallel with revolutionary conditions and changes in the legal order.

Yet Berman reminds us that "the legal institutions of the various nations of Europe, although they became more distinctively national and less European from the sixteenth century on, nevertheless retained their Western character"(1983, 25). No matter how much the old laws changed, a basic integrity remained in structure and form. One such example is the tradition of monarchy that has persisted for more than a millennium and which we discuss in Chapter 4. Thus the fundamental order remains recognizable as certain persistent patterns assimilate into the revolutionary one. Even when a shift occurs in the global structure of the network, a path remains connecting the new structure to the old.

The Western legal tradition is a body of knowledge that is continuously updating. Nevertheless, the patterns of its history constrain the transformative changes it has undergone. As we shall see in Chapters 4–8, even when war, that most violent experience of social discontinuity, swept away the remnants of traditional social structures, a basic source of legitimacy, often a fundamental law derived from the remote past, remained.

During the global financial crisis in 2007–2008, the greater system remained intact, even as numerous components within it, from central banks to subprime lenders and brokerages, faced collapse, investigation, or acquisition at fire sale prices by other actors. The crisis left the system unchanged but altered the structure of the regulatory framework that governs transactions within the system. Indeed, not all phase transitions in social systems have caused collapse; sometimes new classes of activity are created out of the failure of older classes, but the fundamental laws governing the system are unaltered.

A very stable system may in fact be volatile at the agent, or micro, level. In this regard, social systems don't differ from other complex systems. Despite significant turmoil and variability at the micro levels, notes Axtell (2014), complex systems frequently display long-term stationarity and can exhibit aggregate steady states. Axtell discusses social processes where "perpetual adaptation, coevolution, and strategic adjustments are observed at the agent level, while steady states obtain at the macro level" (2014, 1). Agent computing at full scale of the privately invested US economy, which employs 120 million workers, enables him to observe stationary distributions at the aggregate level, despite continuous adaptation at agent levels. He finds continuous agent-level fluctuation, as millions of job seekers change employment in every period and new firms enter the market. Yet the distribution of firm size and the scale of labor flows appear to be constant over time. The survival probability of younger firms also remains constant (Axtell 2019). Analogues in the natural sciences include viruses and bacteria, which undergo many types of equilibria during the average human life span. Within forest ecosystems, too, the proportion of foxes to rabbits can undergo many changes in reproductive cycles; sometimes there are more foxes, and this results in a reduced rabbit population, which in turn changes the population of foxes that can be sustained. All this happens while the forest does not change. Just as in the example of evolving bacteria in a living organism or a forest in a larger ecosystem, it is impossible to deduce a general theory of evolution at the macro scale of a historical epoch simply by aggregating upward from a system's constituent parts.

(3) *A complex system is an "open" system. The fitness or functionality of the components cannot be separated from their environment; nor can it be neatly divided into endogenous and exogenous forces. Openness separates real, living systems from laboratory experiments or models. In the laboratory, one can design experiments whose variables are controlled and operate independently of other variables. In the real world of complex systems, we cannot control what trespasses into our experiment.*

Openness is a characteristic of a living system because all its components, no matter how small or elementary they may be, interact with the surrounding environment, absorbing and transmitting information, resources, and energy. In cells or atoms, the effects of openness are relatively easy to comprehend; but the larger and more conglomerate the system, the more difficult it will be to observe the effects, which are the results of numerous actions and sources.

Social scientists cannot replicate open systems in a lab; nor would they be able to control the random influences of the environments that trespass into their experiments from either the systems' internal or meta-level dynamics. This is why, despite the global dissemination of information about best practices, institutional reform is rarely a smooth process. It is Anderson's broken symmetry at work. The complete "memory" of the transition paths of an evolved institution is likely to be destroyed by random events, and therefore its properties cannot be replicated from a top-down blueprint. Biology offers a helpful analogy: *Jurassic Park* aside, it is next to impossible to use DNA to recreate an extinct species. The mechanism for incubating the extracted or preserved whole DNA and sustaining its growth by sequencing the delivery of nutrition may also have to be recreated, as it too is extinct. Efforts to replicate a mammoth have encountered this very problem; a proxy for the reproductive organs of an extinct variety of the species must be found (Bhullar et al. 2015).

Moreover, the original connections between an institution's structure and function are obscured because the *function* of a surviving structure migrates, sometimes very significantly, from its original use, or it may never have been imagined or known in the first place. The full range of uses to which any innovation, social rule, or societal norm can be put is often discovered long after its initial appearance. Consider the evolution of the World Wide Web since its inception. Or how, in Europe's past, property rights and the rights of people to incorporate had religious derivations connected with collective, rather than individual, well-being. Rules governing female inheritance similarly originated to ensure lineage continuity and orderly succession, and to ensure political stability within Christendom.

Defining the essential institutions for economic development is a far more complex undertaking than economists once conceived. First, because institutions are embedded in their environments, they are themselves open systems. Second, it is nearly impossible to obtain a description of an institutional regime in which memory of the initial conditions is maintained. "A deterministic description of complex dynamical systems," caution Sibani and Jensen, "is prevented by the very large ... degrees of freedom present, usually combined with an imperfect knowledge of their interactions" (2013, 35). In the relationship between agents and structure over many repeated actions the result can be the opposite of what the agents intended.

In its earliest years, evolutionary biology concerned itself with the properties inherent in individual organisms. Today, evolution is understood not only in terms of the internal fitness of a particular species or organism – its study has advanced in ways that blur the distinctions between an individual and a species, and a species and its ecology. In the same way that the cells that constitute living structures are affected by interactions with other cells in the environment they mutually inhabit, the policies and institutions that guide the development of human societies face fitness challenges that have much to do with the changing structures of their networked interactions. As a system becomes more complex, it becomes more singular and has fewer properties in common with other systems. The subjective factors that reflect sensitivity to initial conditions make the consequences of previous choices difficult to surmount, and this reduces the probability that optimal solutions to institutional design problems exist.[17] Being unable to run the sequence of events backward to the initial state, we cannot conclude why an institution takes a particular form.

The evolutionary unfolding of life starts at the level of the simplest cells and ends with mutations passed on among individuals, mutations that are derived from encounters with their changing environments. Just as living ecologies do not have optimal species, open systems lack optimal solutions. No one would say that any particular species – a hawk, a dolphin, a lion, an elephant, or even a human being – is an optimal species toward which all other species should aspire in their particular surroundings. The evolution and fitness of any particular institution, like that of a species, is determined by its relationship with its environment. Research in biology now widely recognizes that external agents, such as bacteria and parasites, affect the dynamic interactions of the cells that produce organs and organisms, and that most mutations in biology are actually harmful.

(4) *A complex system is made up of networks, and networks of networks. Networks are unstable and prone to a wide range of feedback causing reassemblage. A meaningful understanding of networks must include the apprehension that networks exhibit nonlinear dynamics in which feedbacks and interactions are continuous. The differences of structure, meaning how the nodes are linked, will influence how information can spread. Even small differences in structure can alter the diffusion of information and affect how the system behaves.*

A complex systems approach is the ideal tool for investigating networks of historical regimes, comprised as they are of many networks of interacting components. Within any historical regime, an unlimited number of social networks can be envisioned; a virtually unlimited range of dynamical processes is possible. Simplifying complex systems into diagrams of network structure, in which nodes represent the components and lines represent their interactions, helps researchers to recognize the essential features of the interactive configuration that lead to patterns, behaviors, and emergent properties. Contemporary network science is basically an elaboration of how structure arises and influences system behavior. It seeks to identify simplifying rules or statistical properties that networks share. From the clinical models that follow, we can infer the regularities found in a range of empirical examples drawn from world economic history.

A strictly physical network, of course, differs from a social network. The Internet, a collection of physical routers and computers, exemplifies a physical network. The World Wide Web, the information that travels on them, is a social network. Similarly, a trading platform is a physical network, the stock market a social network. Although they have different properties – one is physical, the other is intangible – both networks can be represented by their components, or agents, whose relationships to one another can be depicted in graph form. The agents are depicted as *nodes* or *vertexes*; and their relationships to other nodes in the network are expressed with lines, called *edges*. Graphs can be directed or undirected; directed graphs often employ arrows to specify directions for their edges.

Social networks are made up of autonomous nodes (or agents) whose self-organization into networks can form any variety of pattern, according to the way in which they group themselves relative to their environment.[18] The patterns of interaction among agents in a network determines a network's structure, or *topology*. The number of connections a node has to other nodes is called its *degree*. The *distance* between any two nodes is measured by the number of edges that form the shortest path between them.

Because we are interested in networks of social relations that form historical regimes, we can look at network structure to capture important factors that contribute to the network's behavior. Knowing how agents interact, we can infer structure; and knowing structure, we can infer patterns of information transmission and thus infer collective behavior. How tightly knit a community of agents is, for example, will influence the types of cooperation that might arise, including the capacity for retaliation against misbehavior and the coordination for cooperative engagement, and is important for economic performance. These uses of network analysis to understand agent interactions concerning trust, cooperation, tolerance, communication, the allocation of goods and services, and the diffusion of innovations are already familiar to economists (Jackson 2010).

In the chapters that follow, we are interested in large-scale transformations in structure that occur in the formation of complex systems, such as the emergence of a state, a nation, a legal tradition, or the adaptation of disruptive innovation that changes social organizations and alters the relationships of constituent groups. In the European model, the topology that develops from agent self-organization will also determine how system change occurs through adaptation and coevolution, including through sudden, large-scale disruptions that can reconfigure the system altogether. The Chinese model is an artifice designed to improve governmental efficiency through deliberate centralization; it is also a management tool that offers the possibility to prevent the spread of unwanted innovation with surveillance from a central place. Before we discuss the fifth global property – how both economic systems and complex systems evolve episodically, through phase transitions – we will consider why there is variation, and what "logic" enables structural differences to emerge.

## 2.3   NETWORK REPRESENTATIONS OF COMPLEX SYSTEMS

Similar structures can be found in networks that give rise to entirely different phenomena; the World Wide Web, for example, exhibits a structure with large hubs (websites) that have a great many connections, as do transportation systems, academic citation networks, and marriages among political or economic elites. A vast range of naturally occurring phenomena have deep similarities because they share the property of having network structures that are not random. This is very curious, and not readily apparent. Understanding such regularities in network formation is essential to building a cohesive theory of network connectivity in social systems as well. Several theoretical network models – random, scale free, and small world – have been proposed to capture these regularities.

In a theoretical random network such as that shown in Figure 2.1 (an example of an Erdős–Rényi random network), two nodes

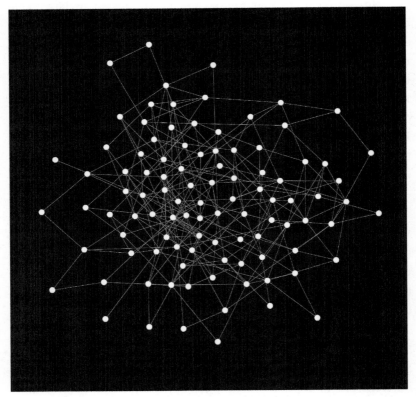

FIGURE 2.1 An Erdős–Rényi random network with 100 nodes. In an Erdős–Rényi random network, a fixed probability is established for the odds that any two nodes will randomly connect. In the above network, the probability is 0.05.

connect randomly. The degree distribution of nodes in Erdős–Rényi random networks is binomial, and it is symmetrical in form without long tails; hence, large hubs with a great number of connections are rare. Random networks can grow very large, but the average path length will remain relatively small. Such networks are of course very unlikely to exist in the real world because in nature or society agents are purposeful and rarely interact purely in a random fashion. But theoretical random models are a useful starting point to understand real-world networks, and there is always some degree of randomness in real-world networks.

More frequently, networks in nature and in society form through an evolutionary process, and this gives the early nodes an advantage for accumulating connections. And because early nodes have already accumulated and have command of more resources, they are also more "attractive" to new nodes, increasing their likelihood of making new connections. This *preferential attachment* mechanism can lead to networks that have highly skewed degree distributions; a few large hubs connect many other nodes.[19] Scale-free models have been used to characterize such networks.

The degree distributions of scale-free networks are said to follow a *power law*, which means that as they grow, their spread occurs in constant, proportional scale. Figure 2.2 depicts a scale-free network generated by the Barabási–Albert model (Barabási and Albert 1999). The model shows that node growth and preferential attachment can give rise to a scale-free network, suggesting that these two mechanisms may underlie the evolution of their topologies.[20] Although perfect scale-free networks with a strict power-law degree distribution are rare in the real world (Broido and Clauset 2018), the existence of large hubs in networks, and the evolutionary process of network formation, are useful for analyzing network behavior and can shed light on their dynamic processes.

Human communications and interactions are also often local and clustered. We might intuit that such local clustering would

FIGURE 2.2 A scale-free network of 300 nodes. The generation of this scale-free network is based on the Barabási–Albert model (1999). The probability of preferential attachment is 0.6.

prevent information diffusion across the whole network. But, in reality, there are many examples of people connecting to total strangers via a small number of steps; many social networks are said to exhibit the *small-world* phenomenon of "six degrees of separation" (Travers and Milgram 1969; Barabási 2003; Watts 2004). Network scientists have used computer models to explain this phenomenon. Duncan J. Watts and Steven H. Strogatz (1998) provided the first model to illustrate how a network can have both a high clustering coefficient that is associated with local clusters and short average path length by adding a few random links to a regular ring network, as shown in Figure 2.3. These random links serve as bridges between clusters and reduce the "distance" for information flows from one node to another,

(a)                                        (b)

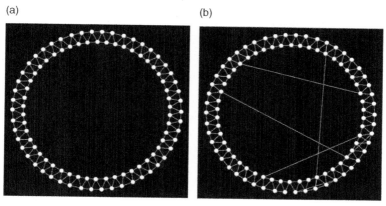

FIGURE 2.3  A regular ring network (a) and a small-world network based
on the 1998 Watts-Strogatz model (b). By adding a few random links to
a regular network, they show that a network can retain high local
connectivity and also have relatively short average path length, two key
characteristics of small-world networks.

enabling the spread of information. Many natural and social networks – for example, the brain's neuron networks, friendship networks, online apps like Facebook and WeChat, and costarring
networks in the entertainment industry – exhibit small-world characteristics, namely high clustering coefficients and relatively short
average path length.

Human-designed networks almost always have certain structures for some intended purpose. For example, transportation systems
often assume a hub-and-spoke structure like that shown in Figure 2.4.
Bureaucratic administrative systems and corporate organizations
similarly operate by means of a hierarchical, hub-and-spoke structure.
While transportation networks are designed to move people or things
efficiently across large areas, organizational networks generally aim to
facilitate communication and management. They can also imply
power distribution, as do social networks in general.

An agent's (node's) "power" or "importance" is implied by its
metaphorical *centrality* in a network. A simple measure of centrality
is the number of connections a node has, called *degree centrality*.

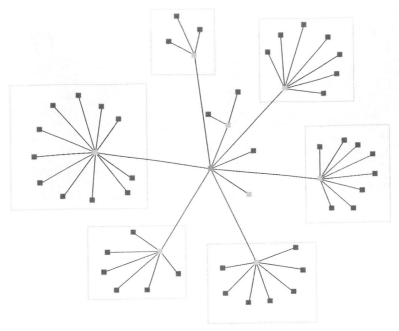

FIGURE 2.4 A simple hub-and-spoke model (Linstedt 2010). In a hub-and-spoke network, the nodes usually have only a few direct connections. This contrasts with scale-free networks, whose large hubs have a great many connections.

Degree centrality can be interpreted as an agent's direct local influence. In contrast, *eigenvector centrality*, calculated using an iterative procedure, captures the idea of how central an agent is according to how central the agent's neighbors are. For example, a CEO in a company may not have a high degree centrality, having few direct connections within the corporation, but usually has high eigenvector centrality, being connected to many others indirectly through their own direct connections. Thus eigenvector centrality can be interpreted as an agent's "global" influence. Another useful measure is called *betweenness centrality*, which represents how often a given node falls along the shortest path between two other nodes. The node with the highest betweenness centrality often has the most control over the flow of information within the network. Nodes whose deletion would disconnect the network are called *cut-points*; should they be eliminated, the network would become two or more unconnected subnetworks.

While a node's centrality may suggest "power," the concept of network centralization describes the distribution of "power" in a network. A network's centralization can be simply measured by the variations of node centrality. Among organizational networks and other human-designed networks, star-shaped networks are the most centralized, with one actor dominating all others. Ring networks and fully connected networks are the most decentralized since all agents share equal centrality. Different organizational designs can lead to different degrees of centralization, which can have implications for power dynamics. Highly centralized networks suggest that certain agents have dominant control; in less centralized networks, the agents share control. There is also a colloquial understanding that a decentralized network is likely to be more robust to system-wide failure and that polycentric models of social organization (e.g., US- or EU-style structures, or the mixed regimes that occupy East Asia) have characteristics of robustness and adaptability.[21]

Network structure, or topology, affects how information diffuses on a network. The existence of large hubs in a scale-free network and the existence of a few bridges between clusters and short average path length in a small-world network can facilitate information flow.[22] They help information originated from any part of the network to travel and spread to other parts of the network. In a star network, information can spread quickly through the central node to all parts of the network, but the central node can also control whether or not to pass on information originated from other nodes. Similarly, cut-points in a network can help information spread across its different parts, but they can also control information flow.

Of course, real-world networks rarely fit perfectly into these theoretical models or forms, and many may have a mixture of the characteristics we have just explored. Nevertheless, the theoretical models and forms allow us to infer the principles or laws that underlie their construction, even without being able to specify their points of origin. And if we know the patterns of interaction, we can infer how the network structure will evolve.

## 2.4 DIFFERENCES IN THE NETWORK STRUCTURE OF CHINA AND THE WEST

Using the theoretical models of the previous section as a point of reference, we can draw certain inferences about historical networks and their behavior. The Chinese bureaucracy and the structure of imperial authority made for a network designed to facilitate administration and governance of a far-flung empire. It had a hierarchical, hub-and-spoke structure, as shown in Figure 2.4, much like the administrative network of a modern corporation. We will explore in Chapters 4 and 6 how the central node (the emperor and the court) was linked to other important nodes (especially the mandarinate), which were local hubs themselves. This network structure enabled the emperor to coordinate the actions of the Confucian officialdom, the military, the local governors, the local gentry, the priests, and the imperial bureaucracy. The network, however, was also highly centralized; the emperor, situated at the top of the hierarchy, had the highest eigenvector and betweenness centralities, and was a cut-point as well. These features of the network had implications for information flows and innovation in the Chinese dynasties, and for dynastic robustness.

The structure of authority in the Western system was very different. The networks that formed to legitimate authority relationships in Europe after the fall of the Roman Empire had self-organized over time, assisted by a tradition of communitarian rule making. Power in Europe was more decentralized within royal dynasties and aristocratic houses that over time became interconnected through marriage and trade to form clusters. Although no single dynasty was so powerful that it could control the others, a small number of lineages tended to accumulate greater power over more area as their wealth and resources grew. They also gained more connections than others to become dominant hubs in the network, and their connections likely provided bridges between clusters. Thus the European authority network should exhibit features of both small-world and scale-free networks.

We reconstruct the marriage network between European royal houses to show that, indeed, the network had a mixture of small-world and scale-free characteristics. We will explore in Chapters 4 and 6 how these features created different behaviors from those in the Chinese system. These features of the European network made it more stable at the macro level. They also enabled information that originated in any part of the network to flow to other parts of the network without a need to pass through a central node. This has important implications for the coordination and spread of potentially disruptive ideas. In both systems, the high centrality of the key actors was a source of increasing returns, so understandably these powerful actors were likely to seek the network's perpetuation.

This brings us to a fifth global property that economic systems share with complex adaptive systems.

## 2.5   CHANGE THRESHOLDS AND PHASE TRANSITIONS

(5) *A complex system evolves episodically; transitions can be abrupt, occurring in fits and starts. Depending on the network's structure, some micro-level transformations may leave the macro system unchanged and even expand preexisting capacity. The larger the system and the more connected its components, the greater the chance that contagion can spread and some extreme event – a phase transition – will reframe the interactions of the agents. Some changes in connectivity can be system preserving, but if a network is a highly centralized hierarchy, it may not be robust against the loss of a central node whose deletion may cause the demise of the previously ordered system.*

The continual coevolution of a network's internal behaviors, functions, and information transmissions, coupled with its connections to increasing numbers of other networks, can reach a threshold when a sudden perturbation of any size can cause a rapid transformation, or *phase transition*. In the natural world, the dynamics of phase transition can take many forms. When water freezes into ice or boils into a vapor, when gas turns to condensate, when cells metastasize, or when molten lava turns to rock – these are all phase transitions.[23] Consider the example of a pond in winter that over the course of a few hours freezes over entirely. Ice crystals have emerged suddenly and simultaneously across the system, which had attained a change threshold of self-organized criticality, "in the sense that all members of the system influence each other" (Jensen 1998, 3). In biology, a phenotypic manifestation of the genetic defect, i.e., the risk of genetic birth defect, occurs when a specific threshold level is exceeded. The financial system also offers examples of phase transition, among them the collapse of global trade in 1929 and the financial system crash of 2007–2008.

Other large-scale "contact" networks – various food webs, the brain, and cellular, genetic, and neural networks – can produce phase transitions such as extinction, epidemics, mutations, and metastasis. Large social networks such as religious sects, social media and protest movements have dynamics that can underlie the phase transitions of opinion formation, fads, and technology and belief diffusion. Cooperation, the transfer of the norms of reciprocity among small groups to broader social networks, has also been described in terms of phase transitions.

While a phase transition can transform the system's topology, it is that same topology, created of its components' interactions, which will determine whether those component networks survive the perturbation, or fail. The resilience to survive a shock depends as much on the system's topology as on the impact of the shock. As noted, phase transitions may also be system cripplers if a critical hub has been removed and the remaining nodes fail to reconnect.

## Network Evolution: The Role of Percolation or Cascades in Economic Transitions and Regime Shifts

The point at which changes occurring within a system cause it to reach a critical state, or *change threshold*, is a research question of fundamental importance in economic history.[24] To gain a better grasp of this question, we must first recall that self-organized groupings of components contribute to the development of network structure, just as that structure contributes to the system's behavior. Topology (structure) and behavior (flow) are key ideas here, and both have to do with the different kinds of phase transitions that are applicable to the evolution of economic systems.

Physicists and mathematicians draw important differences between changes in structure and changes in flow; the former are described as percolation, and the latter as cascades. Percolation can inform about structure, and cascades about flow and the behaviors of the nodes within that structure. Percolation has no flow, but it can be a precondition to host future cascades. Percolations and cascades are models from the natural sciences. Our experiments will be in the lab of historical case studies.[25] The goal is to use one set of models, those from the laboratory of natural science, to help uncover the determinants of history's great transitions.

It is difficult to observe percolation as an experiment in a real-world situation. Its static connectivity is depicted via lattice models that don't even exist in organically or socially arranged systems.[26] So what do the formations of giant clusters in social networks have in common with the mathematical network dynamics of percolation and resulting cascades? As we shall see, in economic transitions the structure and the flow of behaviors also exhibit different dynamic properties. The critical point in a percolation threshold is when long-range connectivity first appears among large, *previously unconnected* clusters, such as when an invention sees market or a tweet goes viral, or a single event such as the immolation that started the Arab Spring has catalytic consequences.[27]

All major social transitions require transformations of the pathways of existing connectivity – some form of *percolation transition* – which enables sweeping contagion to occur. For such phenomena, the network structure, its topology, matters more than the independent activities of a specific set of influential variables – the size of an uprising may matter less than the receptivity of the network to its influence. There exists one paramount rule: structure significantly affects how ideas and behavior spread on a network. The notion that form precedes function is another way to understand the distinct role of a network's topology.

We can think of percolations as those differences in network topology (form) that create sensitivities to new ideas or behaviors that can lead to fundamentally new systems of social organization (function). Once the structural transformations acquire solidity, or stationarity, cascades that take the form of volatile behavioral change can transpire. As a depiction of the structure of a system's underlying connectivity, percolation has analogies in political economy. In fact, we could argue that percolation has generated the most historically meaningful transitions, those leading to fundamentally new systems of social organization. This kind of long-term secular transformation corresponds to Marxist social theory, the idea that socioeconomic change precedes the successful formation of new political and ideological formulas. Marxism itself, with its new political and ideological formulas, diffused rapidly on the global landscape that had been reshaped by industrialization.

The takeoff to sustained modern growth is found in the ongoing formation of webs of interconnected units of production. Eventually they became a massive web, a giant cluster, a network of industrialists and their enterprises stretching across Europe. Industrialization didn't appear at a single moment in time, nor was it characterized by a discrete event or technological input, or triggered by the sequential momentum of investments from the first steam engine onward. It was a structural transformation, but without a tipping point; there was no grain of sand that caused the system to avalanche. In this respect, the quantity and quality of the links were critical, not the timing of a specific trigger or shock.[28]

Other early percolations – changes in the economic structure – that led to changes in beliefs and behavior are the first agricultural revolution (sometimes called the Neolithic Revolution), which transformed human societies from hunting and gathering to farming, and occurred worldwide beginning around 10,000 BCE. A more parochial agricultural revolution of the early medieval period enabled the heavy clay soils of Northern Europe to support a larger population, increasing the returns to capital over that of labor, and making feudal lordship more profitable. Another agricultural revolution, which occurred in eighteenth-century Britain, is closely associated with industrialization and helped precipitate massive urbanization; this again altered the relationship between capital and labor, and changed the structure of social relations and the diffusion of information. Similarly, we can look back at the period spanning the early eleventh through fourteenth centuries, when the spread of commerce in an agricultural and predominately rural environment changed beliefs among dwellers in the rapidly growing Italian city states about the relationship of human agency and the natural world. These beliefs took hold and spread out into the Burgundian heartland.[29] But as with the agricultural revolutions and industrialization, there is no precise date when the diffusion of Aristotelian logic tipped the medieval world into the Renaissance with its acceptance of human centrality in the universe. A percolation may not be recognizable until the remolded structure hosts the cascades that reconfigure beliefs, customs, or modes of conduct.

## What Do Cascades Explain?

Cascades are more readily observable than percolations and more widely understood in social processes. They are easier to identify since these processes usually have discrete temporal elements that are useful for pinpointing and establishing a sequencing, and can be recorded since they transpire during discrete time frames. In epidemiology, the essential concern is the time progression from an initial infection to an outbreak (the percolation transition) that then cascades across populations. Similarly, we can generally date the start of the Reformation from when Martin Luther's *Ninety-Five Theses* were translated from Latin to German and printed for general distribution, just as we trace the cascading Arab Spring or #MeToo movement back to a particular event or tweet.[30] An identifiable trigger initiates sequential action. Cascades are relevant to such questions as changing fashions, beliefs (social norms about same-sex marriage, for example), tolerance, and the acceptance of scientific claims or discoveries. They are frequently noted in processes of diffusion, such as the sudden and unexpected outbreak of uprisings or the success or failure of social innovations.

If we imagine the nodes as individuals, and consider a social movement or a disease moving across their social network, we can envision more easily the cascades of contagion that diffuse along the network's structure.[31] Cascades have been observed as sudden bursts of creativity – in long-awaited reforms, such as the tearing down of the Berlin Wall or the collapse of the Soviet Union; or in the rapid adaptation of new technology such as the telegraph, telephone, radio, television, and Wi-Fi in communication technology, or the steam engine, the internal combustion engine, and eventually jet engines in transportation. Infectious medicine offers numerous examples of cascades in which an identifiable event sets off another that triggers an outbreak. Arctic thaw may mark the first outbreak of a cascading global environmental meltdown. The creation of a major physical infrastructure, such as the Hoover Dam, can initiate a chain reaction and subsequent investments – a cascading effect – that reconfigure the economy of an entire region. The introduction of a new technology, such as the internal combustion engine or the computer, can trigger a chain or cascade of complementary innovations. But while cascades may be more readily observable and understood in social processes than percolations, they cannot be used to describe the underlying process that enables the actual unfolding of *major* transitions such as the Renaissance, the Enlightenment, and the industrialization of Europe.

Cascades of failure and collapse can also occur when failure in one node induces failures in neighboring nodes, resulting in a large number of failures relative to the network size. Such failures occur in power grids, metal fatigue, and in the food chain, and more often than not cause deleterious discontinuous outcomes, such as a widespread power outage, a catastrophic accident, or the loss of a species. Each assumes a given structure that is the precondition for the diffusion of failure. Institutional transitions, such as that from a planned economy to a market economy, may also transpire as a cascade, in which one reform leads rapidly to others.

## Exogeneity versus Endogeneity in Complex Networks

A phase transition occurs because of self-organized criticality *within* the system. At some threshold, the accumulation of snow on a mountainside can trigger an avalanche, or the addition of sand can cause a downrush of the sandpile. Both the snow and the added sand are part of the system, not external to it. Despite the intervening stimulus of the avalanche, the external force of gravity, to which the system is subject, persists. This holds as well for dynamic economic systems, which experience tipping points arising "as a result of their own internal interactions" (Sibani and Jensen 2013), without external stimulus (although the equilibrium system models of conventional economic analysis would require the introduction of one). Financial crises generated by a system's internal dynamics occur regularly in the wake of periods of intensive growth, when investor exuberance maintains the system in a far-from-equilibrium state. Yet when disturbances finally do unfold, the agents typically look for external explanations, turning a blind eye to their own irrational expectations.

That blindness is explained in part because observations of agent-based equilibrium are insufficient approximations of these system-level change processes. Although changes at the local level are consistent with the imperatives set up at macro level, the system's macro structure, its topology, is the result of relationships that over time have shaped actors, organizations, and states. Meanwhile, the participants continue to act locally, with little notion of the globally transformative impacts of their actions. The percolation transition, while it is ongoing, may not be recognizable at the time. Much as tectonic energy builds up over eons and is released by a sudden earthquake, there are many transition processes in economic history that evolved into a critical state over long periods, longer than the life spans of individual agents. The intellectual forces that set off the scientific revolution near the end of the Renaissance, and the Enlightenment, can be traced to tendencies within medieval Christian theology; the political independence of law is traceable to feudalism; the strengthening of dynastic lineages to female rights of inheritance in the West and to the formalization of the harem system of consorts and concubines of Imperial China; the English Industrial Revolution back to increased yields in agricultural; and so forth. Therefore, looking at historical change through the lens of agent-level equilibria, we might not observe the high degree of synchronicity that occurs in large-scale regime transitions when an entire class of correlated institutions disappears, creating space for new types of regime to emerge.

Obviously, the tools of statistical physics can't be used to predict the precise occurrence of societal phase transitions, such as a regime change, a collapse of trust within a network, an outburst of ethnic violence, fashion fads, or the explosive adaptation of a new technology. But even without being able to quantify the laws underlying these kinds of network transitions, we can categorize these phenomena in ways that open important research vistas on unexplored patterns of social organization.

There is little uniformity in how phase transitions operate in different contexts. Systems drive themselves into critical states, but at the critical points, no common characteristic events exist. The complex spatial and temporal structures that characterize one system in transition don't replicate the properties of the critical points of other systems.

## 2.6 TRANSFORMATIVE CHANGE AND NETWORKS IN WORLD HISTORY

In delving into the connections between network topology and network behavior in economic history, there will be deviations from traditional notions of cause and effect because the outcome does not hinge on structure being exogenous; rather, exogeneity depends on where we draw the boundaries of the system. In a complex system, nothing is self-contained. This is openness, remember. The characteristics of a particular network topology, such as small-world, are now well understood, but what triggers the emergence of those characteristics is not. Where do small-world properties come from? Are short average path lengths (those denser local connections) a response to a perturbation, or do agents act in anticipation, creating short path lengths to be prepared for possible changes to the environment? Even without being able to explain why Europe's is a small-world governance structure and China's is a star-shaped network, we can infer that these variations will make certain patterns of development more likely than others.

To identify their critical regularities, we should study networks through their global, or overall, properties. Births and deaths of entire categories of regime types commonly occur in waves of synchronicity; democracy and authoritarianism during the twentieth century, for example, have come and gone in waves. The reason for the synchronicity of fads, styles, beliefs, norms, and patterns of cooperation is part of a much larger question concerning how network structures, and the flows of behaviors within them, originate, interact, coevolve, and differentiate themselves through evolutionary processes.

Network science offers leverage over questions that standard social science models cannot, and enables us to interpret economic change processes in ways that recognize nonlinearity and the connections between structural and behavioral change. With these distinctions in mind, we can gain a deeper grasp of two critically important and strongly correlated phenomena of contemporary political economy: the Great Divergence of East and West, and the global impact of China's contemporary and unprecedented economic transformation.

## Problem Solving and Network Structure

The consequences of network structure for collective behavior are largely unexplored. What underlying economic incentives govern the emergence of structural regularities in the economy? What role does higher-order interdependence play across links within the network structure? We rely on causal mechanisms from economic history that can help us to delve into how various network structures can either constrain or facilitate individual and collective problem solving, and further, how problem solving, in turn, affects structure. Structure arises as a way to solve the information problems that collectivities share, and is also a source of learning by people trying to overcome the obstacles they encounter within their environments – for example, as a means to solve a locally significant optimization problem, such as the trade-off between maximal connectivity and the cost of wiring the network. The relationships between system structures, transformation processes, and agent behavior are largely unchartered. We are nonetheless heading into these waters, but equipped with conceptual tools that have illuminated parallel dynamics and similar change processes.

NOTES

1. In economic historian Douglass North's original proposition, institutions are "the humanly devised constraints that shape human interaction" and the "rules of the game" (1990, 3). This insight led early work in new institutional economics to focus on exogenous constraints (or focus exogenously, given rational choice "game forms"). But it has become apparent that *institutions as rules of the game* cannot, by themselves and through

decree, constrain behavior. North's *institutions as rules* thesis didn't apply the concept of equilibrium, although it was implicit in his rules of the game. The concept of *institutions as equilibria* of strategic games, in which rule-based institutions are the mechanisms by which people are incentivized to follow certain behaviors and practices, is a natural correlate to the original proposition. According to the expanded theory, a "regularity of behavior" is the endogenous motivator that creates and sustains an institution (Shepsle 1979, 2006).

2. For example, to understand economic growth, economists seek an equilibrium in which an economy's capital stock per worker, its level of real GDP per worker, and its efficiency of labor all grow at the same proportional rate. Once the capital–output ratio is equal to its balanced-growth equilibrium value, the economy is on its balanced-growth path.

3. Philosophers Frank Hindriks and Francesco Guala (2015) call for combining the two approaches in one framework, noting that the regularities of behavior to which all members of society agree are difficult to separate from the rules, and that it is unrealistic to say that the rules are redundant and that only actions matter. A *rules in equilibria* approach that recognizes how institutions help players reach coordination and economize on cognitive effort, they insist, is preferable to either the *institutions as rules* or the *institutions as equilibria* approach.

4. A mechanism refers to a process by which something occurs; it is a description of social processes.

5. In Davidson (2012), social revolutions involve a thorough transformation of social/technical relationships.

6. In the Netherlands, the Republic of the Seven United Provinces (1581–1795) was connected to the system of royalty via an elected *Stadholder* from the House of Orange. The Dutch exited the Europe-wide system of royalty after revolting (1568–1648) against the Roman Catholic Philip II of Spain, their lawful, hereditary ruler. The revolt led to the formation of the Dutch Republic (United Provinces), one of the first European republics of the modern era. The *Staten-Generaal* tried without success to find a suitable royal Protestant protector; the United Provinces finally resolved on electing a titular leader. In 1806 the Netherlands reverted and became a constitutional monarchy.

7. Alexis de Tocqueville ([1856]1955) remarked that French economists of the late eighteenth century admired China's centralized political structure and governance by a meritocratic civil service.

8. Examples of thresholds in economics are dynamic system models with multiple equilibria.

9. The term *regime shift* is frequently used in ecology and describes large, abrupt, and persistent changes in a system's structure or function.

10. In a similar vein, Hayek frequently criticized mainstream economics for limiting the notion of competition to a description of an equilibrium state of affairs. He shared with the Austrian tradition doubts about the utility of equilibrium on the grounds that it excludes the possibility of change in the structure of production. Equilibrium analysis minimizes both the role of innovation and the importance of motivation for entrepreneurial discovery. At best, it treats the sources of structural transformation as exogenous. In an equilibrium system, there would be no reason for any one agent to act differently from any other. Instead, Hayek insisted on stressing competition as a process rather than an outcome; and he posited an alternative concept in which competition brings the discovery of new knowledge and helps eliminate errors without there being any systemic tendency toward equilibrium.

11. It is no wonder then that we are always surprised when experts are overtaken by events that they missed, when their habitual frame of reference is to look for stable balances that produce equilibrium. Policy planners rarely possess long-term time series with sufficient data to depict shifts between alternative states or to detect the sources of tipping points. They rarely have data to capture the critical change processes of transition, in part because the administrators of the incumbent regime collect data to monitor system-stabilizing indexes of performance, according to their own stability-seeking priorities. The same reasoning helps explain why data can't be found on products that can transform markets, organizations, and incumbent companies. Markets that don't yet exist can't be analyzed – this is why the data collected to assess the prospects for disruptive innovation of incumbent markets tend to be of little value to those companies that dominate existing supply chains. Corporations have been known to buy up patents and small companies to suppress innovation and inventions. They invest in

analysis to detect innovation that could spell lower profits for themselves. But their success is uneven.

12. Transitions can occur even if the macro-level rules upon which the system's stability is based are not breached. For example, the Renaissance changed the perceptions of the individual in their relationship to nature, and the Reformation to the Church and to the Divine, but the system of social stability based upon hereditary monarchy did not disappear until the twentieth century.

13. Even geological formations, seemingly stable physical systems, exhibit fluctuations before a threshold event such as an earthquake.

14. Holling and environmental scientist Lance Gunderson (2002, 25–62) further link the distinction between resilience and stability to the institutional dynamics of complex systems.

15. For efforts to identify the full range of characteristics that economies share with other complex adaptive systems, see Arthur (2014); Beinhocker (2006); and Johnson et al. (2017).

16. Emergence describes the process through which a system acquires new structures and behaviors that its individual components did not possess. Behavior refers to individual components of the mechanism exhibited by individual nodes of networks.

17. Systems theory differs from complex adaptive systems theory. Systems theory seeks to establish general characteristics or laws that all system share. Complex adaptive systems can exhibit a wide range of unique dynamic behaviors. Consequently there is not yet a theory of complex systems.

18. The behaviors of agents and the patterns their behaviors create are not readily captured by the approximate differential equations of market dynamics.

19. When we say a degree distribution is skewed we compare it with a normal distribution, which has a symmetrical bell-shaped curve and is associated with a random network. Even in a random network, there are some nodes with higher degrees than others. In a network with a highly skewed degree distribution, the likelihood of finding nodes with very high degrees is greater than in a random network with a normal degree distribution.

20. Albert-László Barabási and Réka Albert (1999) first used a computer simulation to demonstrate that a power-law degree distribution can emerge by growing a network through a mechanism called *preferential*

*attachment.* Preferential attachment refers to a node's growth relative to its current degree – the more connections it has, the more attractive it appears to other nodes and the more connections it will draw, and so on. Thus, over time some of the nodes gain greater connection density and command more resources than other nodes, and these become large hubs.

21. Sociologist Linton Freeman (1977; 1978–1979) put forward the concept of *centrality* as important to a network's evolution.

22. Nisha Mathias and Venkatesh Gopal (2001) use a computer model to show how the choice between maximal connectivity and the cost of connecting – which might mean the number of cables or wires in a physical network or the effort put into schmoozing with a number of intermediaries in a social network – can result in various propensities of network topologies. A starlike hub-and-spoke pattern, such as a typical air route network with a few large hubs, is engineered when travelers would want to minimize the number of legs; hence minimal wiring is preferred.
    A small-world roadlike structure, with long bridge links, as well as short average paths, will be engineered when travelers would want to minimize the mileage; hence, a preference for maximal connectivity. Root (2013, 116–17) discusses the trade-off between maximal and minimal wiring in historical regimes.

23. Percolation thresholds and percolation transitions are discussed in Achlioptas, D'Souza, and Spencer (2009).

24. Change in a stable system can be described by a normal probability distribution, expressed as a bell curve, with the highest point on the curve, or top of the bell, being the most probable event in a series of data. All other possible occurrences are equally distributed around the most probable event, creating a downward-sloping line on either side of the peak.

25. Detailed accounts of critical networks that represent the military, political, and economic power of historical regimes are possible using computational capabilities already familiar to many branches of science. The reconstruction over long periods of premodern Chinese and European social networks, the subjects of Chapters 4–6, hinges on sources that are just beginning to be quantified, such as the digitally enhanced network analysis of China's Tang dynasty elites provided by historian Nicolas Tackett (2014). Johannes Preiser-Kapeller (2015), in the Division for Byzantine Research of the Institute for Medieval Research at the Austrian Academy of Sciences Vienna, has used computational methodology to

explore previously unknown patterns in the unfolding of history. The institute has applied the tools of visualization, network, and qualitative analysis to medieval social and spatial networks in a number of case studies. In the project "Complexities and Networks in the Medieval Mediterranean and the Near East" (Preiser-Kapeller 2015), a change of ruler in one year increases the probability of a change of ruler in the five years that follow, for example, the upheavals among the political elites that permanently weakened the Byzantine Empire on the eve of its demise. The importance of stable succession rules to long-term economic growth is discussed in Chapter 4. Eventually, simulations of structure, with data from historical sources, such as correspondence, genealogies, the signatures on treaties, the role calls in ancient assemblies, and the commissions of military officers, will clarify how ideas and opinion flow through society. Even without numerically precise graphs of the network connectivities of historical regimes, we do have thousands of recorded observations by both contemporaries and historians to work with that can help us identify certain characteristics of regime stability and resilience to change.

26. A percolation transition can transform a system's structure by creating a giant system-wide cluster (Lee, Cho, and Kahng 2016). A percolation transition is identified in Achlioptas, D'Souza, and Spencer (2009); Chen, Zheng, and D'Souza (2012); and Chen and D'Souza (2011). As the individual components connect gradually to one another and form more and larger groups of clusters, the system itself, on a macroscopic scale, edges toward a critical threshold; at that point the nodes form a giant cluster of connections, with new linkages emerging simultaneously across all levels of the system until every node is connected to every other node. Can China's rise affect such a system-transforming percolation of the system of international relations?

27. The condition for a percolation threshold is met when the average degree increases to 1, and this occurs when a certain density of connections is reached.

28. Karoly Mike (2017) discusses the role of economic theory in economic development and emphasizes that institutions largely independent of the economy – in religion, science, and the arts – can critically influence production and exchange processes, and responsiveness to innovation.

29. Unlike other identifiable moments in history, such as the purported nailing of the *Theses* on the church door at Wittenberg (commemorated each year as Reformation Day), the tearing down of the Berlin Wall, a tweet from Tahrir Square, or the appearance of a primary case in infectious disease, we cannot date the exact onset of the Renaissance or the Enlightenment. But when they were named and first observed in scholarly literature can be dated.

30. The famous episode of Luther nailing his *Ninety-Five Theses* to the door of All Saints' Church in Wittenberg on October 31, 1517, is likely apocryphal. But we do know that his ideas spread rapidly throughout Germany and Europe. The contagion began in January 1518, when friends of Luther translated his *Theses* from Latin into German, after which they were printed and widely distributed in pamphlet form.

31. Whether the contagion is passed to neighbors will be determined by probabilistic rules. These can be studied statistically by determining, for instance, the largest percentage of nodes that are infected at the peak of the outbreak (communication with physicist Eduardo López, March 24, 2018).

# 3 Human Evolutionary Behavior and Political Economy

A considerable literature on the economics of networks addresses different types of diffusion, such as the spread of behaviors, opinions, ideas, fads, learning, innovations, and diseases. Researchers utilize various methods, including field experiments, laboratory experiments, and econometrics (Bramoullé, Galeotti, and Rogers 2016). Theoretical work in network formation has explored behavior in the context of repeated games. In a more practical vein, research in societies where formal institutions do not function effectively finds that social networks are likely to fill the gaps, coordinating a wide range of activities. These studies, mostly field experiments, allow researchers to better understand why individuals join groups and how they are affected by the preferences of others through peer monitoring, enforcement, and risk sharing within communities.

As Chapter 2 explained, different kinds of linkage patterns, such as small-world or centralized connectivity, account for differences in information diffusion in complex systems. Understanding of the connectivity patterns can be broken down further into two related issues. The first is the formation of structure and the properties of connectedness that are related to network topology, which was the topic of the previous chapter. The second is connectedness at the level of behavior, essentially how the actions of each individual agent have consequences for the outcomes of every other agent in the network and across the system.

We have been learning that policies and practices aimed at reducing poverty are most successful when they engage peer-to-peer incentives, and when they go beyond individual assistance and help peer groups lead their own changes. Programs that strive to build the capacity of communities to improve general well-being by engaging

peer-to-peer monitoring and emulation have been the standout performers in the development field, regardless of the cultural milieu in
which they are introduced. In this chapter, we will explore why programs for reforming institutions and improving general welfare in
areas as diverse as poverty alleviation, workforce development, entrepreneurship, criminal justice reform, early learning, and child welfare
are more likely to succeed if policy reforms align with core elements
that govern group cognition. We will also learn that those same properties that contribute to small-group survival can impair our ability to
cope with a rapidly changing environment.

## 3.1    LATER IS DIFFERENT

At the end of the Cold War, when Francis Fukuyama declared history
to be over, the global hegemony of democracy and market economies
was gaining considerable validation from empirical trends, and
seemed absolute. The Soviet Union was near collapse, socialism in
Sweden was undergoing a structural crisis, French socialism had suffered reversals, and there was democratic consolidation in Japan, the
Philippines, South Korea, and Taiwan. In 1989, events seemed to be
consistent with the logic that countries in transition could proceed in
one direction only, toward liberal democracy, whose rivals on the
world stage were being routed.[1]

Yet one has only to look at the dynamics of institutional variation in fast-growing, highly interconnected states in the developing
world to see that political reform frequently lags behind market-led
economic growth. Many fast-growing economies and modernizing
societies have not made a transition to democracy, suggesting that
the link between the two is, at best, tenuous and, at worst, teleological
(Root 2013). The pernicious effects of the "end of history" tautology
can be seen in the record of failed US military interventions that had
aimed to promote a particular vision of modernization.

It turns out, this concept, the end of history, conflicts with
much of our knowledge of natural systems – that they exist in a time-
bound framework and that the arrow of time creates path

dependencies that shape the formation of all living things, including institutions. The consequences arising from social, political, and economic processes that operate at different timescales may be difficult to reconcile or surmount for long periods, even decades. In data processing, the time it takes to receive new data will alter the overall content. In agent-based simulations, a lag in the arrival or performance of one variable will affect every other agent on the landscape. If one agent is delayed and another agent is not, their relationship will be altered and they will not be on equal terms. This will affect the subsequent context and outcome of their interactions.[2] Political scientists John Padgett and Walter Powell observe that "in the short run, actors create relations; in the long run, relations create actors" (2012, 2). Living organisms would all be the same if time were not present to craft and form behaviors and structures so that every organism, every creature, every place, every country, every philosophy is different. The variations contribute to global development. They may in fact be its central drivers.

## 3.2   EVOLVING PROPERTIES OF GLOBAL CONNECTIVITY

Evidence is accumulating that the global political economy is not moving in only one direction. In some nations with little progress on political liberty, living standards are rising to those already attained by the first generation of industrializers.[3] In countries as diverse as China, Saudi Arabia, Russia, Singapore, and Turkey, the economic gap with the West is closing – but not the gap in political freedom or human rights. Meanwhile, the same China that enjoys the advantages of international law and organization continues to contest the legitimacy of the international order's core liberal values. Much of the former Soviet Union has relapsed into authoritarianism, and the end of dictatorships in certain Muslim countries doesn't necessarily mean that pluralistic democracy is the preferred alternative. Political Islam is finding a safe haven in an economically open Turkey, and Turkey's example is shaping the aspirations of emerging democracies throughout the Middle East, making liberal economic reform unpopular and politically unfeasible. The under-lying societal dynamics of these hybrid regimes bear little resemblance to prior democratic variants, lacking such essential traits as competitive and multiparty elections, the right of assembly, an independent judiciary, and a free media. They remain closer to the autocracies they once were than to the liberal states it was hoped they would become. Moreover, the emerging middle classes exhibit forbearance of authoritarian rule, skepticism about political equality, and indifference to environmental sustainability.

The dominant models of political economy can explain some global convergence, but not the prevalence of different paths to modernity that hold many variations of democracy and authoritarianism. What behavioral subtleties are the dominant theories missing?

## Interaction, Coevolution, and Specialization As Drivers of Development

Discovering what happens in an environment when interconnectivity increases is not only a critical question for contemporary global policy, it is one that scientists who study living systems in nature grapple with as well.[4] In fact, the experience of many cultures with open markets is more consistent with the logic of niche construction theory in evolutionary biology than with the logic of microeconomics that has pervaded political economy analysis. At the very least, microeconomics is an insufficient basis for understanding long-term historical change.

Microeconomics, for example, postulates that competition in a market of many players will promote convergence toward a single set of optimized goods, and that growth occurs as more efficient social technologies, institutions, regulations, or firms supplant variations that are less efficient at providing the market, i.e., consumers or regimes, with the optimized products it demands. The market prefers optimized products; thus, it converges toward the most efficient producer of those products. In this view, deviations from best practice would be eliminated by competition, leading all firms, industries, and societies toward the same endpoint, or what biologists sometimes call a "fitness peak."

Niche construction theory, however, looks at the specific set of biological traits of a population (genotype, species) that enable it to exploit the resources of the environment (Odling-Smee, Laland, and Feldman 2003).[5] With this new theoretical perspective, evolutionary biology is no longer only about survival of the fittest. The logic of niche construction reveals that in densely connected ecosystems, growth leads to variation; convergence and divergence coexist. Growth creates opportunities for alliances that can enable the proliferation of diverse behaviors, ranging from the predatory and parasitical to the symbiotic. Such seemingly wasteful or suboptimal strategies exhibit ecological resilience, and in natural environments, the symbiosis of parasites and their hosts are actually viable and may even stabilize the larger system. Nature ensures ecological resilience through variation – not convergence to an optimal model.

This concept of the *developmental sequence of growth* in nature-made ecosystems contrasts with the explanation for growth in microeconomic theory. Yes, the number of interactions accelerates growth in both, but the most favorable strategy for evolution is not to eliminate variety, but to increase it. A species that secures a niche for itself creates evolutionary space for others to find new strategies for their own survival. This same logic, that as markets increase in size they promote growth by increasing variety, can be applied to microeconomic reasoning.

John Holland (1995; 1998), who began his inquiries while a computer scientist, and evolutionary biologist Stuart Kauffman (1993) applied niche construction to social organizations. Seeking to explain how developmental processes within a single industry can affect a multitude of other industries and trigger a macroevolutionary change like the Industrial Revolution, Kauffman hypothesizes that "the goods and services in an economy themselves offer new opportunities to invent yet further goods and services. In turn, new goods and services drive older goods and services out of the economy. Thus, the system transforms" (1993, 395). In the same way, "new species of molecules, or goods and services, afford niches for yet further new species, which are awakened into existence in an explosion of possibilities" (Kauffman 1995, 26). It follows that as the interrelatedness associated with globalization increases market size, novelty will arise via competition among many players for resources, and that this will drive adaptation toward specialization and variation, i.e., niche construction, creating new capabilities that in turn introduce new strategic options. The "novel molecules produced in one venue ultimately impinge on another and afford the possibility of novel reactions leading to a further increased diversity" (Kauffman 1993, 393).[6]

There are four relevant components of niche construction theory. First, new relationships form among incumbents and newcomers. Second, new specializations or refinements of existing strategies in one environment may appear suboptimal in another.[7] As connectivity increases and adaptations proliferate, each additional niche can foster the possibility of new sets of interactions and exchanges, and new niches. Third, local resource distribution in an ecosystem alters the subsequent evolution of the ecosystem as a whole, such as when a first mover's advantage yields increasing returns to scale to a particular variant. And fourth, development within a population (microevolution) can influence change at a system level (macroevolution).

## Optimization Is Constrained by Topology in Any Agent-Based Environment

According to the logic of niche construction, and evolution more generally, it matters a great deal where an agent or population is situated within the system it inhabits, and where an agent begins its fitness climb.[8] To study the evolution of a system, biologists frequently use computational agent-based simulations of evolution, called *fitness landscapes*, to visualize how the "survivability" of a population evolves according to the environment's topology, which is in turn created by interactions within it. The highest peaks on the landscape represent the agents' maximum fitness levels. Agents have niche positions in the larger landscape, or environment, that they share with other populations, and generally seek the highest local peak that will not put their own survival at risk.[9]

Biologists describe fitness landscapes in terms of variation, ranging from smooth to extremely rugged. Rising above a "flat world" landscape, the rugged crests represent the local fitness peaks, and the deep valleys found between peaks represent the lowest fitness. On a smooth landscape, with a flat, open view of the horizon, all paths lead to the highest peak. Regardless of the paths selected, the adaptive walks of all populations on a smooth landscape will conclude at the same endpoint.[10]

Few populations find themselves in a position to have an uninterrupted view of the highest fitness peak in their landscape. Most landscapes are jagged and rugged, with lots of peaks and valleys of different degrees of difficulty. For populations, be they nations, organizations, or firms making their fitness ascents on rugged landscapes, predicting an attainable evolutionary outcome is far more difficult. Rugged landscapes have many local peaks, and only some paths lead to the highest fitness. Within its landscape are numerous conditions, including the height and range of the local peaks the population must climb, the interactions of its landscape with neighboring landscapes, and even the prior behaviors that placed it in its current position, and all these will determine the options and strategies that populations can pursue in making an adaptive upward climb. Local fitness peaks are more common, but having embarked on a path that leads to one local peak, a population may become "stuck." Figuratively, a population cannot reverse course and climb down the local peak in the hope of finding a better path; any motion away from the peak results in a lower fitness, and thus a population will not take it. Nevertheless, a population will adopt survival strategies based on its position within its landscape, and will most often move uphill only toward *its own* local fitness peak.[11]

When applied to the question of institutional selection and regime transition, the concept of the fitness landscape can help us visualize why current institutional choices are not independent of prior choices. The ruggedness of fitness landscapes explains why the optimal choice, the one that leads to the highest fitness function, might not be the one chosen. Fitness landscapes enable us to visualize why not every population can choose from the same number of good designs or policy choices to maximize its fitness, and therefore why evolutionary outcomes that began on different landscapes will not produce convergent outlooks. Populations will not see the same sets of alternatives due to the different impediments that arise from the differing degrees of ruggedness in their fitness landscapes.

Applying the notion of fitness landscapes to global political economy brings to the forefront certain obstacles that constrain strategic decision making, but which are otherwise overlooked by the dominant economic models. It also forces us to consider why the context of the larger system actually matters to the set of agents that forms a local population. One of the concepts we can visualize much better is that a regime's characteristics cannot be separated from the landscape in which it must operate. This way of thinking differs from most microeconomic models that isolate a part of the system and then aggregate upward to identify the system-level properties. Thinking in terms of fitness landscapes should also enable us to envision why competition in globalization will not lead all populations to some optimal set of solutions or presumed ideal endpoints, their global fitness peaks.

Microeconomic theory as applied to the global economy is often used to bolster the prediction that external competition, in an environment of market liberalism, will drive all firms and nations to similar regulatory structures, similar standards of living, and, eventually, similar systems of domestic governance. To attain this peak, again according to the logic of microeconomic theory, competition will enable the best organizational norms to be selected; this will lead open market economies toward a convergence of social values epitomized by a global middle class with the same culture of efficiency and the same social aspirations. A complex systems approach leads to a different conclusion: that market liberalism poses differing challenges for different populations.

In sum, the challenge of global development can be expressed in terms of a fitness landscape:

> In a coevolutionary system, we need to represent the fact that both the fitness and the fitness landscape of each species are a function of the other species. Thus, in general, it is necessary to couple the rugged fitness landscapes for each species, such that an adaptive move by one species projects onto the fitness landscape of the other species and alters those fitness landscapes more or less profoundly. Over time, each species jockeys uphill on its own landscape and thereby deforms the landscapes of its ecological neighbors. Any such move by one species may increase or decrease the fitness of each neighbor on the latter's landscape and alter the uphill adaptive walks accessible to that neighbor.
>
> *(Kauffman 1993)*

This approach describes the special challenges globalization poses to developing nations; but the incumbent West must also be ready for ideological and cultural challenges from non-Western developmental trajectories. To provision a legal infrastructure for the future of global capitalism may require sidestepping the implausibly complex regulatory systems of incumbent industrial economies. The benefits of overly elaborate systems will exceed the costs they impose on enterprises and people far down the value chain.

## 3.3  EVOLUTIONARY SOCIAL PSYCHOLOGY APPLIED TO AGENT BEHAVIOR

A policy challenge for the development of human behavioral political economy is to offer realistic models of agent behaviors, particularly with regard to development assistance.

Advocating for foreign aid, President Harry Truman in his second inaugural address, referred to all the benefits to be had if we could transfer "our inexhaustible stores of technical knowledge" to underdeveloped countries (1949). The Truman administration's idea was one of "the few real innovations which the modern age has introduced into the practice of foreign policy" (Morgenthau 1962, 301). It seemed natural to Truman that countries hoping to modernize would welcome the opportunity to copy from the best practices of successful nations, but evidence of its transformative capacity remains disappointing.

To implement this agenda, development practice has taken the form of a star-shaped network. Small numbers of experts distribute information to larger specialized groups of locals, but rarely will knowledge circulate equally throughout the system. And despite an elaborate transmission belt comprising bilateral and multilateral institutions, as well as nongovernmental organizations, it has proved difficult to replicate in one environment the chain of development that occurred in another. Convergence of both economic and political openness has been delayed, even among fast-growing economies where technical knowledge about managing financial flows has been transferred successfully.

A recognition that the acquired beliefs of local culture, community, and institutions are the frame through which people view essential issues and solve problems has led a number of scholars toward the field of evolutionary social psychology (ESP). Together with ideas of bounded rationality that already pervade the global political economy analysis of institution building, ESP is being used to explore empirically the complex evolutionary dynamics of learning and knowledge acquisition.[12] It illustrates the ways that people solve their problems by drawing on their own cultures. It also instructs us as to why it is so difficult to transfer strategies, norms, or institutions across cultures. A population is more likely to refer to its own cultural history and traditions – and to reinforce its differences by doing so – before accepting a solution from other populations. These patterns of evolutionary learning will impair our faculties for coping with an increasingly pluralist and interconnected world.

The approach to social learning explored by biologist Peter Richerson and anthropologist Robert Boyd in *Not by Genes Alone: How Culture Transformed Human Evolution* (2005) is inspired by evolutionary biology that places genetics in the broader context of population history and ecology. With this approach, they clarify why populations copy rather than learn from personal trial and error. Copying reduces social learning costs; copying existing ideas saves time and effort. However, they also note, individuals adapt by copying the behaviors of people like themselves, whose circumstances are similar to theirs, regardless of whether the individuals are making the best decisions. The poor and less educated, especially, who have limited means to bear the costs of a direct evaluation of choices, will imitate local models, not those of distant societies or change experts whose situations are far removed from their own.

And therein lies a paradox. When individuals or groups confront conditions not previously experienced in their lifetimes, by copying the behavior of their neighbors, they are apt to engage in grossly maladaptive behaviors. During periods of abrupt social change, when the environment changes faster than the response time allotted to the individual agent, local information is likely to be insufficient. "No matter how error-prone your best guess is about what to do," note Richerson and Boyd, "you are bound to do better than imitating someone whose behavior is surely out of date" (2005). When the environment is under stress, what was once adaptive suddenly becomes maladaptive and puts the survival of the group at risk. Thus, adaptations shaped by local cultural norms may amplify global polarization, and successful local models may be maladaptive globally.

In this vein, pioneering efforts that applied evolutionary theory to social systems led political scientist Robert Axelrod to conclude that the tendency to bond with those one feels most like homophily can interfere with the diffusion of optimal designs that characterize the most efficient societies. Polarization results when people learn from those most like themselves; indeed, their differences from other groups are retained and even amplified (1997, 205).

In *Positive Linking*, British economist Paul Ormerod (2012) explains how cognition takes shortcuts. In the face of uncertainty, agents use heuristics, such as copying, and these reinforce the network effects that reduce individual search costs; they also cause the herd mentality that substitutes for exacting cost–benefit calculations. When people copy, they remove the burden of thoughtful assessment and rigorous comparisons. This reduces the range of available options and makes the selection of objectively inferior alternatives more likely. It reduces not just individual search costs, but the likelihood of finding a qualitatively better alternative, and increases the probability that an inferior alternative will become mainstream. Ormerod's insight illuminates an earlier argument raised by economist Lant Pritchett (1977), who observed that incomes among developing economies tend to cluster toward the standard of neighboring countries with which they share intrinsic cultural and historical characteristics.

The paradox of suboptimal selection doesn't disappear as societies become more affluent. It persists because, Ormerod tells us, as consumers gain an ever-increasing variety of services and products from which to choose, they have relatively less time to make informed choices. Faced with uncertainty and time constraints, they seek shortcuts; it's easier to observe what other consumers have chosen than to conduct a comprehensive search. A product can emerge as the most popular with only a slight advantage early in the search process. The initial consumers might make decisions based on vivid and memorable first impressions, even though the choice may not be the best available. Thus, patterns of cultural diffusion in both developing and developed societies share a common element.

The limits of conventional concepts of agent rationality have caused global change experts to overestimate the pull of liberalism and underestimate the pull of China. ESP, by contrast, may help explain why the diffusion of norms based on individual rights doesn't find fertile soil in fast-growing, modernizing societies, such as China's. With its long history of self-governance to draw upon, there are abundant local models to guide future choices. This same dynamic of institutional adaptation also illustrates why China's experience may be a strong attractor for other developing nations. It is sufficient that the China model is a more familiar starting point than a Western alternative, and more easily copied by other emerging nations (Root 2013).

A model developed with the complex adaptive systems approach would acknowledge cognitive limitations and consider the tendency of individuals to imitate successful behaviors in their own populations and measure their payoffs relative to that of their local interaction partners. This way we can address cultural diffusion by producing a realistic model of how collective learning can produce populist trends such as the rise of political Islam, Vladimir Putin's popularity, Brexit, and economic nationalism in the United States. These trends illustrate how leaders build political coalitions by resorting to declaratory history, i.e., models based on past lessons, rather than relying upon scientific analytical frameworks to explore future opportunities.

## Cascades or Percolations in the Modernization of India and China

ESP gives us many reasons to believe that enduring economic transitions are time-dependent, and that differences between the first movers and the latecomers in global development will be persistent and difficult to overcome. This is because once an institutional adaptation occurs, the increase of utility that its benefactors derive creates strong vested interests in them for it. A future lower-cost option, or one that offers superior performance, may be passed over (Arthur 1989). Thus, political scientist Paul Pierson (2000; 2004) attributes both the perplexing continuity of suboptimal institutions and the slow pace of reform to the increasing returns to scale captured by groups that enjoy first-mover advantages.

When we compare the beginnings of post-colonial India with the beginnings of socialist China, we can speculate that the radical stages of China's Marxist revolution may have eliminated intractable institutional legacies, such as the binding of feet or mass illiteracy. However, early accomplishments were followed by policies that reveal the self-reinforcing effects of locked-in self-interest, with the result that high incomes need not lead to democracy in China's future. Pre-democratic interest groups have become entrenched. As the one-party system matures, its fitness will increase, but only to a point that the CCP can protect its governing niche from domestic competitors. Thus lock-in will slow the adaptation of new governance norms and amplify the evolutionary processes of differentiation from Western liberal values. Sustained economic performance is confirming that the party knows best, thereby contributing to the normalization of the one-party system, sustaining the interests vested in networks of state control of the economy (Cheung 1982).

India's post-colonial trajectory also illustrates how variations at nascent stages can have large impacts that may require a large change at later stages to reverse. India's first prime minister, Jawaharlal Nehru, failed to make India the democratic example for other aspiring nations. He compromised this long-term goal in order to ensure a Congress Party victory over his political rivals. He exploited the existing patron–client system for immediate payoffs to the Congress Party, instead of trying to create a new concept of social affiliation based on citizenship. This led the party to ally with local "big men," locking in the preexisting social inequities and patron–clientelism of an earlier time. Even today, the basic rights and responsibilities of citizenship are unfamiliar to large segments of India's population. India's administrators are often less accountable than those of the more autocratic officialdom of China, and the patterns of traditional patronage at the village level work hand in glove with massive corruption at the national level. The modernization experience of both nations reveals how, during the early stages of transition, structural reforms of institutions are likely to converge quickly with the underlying cultural norms. Successful economic transitions, such as from a planned economy to a market economy, may resemble a cascade model, but the underlying network structure must first be transformed in order for the cascade to happen. Compared to India's more gradual approach to tackling societal hierarchies and to building human capital, Chinese communism, by changing the underlying structural conditions in which the economy sits, has enabled cascades to happen that transformed behavior.

## Why Local Diversity Resists the Optimization of Global Public Policy

The West's good governance agenda is conceived as an optimization process of developing-nation hopefuls seeking the most efficient path to a fixed endpoint. This approach has shown limited effectiveness in reducing the risks of persistent ungovernability and policy failure in emerging regions. The tendency to benchmark local progress against global "best practices" is difficult to reconcile with the novelty that results from the multiscale dynamics of political, social, and economic processes operating at different speeds. It incorrectly turns global development into a race of "catching up," and of correcting inferior choices via convergence to a universal formula of optimal political and social organization.

However, if we view the economy as a complex system, it matters little if one nation outperforms another by objective measures, such as GDP, or by indexes that measure transparency, civil society participation, or the rule of law. No single attribute, strategy, or type can solve all local optimization problems; and locally adaptive responses may not result in globally optimal structures. Should all populations define efficiency by the same criteria and pursue it with the same policies, for example if they all invest in the same new industries, they may compromise a healthy diversity and compound risks to the stability of the shared global environment.

## 3.4 PREVENTATIVE CHAOS: ECONOMIC OPPORTUNITIES HIDE IN GLOBAL FRACTURES

Every day, in scholarship and in the media, the rise of illiberalism is depicted as laying siege to the liberal international world order. The center does not hold; populism and illiberalism are tearing it apart by rejecting international cooperation. Yet the list of regimes and policy options that qualify as illiberal and populist have little in common with one another. Numerous processes – path dependence, lock-in, sensitivity to initial conditions, self-organization, emergence, positive and negative feedback, and learning by copying – are in play as national leaders seek to establish state power in ways that enhance their own power, and to engage in the global economy by discovering dynamic synergies with local institutions, local resources, and social capacity.

There can be no global formula for success to resolve all that is dividing world cultures, be it privilege, immigration, harassment, religion, the stigma of mental health and disability, race, or sexual identity. Successful responses must account for the prerequisites peculiar to each society and culture. The art of governance is to design institutions that are compatible with, but go beyond, the logic of social relations already in operation. A relatively small local difference can have a giant influence on policy outcomes. Investments in manufacturing steel, for example, have been successful in South Korea, but not in Nigeria; although Nigeria has far greater sources of iron ore, it lacks moral consensus on what constitutes good governance. State development banks in Argentina failed, but institutions with the same charter thrive in East Asia. Grameen Bank's formula for microfinance and community banking that has succeeded in Bangladesh falters in India, just across the border.

The application of ESP to political economy offers a framework to avoid reducing long-term historical change to a conflict between liberal and illiberal values. It can enable a better understanding of what makes each society exceptional, and ultimately offers concepts to trace the sources of creativity in the different paths toward economic and social development. The diversity of nations and the differences in the ways populations pursue freedom and dignity will persist, despite heightened interconnectivity, and will produce multiple modernities and reinforce multiple identities. To mix, mingle, and become more diverse is a primary lesson of globalization. Instead of emulation and the top-down inculcation of norms, powerful, self-reinforcing micro-change processes may combine to propel developed and emerging economies, and old and new nations, to different political outcomes.

The aspiration that all countries should try to adopt the same model of globalization may in fact carry its own seeds of destruction. A world economy that is in sync can only reduce volatility for a limited period. Synchronized growth may very well lead to synchronized market failure. As national economies become increasingly integrated, the failures of one economy can surge like an avalanche across the system. This happened in 2008, when the failure in US mortgage-backed securities spread with amplifying consequences. Yet during that downturn, China, whose economy was disconnected from global norms and calibrated to a different setting, was able to sustain its partners. Similarly, India was less affected by the crisis of 2008 because it had fewer linkages with international financial markets, but it also had fewer trading partners.

Is there a point at which extensive global economic integration can lessen the effects of the first episode of contagion? Is it possible that the next generation of economic opportunities will be discovered as result of a pluralism of liberalisms, with different countries experimenting with a diversity of constitutional, religious, and economic arrangements? The idea is similar to what occurs in a diversified investment portfolio, though on a much greater scale. The impact of an initial failure in one economy, the theory goes, could be mitigated by diversification among the portfolios of different sectors and actors, reducing their sensitivity to a failure of any particular link. But there is a trade-off: increased risk sharing among national economies and firms reduces sensitivity to one's own investment choices, and this adversely reduces the potential gains from innovation and risk taking more generally (Elliott, Golub, and Jackson 2014). If a sweet spot exists, we still do not know where it is.

A "fractured world" that does not respond to top-down directives may in fact hold an answer for that sweet spot. Hidden among the fractures might be the next generation of opportunities for renewal and innovation. A variety of countries insistent on finding their own solutions tailored to their own environments, driven by domestic populism or simply necessity, may find the balance that might prevent future economic meltdowns of the entire global economy.

The breakdown of Cold War hierarchies, such as the tendency for trade to be north–south, will be described in Chapter 9, and underlies some of the most important changes in recent global history. As hierarchy in the system diminishes, the global political economy becomes an ecology in which increasing numbers of "species" with well-separated traits compete for resources and must adapt strategies and devise niches in which they can survive. During this period of transformation, one dynamic observed in complex ecological systems is evident. While heightened interconnectivity might offer an individual genome an opportunity to increase its fitness by copying a higher-order example, a successful species more easily attains its survival by protecting its own niche, rather than by copying the strategy of another. Understanding these principles of change in international organization makes the concept of a pluralistic world order both more appealing and more realistic. However, our cognitive evolution – the way we acquire beliefs from local models – does not adequately equip us to cope with the challenges of a hyperconnected world. Frameworks for belief formation that are derived locally do not prepare us to solve problems that originate globally.

NOTES

1. Twenty-five years after proclaiming history to have ended, Francis Fukuyama, writing in the *Wall Street Journal* (2014), conceded that it is

not the "end of history" yet. Models of national development whose strictly materialist focus makes them seem robust today will ultimately lose their appeal, failing to address the inherent human drives for recognition and self-expression. Even China, the "single most serious challenge to liberal democracy in the world today" (Fukuyama 2011, 56–57), will converge, he predicted; its path will be multigenerational, taking more time than originally anticipated, but nevertheless inevitable. No matter how effectively its one-party state fulfills materialistic needs, its failure to satisfy other, universal needs will make its influence on the world stage transitory: "The emergence of a market-based global economic order and the spread of democracy are clearly linked. Democracy has always rested on a broad middle class and the ranks of prosperous, property-holding citizens have ballooned everywhere. ... Once societies get up the escalator of industrialization, their social structure begins to change in ways that increase the demands for political participation."

2. One example is the "rich get richer" phenomenon that Vilfredo Pareto (1848–1923) described, which has been observed in agent-based models such as that in Sugarscape (Epstein and Axtell 1996).

3. Macroeconomic and democracy data have been moving in opposite directions. Between 2000 and 2016, world GDP of non-OECD countries rose as trade as a percentage of world GDP grew. GDP growth of non-OECD economies consistently surpassed that of OECD countries, in some years by significant margins. Infant mortality in non-OECD countries dropped and life expectancy increased. Nevertheless, civil liberties declined, and rule-of-law indicators and political rights stagnated in some of the fastest-growing economies. Freedom House reported that 2017 was the twelfth consecutive year in which global freedom declined, dispelling confidence in the linkage of economic and political development. "Political rights and civil liberties around the world deteriorated to their lowest point in more than a decade in 2017," the report concludes (Freedom House 2018).

4. On connectivity and diversity in evolutionary biology, see Sibani and Jensen (2013).

5. In global economics, an analogy would be South Korea's large, export-oriented *chaebols* that arose locally and naturally from within the social structures of premodern Korea. These conglomerates exemplify how

a country can attain global competitiveness by strengthening its local institutional uniqueness. A number of institutional and cultural preconditions existed that allowed the deployment of surplus revenues from oligopolistic competition at home to be channeled into competitive strategies and products desired globally.

6. Kauffman offers a hypothesis about how ecosystems coevolve to the edge of chaos. In a coevolutionary process, "each organism myopically alters the structure of its fitness landscape and the extent to which the landscape is deformed by the adaptive moves of other organisms, such that, as if by an invisible hand, the entire ecosystem coevolves to a poised state at the edge of chaos" (Kauffman 1993, 261).

7. When increasing numbers of species with well-separated traits compete for resources, they all must adapt strategies and devise niches in which they can survive.

8. There is no principal-agency relationship in an agent-based environment. These are environments without a central controller, or agent, who has a deterministic or dominant interest in the outcome. The environment is self-organized out of the interactions of all the agents.

9. Fitness landscapes are explored in Gavrilets (2004); Reeves (2005); Richter and Engelbrecht (2014); and Svensson and Calsbeek (2012). For examples of fitness landscapes applied to social science, see Axelrod (1997).

10. This can be represented as a Mount Fuji type of peak in which the landscape rises evenly on all sides.

11. In biology, a population sends out feelers, mutations, that go off in any number of directions; if a mutation succeeds in occupying a higher peak, selection will pull the population in that direction. But very few mutations find a path that leads to the highest peak.

12. Institutional choices reflect bounded rationality among decision makers in *Institutional Choice and Global Commerce* (Jupille, Mattli, and Snidal 2013).

# PART II  An Analysis of Historical Regimes

# 4  Network Assemblage of Regime Stability and Resilience in Europe and China

In this chapter we explore the first of five great transitions: the creation in Europe and China of institutions of dynastic succession. In both China and Europe, unlike other known historical meta-regimes, such as the Roman, Ottoman, or Mughal empires, rule-based systems were established for clear, orderly, and incontestable lines of hereditary succession that, from the ninth century onward, afforded great dynastic longevity.[1] The sacred embodiment of kingship was also reformed, according to the great French medievalist Marc Bloch: "No longer, as among the early Germanic peoples, did the sacred character [of kingship] extend to a whole line; it had become definitively concentrated in a single person, the head of the eldest branch, the sole lawful heir to the crown, who alone possessed the right to work miracles." (Bloch 1973, 48).

It is axiomatic in comparative economic history that Europe's decentralized and competitive state system, comprised numerous dominions, was key to its developmental divergence from China, which was under the rule of successive single dynasties. This chapter references advances in network science to show why it is not enough to say that Europe's dynamism stems from its decentralized political competition. Interstate rivalries and war also featured significantly across China's geopolitical landscape, and political competition there produced severe periods of disruption and collapse without parallel in Europe (Andrade 2016). Yet with each restoration of order came a return of imperial rule and governance by an imperial bureaucracy educated in Confucian classics.

The historical regimes in both China and Europe (and, in fact, all historical regimes) are multiscale systems in which different orders of hierarchy exist and intermingle, giving rise to change processes across levels. The interactions and coevolution within these multilevel environments form the system's *hypernetworks* and produce system-level dynamics as well. A hypernetwork is the shared element among the levels of a system; its structure can be hub-and-spoke (starlike) or entirely decentralized. Here we look at the two very different regime structures in China and Europe, both of which evolved around the dynamics of hereditary dynastic succession.[2] As a multiscale system, a social system can have multiple hypernetworks; this chapter concentrates on one. The papacy is another, parallel Europe-wide hyper-network and the two systems were closely interconnected; royalty depended upon anointment bestowed by the consent of the Church, and the papacy needed allies among the monarchs.

This chapter advances two central claims. The first is a methodological one, showing that patterns of long-term historical change are best studied at the system level rather than through a traditional equilibrium framework grounded in models of individual behavior. The second, an empirical claim, is established by comparisons of China's hub-and-spoke hypernetwork with Europe's multi-hub hypernetwork to show that their different patterns of interconnectivity forged their respective capacities to weather intermittent socioeconomic transitions.

We will demonstrate how different hypernetwork structures in China and Europe played major roles in the state development of each and resulted in differences in the system-level properties of stability and resilience. We define stability as the capacity of a system's components, its subsystems, *to revert to functionality despite disruptions*. Resilience, on the other hand, refers to the capacity of the system itself to accommodate and absorb great, intermittent local-level stresses and *transform itself*. We find that loss of resilience is proportional to the removal of major hubs or nodes. If just one hub controls the system, the risk to stability will be magnified.

Only recently have scholars of institutional change and economic development come to recognize that the central questions of how social institutions emerge, adapt, and evolve echo debates long occurring in the natural sciences, in fields as diverse as neurology, ecology, and physics, where it is understood that ecosystems are complex adaptive systems. Social scientists are now starting to apply this understanding to the connections between a system's microscopic and macroscopic components.

## 4.1   IDENTIFYING HYPERNETWORKS IN EUROPE AND CHINA

This historical analysis can deepen our understanding of how *disequilibria* at agent levels – seen in shifting borders, revolutionary pacts, codes of ethics, the rise and fall of royal houses, and other actions and interactions occurring within that complex system – do not necessarily disrupt aggregate stationarity of the hypernetwork structure. Despite fluctuations within a particular nation state or states, the resilience of the macro can remain unchanged. Like the backcloth of an opera, the hypernetwork remains stationary and unlikely to be unaffected by the drama onstage. However, hypernetworks are also sensitive to interactions and evolution, and the patterns of interconnectivity that form a hypernetwork render it vulnerable to system-level shocks, such as that which occurred to Europe's intermarried royal families as a result of World War I.

European dynasties came and went, and any part of Europe was subject to invasion by any other part. Yet Europe's hypernetwork of relationships between interconnected royal families provided continuity across the continent that transcended the nation states. Its connectivity would break apart, its resilience collapse, only with the removal of all the major hubs. In China, as well, dynasties rose and were toppled, and their collapse brought periods of chaos; yet the hypernetwork structure reappeared time after time (and continues today) in its familiar hub-and-spoke form. The robustness of regime dynamics resides in the structure of the hypernetwork – in the patterns of connectivity among the system's hubs – rather than from an accumulation of local affects or simple aggregation of agent-level equilibria (Johnson 2013).

## Hypernetwork Structure and Resilience: The European Example

As we will see, there were advantages and disadvantages in the network designs of China and Europe, as illustrated in their sociocultural evolution over many centuries. Europe's state resilience lay in the connected dynasties ruling across the continental "fabric." The aggregate hypernetwork structure that those dynasties formed kept Europe from transitioning into instability when abrupt shocks disabled a particular royal lineage. Even if a royal house fell, the remaining hubs would self-organize by "rerouting the traffic" on the network. Thus, for example, the royal House of Plantagenet, the royal Houses of Tudor and Stuart, and the House of Hapsburg all became extinct, but dynastic rule persisted. Understanding this ability to reconfigure without system-level breakdown is essential for explaining the dynamics of Europe's long-term development trajectory.

Europe's cultural continuity thus resides in its small-world network connectivity, a hierarchy of many small nodes held together by a few larger hubs that are themselves connected to a small number of yet larger hubs. In such networks, if one hub is destroyed, the remaining nodes diffuse and reconnect to a neighbor. The smaller nodes of the many different subunits are not isolated, and the behavior of the system, even under extreme stress, is not entirely random, lending resilience to the system as a whole. Links to a few highly connected hubs prevent the smaller nodes from falling into isolation.

Like the CEOs of large corporations, Europe's royal families bridged the various subunits to unify the many discrete functionalities. This network structure of decentralized yet interconnected hubs enabled Europe to adapt to a changing environment, survive disruptive events, and accommodate coevolutionary changes across local systems. The Christian Church during the Middle Ages played a critical role in facilitating the durability of royal clans. It prohibited polygamy and marriages up through a sixth canonical degree of consanguinity (or sixth cousin) for all members of the population, except for nobility, royalty, and, later, the merchant elites. This proscription undermined the marital cohesiveness of all kinship groups, with the exception of elite families, allowing those families to tighten their grip on power. Later, in the nineteenth century, the constraints against marriage within kinship groups were adopted by nation states and enforced by secular authorities.

Europe experienced its first catastrophic breakdown after the highly centralized Roman Imperium broke apart in the fifth century. The end of the imperial system led to the evolution of a new forms of government across the continent. Based on Germanic feudalism, over the centuries they gave rise to the consolidation of states into disparate sovereign units. No center remained; instead, the continent's dynamism shifted from one region to another. Regimes came and went, and advantage shifted from one royal house to another, without any one hub becoming strong enough to secure a monopoly on victory. A shift of power from one set of dynastic lineages to another did not entail continent-wide demographic catastrophes.

This network of princely and royal houses governed continuously, and the hypernetwork generated by this system of dynastic succession persisted, despite a wide spectrum of observed microequilibria at agent levels, where profound variations in outlook existed, technologies changed, and formal institutions were often repurposed, deviating from their original functions. An innovation by one dynasty was parried by a counterthrust from another. Although intermarried, the Hapsburgs, Bourbons, and Hohenzollerns continually competed to contain one another's ambitions. The smaller networks created by each hub were not necessarily highly stable, but the small-world network of the great families outlived these variations. This kind of network structure protected the system from random failure, and because the ecology they inhabited survived, Europe's interconnected monarchies remained intact as a governing class, exhibiting both continuity and change over a millennium.

Moreover, what this kind of a hypernetwork loses in stability, it gains in resilience, i.e., the capacity to accommodate and absorb great

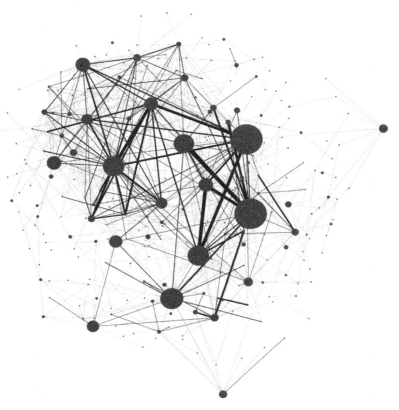

FIGURE 4.1 The marriage network between European royal houses from the fourteenth through the twentieth centuries. An edge is established when there is a marriage between two royal houses. The thickness of edges represents the number of marriages between two royal houses (1–92). The size of a node represents its degree, i.e., the number of houses with which it has a marriage relationship (0–41). The network includes 239 nodes and 622 edges, excluding self-loops (marriages between members in the same house). The nodes also include nobility, popes, bishops, and electors. Bishops and popes were expected to be celibate, but some had children for the express purpose of establishing alliances, and these are included. The marriage network resembles a small-world network. Using Python, 100 random networks with the same number of nodes and edges are generated, and the clustering coefficient and the average shortest path are calculated for each simulated network. This network has an average shortest path length of 3.3857, comparable to that of a random network of 3.4844, but with a much higher clustering coefficient of 0.2010 relative to the 0.0218 characteristic of a random network.

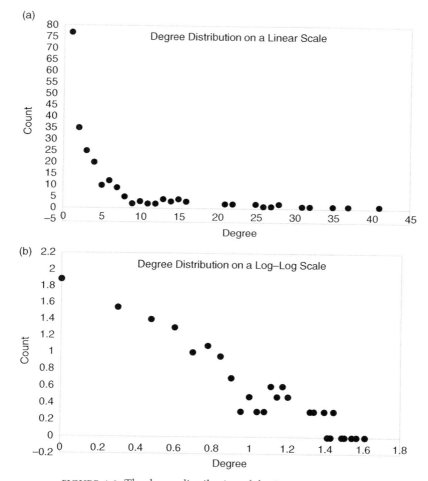

FIGURE 4.2 The degree distribution of the European marriage network between royal houses (a) on a linear scale, and (b) on a log–log scale. The marriage network resembles a scale-free network to some degree. A scale-free network has a highly skewed degree distribution with a long tail, strictly speaking, following a power-law distribution.

intermittent stresses. With its distributed "mesh-like architecture," enough redundancy exists to enable communication between remaining hubs, so that actions and ideas can spread among them. Even when intermittent and episodic transformations occur at the agent level, the macro-stability of the system is not disabled.

## The European Authority Network

Figure 4.1 is a composite representation of European dynastic marriages from the fourteenth through the twentieth centuries. The network exhibits mixed features of small-world and scale-free networks. It has a highly skewed degree distribution, with a few large hubs, prevalent in scale-free models, though it is not a perfect power-law distribution (see Figure 4.2). It also exhibits small-world characteristics because it has an average shortest path length comparable to random networks, but with a much higher clustering coefficient (Figure 4.1).

This network helps explain why describing Europe solely in terms of decentralization gives short shrift to the patterns of hub-based communication that enabled lateral communication across the network. In the network, communication channels to larger nodes or hubs are highly skewed, with a few highly connected hubs linking the smaller nodes with one another. For the system to collapse, a large number of the major hubs must be destroyed; otherwise the traffic will reroute among the surviving hubs.

## Hypernetwork Structure and Stability: The Chinese Example

China's regime structure, i.e., an emperor at the center of a hub-and-spoke structure of governance, produced a hypernetwork of a different kind; its strength resided in the great efficiency with which information circulated from one end of the empire to another. But the hypernetwork structure also made the state more vulnerable to massive shocks. In times of great disruption, as in Europe, only the links that were connected with other links could hold the empire together, and China had few of these. The resilience of the European model also resides in a capacity to more easily add or subtract connectivities. Just adding a small number of random connections alters path lengths among the remaining nodes. Being less adaptive, China experienced less variation and was at a greater risk of ossification.

Dynastic collapse had extensive social and economic consequences, and the rebuilding process was exhaustive. Nevertheless, the institutions of China's dynastic system invariably reappeared. In this sense, the Chinese dynastic system exhibited *stability* rather than resilience. (Recall that resilience depends on the redundancy of hubs, and China had just one central hub.) The contemporary sinologist Yuri Pines explains that "the peculiar historical trajectory of the Chinese empire is not its indestructability – it witnessed several spectacular collapses – but rather its repeated resurrection in more or less the same territory, and with a functional structure similar to that of the pre-turmoil period" (2012, 3). *Why* that structure reappeared as the preferred option to rebuild a collapsed empire is discussed at length in Chapter 6.

The definition of *resilience* in common use by ecologists and others who study complex adaptive systems applies here. Resilience is the ability of the macro system to absorb subsystem disturbances while retaining its own system of rules and procedures. But resilience at the hypernetwork level also shapes the capacity of the microsystem, the regime. This regime stability was a characteristic shared by China and Europe at the macro levels, but at the micro levels, China experienced far less variation. What made the European system more *resilient* was that its hypernetwork survived dramatic local transitions intact.

## 4.2   RESILIENCE AND STABILITY TRADE-OFFS IN CHINA AND EUROPE

There were trade-offs between stability and resilience in both Europe's and China's hypernetworks. As noted previously, in the case of Europe, one such trade-off was redundancy, both in communication channels between the multitudes of political jurisdictions and in institutions. The resilience of the state system generally resided in the adaptive capacity of its distributed network structure to survive drastic events. Yet in a paradox of small-world network structure,

Europe proved to be both highly unstable and highly resilient.[3] Its great instability derived from its decentralized network comprising many dense connections; difficult to manage, the system was prone to disruptive large events that could eliminate one or more hubs.

By contrast, China's hub-and-spoke system of governance exhibited great efficiency in maintaining communication and continuity among the government structures of a far-flung empire, which helps explain its recurrence with each successive dynasty. A study of social networks by Ronald Burt explains how centralized (hub-and-spoke) networks outperform decentralized networks (1992). They support effective decision making, Burt argues, by strengthening the leadership's decision-making capacities. They provide greater opportunities for information access, timing, and monitoring, making management less costly in terms of energy, time, and resources.

In China, fewer redundant contacts increased the efficient flow of information to the center and required less effort to maintain clusters of influence. Instead of maintaining relations with the entire network of contacts along its spokes, the central decision maker, the emperor, could preserve resources to reward the primary contacts delegated the task of maintaining the total network, and utilize the conserved resources to expand the network to include new clusters of influence.

Whatever trade-offs arose between the properties of stability and resilience in these respective hypernetwork structures, they were ultimately made according to widely different adaptive values, i.e., according to the properties that most ensured the perpetuation of the hypernetworks. Thus, redundancies in Europe's scale-free network system absorbed considerable scarce resources but lent resilience to the macro system. China utilized a far more efficient system of communication, but with the attendant risks of a lone central hub and its reliance on imperial bureaucracy.

In China the dynasties themselves lasted generations, if not centuries. Yet should the throne fail, the "transitions" were not peaceful. The disrupted communication channels would render the entire polity more susceptible to collapse; the remaining nodes, much like isolated islands, were unable to communicate. This made imperial China vulnerable to intervals of extreme disorder since subsidiary systems of governance had to be rebuilt and replaced. Each dynasty's collapse disabled the center. Rebellion from within and invasion from without produced cycles of decay of long duration, in which the central rule of the mandarinate retreated or disappeared entirely. During these transitions, the underlying economic and social conditions of the population deteriorated on massive scales.

## 4.3 THE ENDURANCE OF DYNASTIC LORDSHIP IN EUROPE

The great instability of its particular regimes makes Europe seem weak and vulnerable to easy conquest; its intrastate governance seems far less robust than China's. However, the small-world network structure of the aristocracy acted as the source of system-wide continuity. In such small-world networks, most of the smaller components (nodes) are not themselves linked to many others. But as we shall see, a small number of high-connectivity nodes link many of the nodes to *any* other node, and to other high-degree nodes. They derived their social power from the length of their connectivity to other high-degree nodes, rather than to the density of their connectivity to a larger number of smaller nodes.

### Europe As a Small-World Network

The industrialization of Great Britain exemplifies the remarkable small-world continuity, balancing aristocratic entitlements with the ambitions of the rising industrial elites. Even after systems of production were transformed, no such equally dramatic events or clearly decisive changes to the social structure of authority occurred (Southern 1953, 13). "[T]he aristocracy successfully maintained its power during all the vicissitudes of three-quarters of a millennium," notes historian J. H. Hexter, "during which almost everything else changed, quite drastically" (1961, 19). The knightly aristocracy, along with the monarchy, surrendered its primacy in Britain's social ordering only after World War I (Cannadine 1999).

The evolution of royal families fanning out across Europe allowed for multiple connections among regions and systems, and serves as a prime example of hypernetwork activity. When World War I broke out in 1914, monarchs ruled most European states, and almost all the royals were related to one another in a kind of small-world network; Queen Victoria's direct descendants sat on the thrones of Britain, Denmark, Greece, Germany, Norway, Russia, and Spain, earning her the sobriquet "Grandmother of Europe." The social and economic effects of industrialization did not deter the crowned heads of Europe from consolidating their national powers and alliances.[4]

Of the major European nations, only France and Switzerland were outliers. Switzerland did not fight in World War I, and France entered the war as a republic. "Except in France the kings remained the divinely ordained 'centerpieces' of Europe's authority systems," writes historian Arno Mayer in his magisterial study of the end of the old order in Europe (1981, 11). He notes that "even in France, where the ancient regime was pronounced legally dead between 1789 and 1793, it kept resurfacing violently and lived on in many ways for more than a century" (1981, 6). Four failed efforts to restore monarchical government occurred during the nineteenth century, and royalist sympathizers in France were abetted by supporters across the continent.

The collection of royal dynasties, spread out across Europe as a hypernetwork, shaped the territorial evolution of European states and gave order to the whole system. Describing the system as decentralized without considering the patterns of communication among the nodes of various sizes reveals an incomplete framework. Yet most scholarship of European state building focuses on the nation-state level, emphasizing competitive state-level fragmentation rather than a system-level focus.

## Marriage Networks among Royal Houses

It is remarkable that during the late medieval period, circa 1500, Europe comprised more than 500 distinct dominions – sovereign or quasi-sovereign jurisdictions that were largely independent political units. Yet no matter how fragmented feudal Europe was to become, no town or village could ever legally claim to be the subject of more than one kingdom. Despite the intensive selective pressures on European societies to compete by constantly updating their political, economic, and military structures, at no time until Napoleon did a usurper ever claim the status of royalty. The royal dynasties that dominated the European stage until the early twentieth century trace their origins to the Germanic kingdoms of the early Middle Ages. Although many independent powers arose, only to fall into decay, it is a testament to the strength of the monarchical tradition that none, even at the peak of power, ever dared to claim a royal title. One reason for this, already noted, is the coevolution of the sacred embodiment of kingship with the legal and customary formulation of hereditary succession. The embodiment of the crown's sacred role could only be exercised by the head of the oldest branch of the lineage. Bloch underscores that "no great feudatory, however powerful he might be, ever dared to demand the most sacred part of the ceremony of being the 'Lord's anointed,' a status found only among kings and priests" (1961, 400). The belief in the hereditary vocation of a dynasty prevailed, ensuring that when a king died, the kingdom remained.

The Germanic kingdoms of the eighth and ninth century laid the basis of Western Europe's political evolution, which would establish the borders of both medieval and modern Europe. Bloch notes that

> thus the feudal era witnessed the emergence of the first lineaments of a political map of Europe. . . . [It] also debated those problems of frontier zones which were destined till our own day to be responsible for the spilling of both ink and blood. . . . [T]he most

characteristic feature of this geography of kingdoms was that
though their territorial limits fluctuated, their number varied
remarkably little.

*(1961, 399)*

This phenomenon, found among the crowned heads of Europe,
in which every royal house was connected in some way, if only
remotely, to every other is not merely a curiosity in the history of
the continent. Via their elaborate protocols of intermarriage, the
small-world hypernetwork that developed formed a strategic ecology
and lent stability to society, enabling state formation (Sharma 2015,
155). Over time, and in large measure due to the efforts of the Church
and its support of the combined practice of primogeniture and female
inheritance, the various political entities and principalities were concentrated into the hands of a few royal families. The logic of dynastic
succession was the primary driver of the territorial consolidation of
these fragmented units. War was an instrument used to accelerate or
decelerate progress, but the big gains, such as the unification of
Britain, France, and Spain, were achieved through dynastic
accumulation.[5] The Germanic territories of the Holy Roman Empire
only adopted primogeniture later in the eighteenth century, and this
deferral may have contributed to their continual fragmentation.

The legal framework of dynastic marriage was established with
the blending of property rights and political power. The same laws,
norms, and customs that governed the transmission of landed property also held and transmitted political power. This intertwining of
public authority and property allowed for the orderly transmission of
the office of the head of state from one generation to the next. Most
important, these laws, behaviors, and customs transcended regional,
sectarian, and political boundaries. They were prevalent throughout
the European continent, extending from Britain into Russia.

The papacy played a central role in the cultural and ideological
cohesion of Europe. The Church hierarchy is best understood as
a parallel hypernetwork within the larger European ecology. The

Church's independent stature ensured that the right to justice became part of the value system of Western Europe, for the Church insisted that no monarch could deny the right to justice of even the humblest servant.[6]

Royal marriage was the pivot upon which the European system of international relations rotated, and "each shift of power directly or indirectly involved every unit, every country" (Elias 1983, 300). The higher-degree linkages and rivalries between royal houses propelled the formation of states and their interrelations – and the "institution of dynastic succession, driven by the contingency of birth, marriage, and death in the leading princely families of Europe, determined the distribution of power in Europe" (Sharma 2015, 169). Intermarriage was the prevailing means to secure, maintain, and extend power among reigning families from the medieval era until the outbreak of World War I. Contrary to the oft-repeated remark of sociologist Charles Tilly that "war made states and states made war," the major states of Europe were born of dynastic accumulation. The map of modern Europe is roughly the product of dynastic marriage (Brenner et al. 2003).[7]

## The Paradox of Maladaptive Institutional Resilience

Dynastic succession itself is not a hypernetwork, but an *institution* through which the hypernetwork of royal families perpetuated itself.[8] The network of royal houses can be interpreted along three dimensions: first, a rule-based dimension (or *house rules*), albeit more customary than formal, which describes how dynastic property is to be transferred; second, an *equilibria dimension*, of strategic games created with self-reinforcing behavior; and third, a system of symbolic representation in which *status is itself an institution*, regulated by society's symbolic order. We have discussed the first two already; only the third one remains to be discussed.

Stable systems can generate unintended long-term consequences in the form of feedback loops and path dependencies, but the resilience of a system can also be maladaptive. For example, while dynastic succession facilitated the territorial and administrative consolidation of continental Europe, it also incited continuous warfare.

"Consider the consequences if a system were highly resilient," note Holling and Gunderson (2002). "Is that entirely a desired condition?" Remember, resilience in complex systems is the capacity to absorb and recover from perturbation; in the face of large disturbances, variables would shift and move, but the system would maintain its control and structures. In the case of Europe, the resilience of the monarchy as the source of political authority on the eve of World War I jarred with the structure of a society changed by a century of increased regional and global industrialization and capitalism. The efforts to preserve dynastic lordship at the opening of the twentieth century exemplify how the resilience of a particular social order can prevail *without* possessing needed welfare-enhancing properties.

## The European Ruling Elite and Militarism

When war broke out between Germany and Britain in 1914, the monarchs of Germany (Kaiser Wilhelm) and Great Britain (King George) were first cousins, as were the king and Russia's Czar Nicholas. Considering these shared genealogical connections among the princely dynasties of Europe, why was war unavoidable?

The monarch was the functional and symbolic leader of the army, and the conduct of warfare defined rank, title, and status, making military prowess a fountainhead of legitimacy, to the traditional society of orders. Thus, Joseph Schumpeter in *Imperialism and Social Classes* explains that imperialism developed on the continent because of the perennial belligerence that was instinctive for the monarchy; its heritage included a "war machine, together with its socio-psychological aura and aggressive bent, and because a class oriented toward war maintained itself in a ruling position" (1951, 129).

In Schumpeter's account, militarism, war, and imperialism are embedded in the European state system because the legacy of prowess in warfare was how Europe's crowned cousins justified the honors of their office and exerted their superiority over lineages of common stock. Even when at war, they followed codes of honor to respect the esteem of their office, avoided taking each other hostage, and did not impose changes or dictate the internal institutional structures of a defeated rival. Schumpeter's observations echo those of US President Woodrow Wilson, who posited the same explanation for the Europeans' perpetual tendency to be at war with one another, and who further believed that this propensity would not end until the "pretensions" of the elite genealogies that sustained it were "checked and nullified" (1917).

Mayer claims that prior to World War I, a militarist revival was under way in which the kaiser, the Austrian Hapsburgs, and Russia's Romanovs sought to form alliances to preempt their loss of status and restore the Church and the army as the bastions of social order (1981). The crowned heads of Europe, Mayer believes, feared class mobilization more than war; the latter, they imagined, would restore the society of orders and revive Old Regime civil and political institutions.

## The New World As Destroyer of Europe's Ancient Order

To explain the origin of World War I, historians weigh the domestic issues of militarism and nationalism against external pressures, i.e., the system of alliances, war plans, and the accumulation of crises prior to 1914. But the European hypernetwork structure is itself a plausible explanation for why a small perturbation like the assassination of Archduke Franz Ferdinand in Sarajevo on June 28, 1914, would have been enough to push the entire state system into a crisis. Network science explains how, in a highly interconnected network of interrelated royal families, a small, localized event could trigger a cascade of military responses that swept across national boundaries. This is because in highly connected networks, what happens to some nodes can set off waves of interactive responses.

Yet being prone to contagion does not explain why a small perturbation could have caused the sudden demise of the *entire* system. Thus, another factor becomes paramount – the structure of the hypernetwork itself was transformed.

The peace repositioned the United States, transforming it into a principal hub of the Western political system. From having been a peripheral player, the United States sought to redesign the system around a new strategy for global order premised on its preference for democratic universalism. President Wilson was not content with merely redistributing the spoils of victory among the surviving lineages; he sought to use the newly acquired position of the United States as a powerful hub to reduce militancy and imperialism, and transform the landscape for the surviving royal houses. This changed the logic of network affiliation and led to the emergence of new organizations and regional communities. He persuaded the allies to refuse to negotiate with any German government that had ties to the kaiser's army.[9] He insisted that the new nations, carved out of the fallen empires of Turkey, Germany, Austria–Hungary, and Russia, were to be representative democracies.

The peace redefined the basis of regime legitimacy to be in conformity with the democratic values and aspirations of all nations for statehood. However, the subsequent failure of the US Congress to ratify the League of Nations treaty and America's retreat into isolationism contributed to the inability to institutionalize the Wilsonian ideal of a liberal world order. Instead of strengthening international law and organization under the auspices of liberal institutions, the victors at the Paris Peace Conference allowed self-interests to set the terms of the peace. With the abdication of Kaiser Wilhelm II, Germany's hub of political organization was decapitated, and the empire descended into lawlessness that spread across Europe. The demand to reframe the basis of regime legitimacy clashed with Westphalian ideals that recognized the primacy of sovereignty.[10] It took another world war to fully integrate Europe into the liberal world order led by the United States.

When the twentieth century began, only France and Switzerland, and the short-lived San Marco, were republics. Yet within a single generation, in both China and Europe, dynastic succession ceased to be the institution underpinning the orderly transmission of power. By the end of World War II, the surviving royal houses of Belgium, Denmark, Luxembourg, the Netherlands, Spain, Sweden, Norway, and the United Kingdom were vestiges of their former selves. In China the postwar restoration of central power spanned several decades, during which its people experienced warlords, a nationalist revolution, and eight years of Japanese invasion, followed by four years of civil war.

Using network science, we can draw two key insights from the persistence of Europe's royal Old Regime elites and values before World War I, and their sudden disappearance after the two world wars. The first is that national institutions and elite social behaviors are embedded in a much larger environment and do not exist in isolation from it. Second, the resilience of the system of distributed monarchies exceeded its social utility as the predominant system of governance and statecraft, and this may have been one of the reasons for its violent end in World War I and the disorderly transition, including World War II and the redrawing of political boundaries worldwide, that followed.

Despite their important respective strengths and vulnerabilities, the demise and re-formation of the hypernetwork of both the Chinese and European systems in the early twentieth century came from changes in the structure of the *global* network caused by the changing relationships among the principal hubs that created new sets of interconnections within the international system. In Chapter 9, we will consider another transition now under way, as the structure of the system of international relations drifts from a system linked via a few primary hubs toward a far more distributed system in which lateral relations among subsidiary or peripheral actors are increasing in density. The stability principles of the new system are still too preliminary to model or predict.

## 4.4   DECAY AND RENEWAL OF CHINESE DYNASTIES

The longevity of China's dynasties is one of the wonders of history. So, too, is the continuity of Chinese culture. The continuous feedback between culture and institutional structure is the subject of a sophisticated literature that combines the insights of sociologists, economists, and historians. Insights from network science allow us to explore new possibilities for understanding this puzzle.

China entered the twentieth century with its ancient protocols of dynastic succession as the pivot of social order; the administrative continuum that carried China through the centuries was composed of a structural apex, with a single dynasty at the top, supported by an imperial bureaucracy as the mechanism of coordination and national integration with entry via the examination system. Nobles, landlords, merchants, lawyers, and priests enjoyed minimal autonomy and few opportunities for institutional representation. The most lucrative opportunities for profit and gain were through the state. The combination of officialdom and a standing army under civil authority, writes Samuel Edward Finer in *The History of Government*, distinguished China's palace-style governance from that of other empires in recorded history (1997, 756).

The Roman imperial traditions were never to be reconstituted in Europe, but in China, the Han dynasty (206 BCE–220 CE) became the prototype of all subsequent regimes. The Han dynasty introduced an imperial university for official appointees in 124 BCE; by 1 CE, official scholars began to administer examinations for entrants to government service, and justice was vested in organs of the central administration rather than local judiciaries. After the 350 years of division and disorder that followed the Han dynasty's collapse, the Tang dynasty (618–907) reconstituted what the Han had initiated, strengthening many of the characteristic institutions, notably the central officialdom that enabled the subordination of the military to civil leadership. The civil service system attained its pinnacle under the Song dynasty (960–1279), which perfected the examination system

developed during the Tang.[11] As a further refinement of rule by officialdom, the Song prohibited relatives of officials to conduct business
with one another, and relatives of the empress or other imperial consorts were barred from becoming high-ranking officials. Without attributes of autonomy – such as hereditary titles of nobility, guaranteed
officer status in the military, and estates passed on over many generations – there were no consolidated class liberties that could constitute
a brake on the development of a unified and absolute monarchy.

The protocols of dynastic succession also took definitive form
during Song rule and persisted until the downfall of the imperial
system in 1912.[12] In earlier periods, usurpation of the throne by generals, empresses, and even civil officials was common, but, as Edwin
Reischauer and John Fairbank (1958) note, never again after the Song
instituted the system of dynastic succession.[13] Dynasties might fall
by invasion, and members of the royal family could murder each
other, but a "non-royal" usurper could never again capture the imperial throne.

In China, the hub-and-spoke system, with its reliance on imperial bureaucracy, continued to reappear. Even after prolonged and violent transitions, each successive dynasty rediscovered in Confucian
officialdom a means to integrate the bureaucracy and restore stability,
establish homogeneity of values, and ensure that officialdom, not
privately accumulated wealth or military prowess, was the channel
for social mobility. Ruling dynasties that failed to adopt it, such as the
Mongol-led Yuan (1279–1368), which deviated toward a more explicitly tribal order, were relatively short lived. The Ming (1368–1644)
and the Qing (1662–1911) dynasties reverted to and strengthened
officialdom.

## China's Politically Induced Cycles of Economic Decline

Chinese history is often told as a continuum of dynastic cycles of
decay and renewal. Popular accounts carry a moral lesson: successive
dynasties rose from the ashes of their predecessors to attain peaks of
cultural and engineering excellence, followed by corruption, factional

quarrels, blind ambition, and moral decay that caused them to lose the Mandate of Heaven. A period of disorder resulted, and the Mandate of Heaven was bestowed on a new dynasty.

More sophisticated accounts of Chinese history do not reject the idea of dynastic cyclicality but add an assessment of economic and administrative failings. Reischauer and Fairbank explain that when affluent central governments engaged in costly projects – palaces, roads, canals, and walls – the nobility and bureaucracy prospered and grew in numbers (1958, 117–18). Defending the larger empire also became costlier. The peasant farmers supported elites, who paid few taxes, causing expenditures to increase against declining revenues.

Revenue from the land tax, the chief source of government revenue, became progressively smaller over time as land was increasingly shielded from taxation by various subterfuges that involved the complicity of landowners and tax collectors (Fairbank 1948, 96). The peasants were left to bear a heavier burden, triggering endemic revolts often led by fanatical religious leadership; local resistance multiplied, despite efforts at repression. Eventually, disorder spread, frontier defenses crumbled, unpaid soldiers defected, and the center weakened and collapsed.

Finer observes that "the collapse of each of the great imperial structures ushered in similar dismal periods of disunion, carnage, warlordism, and court dissension, followed by the predictable barbarian invasion and conquest" (1997, 744). After the dissolution, partition, and conflict that followed the demise of the Han dynasty in 220, the Tang dynasty restored unity to last some 300 years, only to collapse like the Han dynasty. Its demise spanned a quarter century in which violence affected most parts of the empire, and the great administrative lineages that served the Tang dynasty were victims of wholesale slaughter.

Nicolas Tackett describes how the fall of the capital Chang'an in 880 and its destruction in 904 were decisive contributors to the demise of the Tang dynasty (the capital was renamed Xi'an and repopulated in the twentieth century). He explains that "the Tang regime had essentially been decapitated" and "provincial authorities began to act autonomously," and concludes, "The disintegration of the old capital entailed the demise of an entire cultural universe" (2014, 240–241).[14] After the sack of Rome, the European capitals that arose during the Middle Ages rarely suffered episodes in which everything was demolished. In European history, the destruction of an entire ruling aristocracy, even during the French Revolution, was never as thorough as the collapse of the Tang dynasty.

Nearly a century of intense warfare accompanied the transition from the Yuan to Ming dynasties (1350–1450). The chaos caused by the Manchu conquest and defeat of the Ming spanned the period 1550–1683 and cost an estimated eighty million deaths, with warfare continuing into the early eighteenth century. The wars associated with dynastic succession were of a length and intensity that had no parallel in the dynastic wars in Europe.

China's dynastic transitions can be observed in its nation-wide demographic patterns, which follow political transitions. Population numbers blossomed during the Song dynasty, only to decline dramatically to about half of their peak during the Song collapse and the Mongol conquest. The numbers did not recover during the Yuan, which coincided with the Black Death. Population numbers reached a new peak during the Ming period, increasing threefold over the 1291 level. Again, a drastic decline occurred when the Ming collapsed and the violent Qing conquest overtook it, "in 1644 the Chinese population was only about 80 percent of its 1630 level" (Xu, van Leeuwen, and van Zanden 2018, 332).

A similar history of reversion is not so prevalent in European cultural and religious sentiment. Indeed, unorganized bands of soldiers plundered parts of France in the sixteenth century, the Thirty Years War destroyed many regions of Germany, and the Napoleonic Wars engaged almost the entire continent, but none of these ever caused the overarching system of connected monarchies to collapse or a continent-wide elite to be devastated and systematically eliminated.

A descent into chaos caused by a fundamental change in the control of dynastic elites had been avoided since the fall of the Roman Empire.

Europe's population trends exhibit primarily ecological or biological Malthusian dynamics, rather than political dynamics as in China. Yi Xu, Bas van Leeuwen, and Jan Luiten van Zanden conclude that Western European population patterns are more consistent, that

> we see a much more gradual growth, only once interrupted between 1300 and 1400 – by the Black Death. ... Steep declines in Chinese population levels are linked to transitions from one dynasty to another and/or large-scale social-political unrest. ... Comparable declines in European populations did occur – during the Thirty Years War (1618–1648), for example, large parts of Germany and Poland were depopulated – but on a much more limited scale, due to the smaller size of European political entities. ... In China warfare was ... linked to changes in dynasties, but it seems to have had much greater consequences for the demographic development of the region.
>
> *(2018, 233)*

## Stability of Dynastic China

Identification of the properties that reside in the hypernetwork, and of the trade-offs between stability and resilience, can help to describe one of the peculiarities of the trajectory of Chinese history: the entire hub-and-spoke system of governance was resurrected "in a more or less similar territorial framework and with a mode of functioning similar to that of the preceding unified dynasty" (Pines 2012, 11). Replication occurred even when the new dynasty was led by a foreigner.

Why was there such persistent reversion to the same system, with its authoritative bureaucracy, articulated social hierarchy, and an uninterrupted educational curriculum, despite the "tremendous changes in demography and topography, in ethnic composition of the ruling elites and socioeconomic structure, in religion and means of artistic expression" (Pines 2012, 2)? China scholars offer many answers. A widely accepted explanation places the question in its sociological context and emphasizes the emperor's need to weaken clan loyalties. The essential role of officialdom established governance via an impersonal institutional form. The exam system that permitted entry into the mandarinate inculcated loyalty to the prince as supreme within the state. The members of a meritocracy recruited by examination were more likely to be loyal than were the landed gentry, since they derived their status from serving the state.

A centralized officialdom also enabled the emperors to maintain, provision, and conscript a standing professional army. Rather than depend on a nobility with an independent landed base in the form of fiefs, as was the case in Europe, the Chinese emperor, through his government, used conscription as the predominant means of recruitment. Officers were commissioned on the basis of merit, not inherited status. This further established the supremacy of the emperor, diverting loyalty from local clans to the state. Tackett observes, "Under the Song dynasty, a culture of merit came to eclipse the aristocratic ethos of earlier times, largely precluding any resurgence of the old order" (2014, 3). The families that came to dominate society and politics did so on the basis of talent, education, and formal nationwide exams (Hartwell 1982), while Europe's premodern governing elites came to distinguish themselves on the basis of blood. Thus it has come to be well recognized by social historians of China that meritocracy in public administration is one of the most significant distinctions between Chinese and Western societies over the course of premodern history.

The endurance of Chinese culture (in its broadest definition), and the limited value it allocates toward defending political freedom, are puzzles that continue to intrigue China scholars. Is the tenacity of Chinese culture what predisposed generations of Chinese to restore the imperial order with similar governing structures? China's cultural and linguistic continuity survived the Mongol and Manchu invasions.

Did this endurance make the imperial order seem to be the "normal and normative way of sociopolitical conduct," as Pines (2012, 3) argues? Does political culture have a self-organizing capacity? If so, what are the mechanisms of its persistence? And which comes first, culture or political institutions?

The concept of path dependence offers a way to answer these questions and to think about the seemingly irreversible Chinese cultural forbearance of authoritarian rule. In complex systems, initial conditions matter. Once a network grows into a common state of dependence on a central authority, no successor form of that network will develop the capacity to administer itself. Once the component parts grow sufficiently isolated through estrangement from one another, they lose the capacity to act in concert – until a unifying agent steps in. Thus Alexis de Tocqueville in *The Old Regime and the French Revolution* observes that it is far easier to estrange than to reunite a social order in which the parts have been reduced to the status of isolated units ([1856] 1955, 107). Once a centralized hub-and-spoke system is constructed, the lower-level nodes are no longer obliged to maintain contact, and become unable to join forces should the need arise. Conversely, when a system is populated by multiple monarchs, they have an incentive to provide mutual protection to ensure that no single dynasty or monarch takes primacy and gains a privileged position by rising above all the others.

## 4.5 TECHNOLOGICAL PROGRESS AND NETWORK RESILIENCE

This assessment of network dynamics makes it possible to go further than traditional perspectives and to advance the claim that Europe's hypernetwork design made it far more capable of emergent complex behavior. Even in the absence of a central or exogenous coordinator or control agent, Europe could undertake ambitious leaps in the development of new social structures and activities. Due to the "mesh-like" network structure of the system, interactions among nearest neighbors could extend across the shared connectors and the wider system. All members of the system could influence one another without having to share information passed through a single unifying center.

The ease of organizing lateral communication may have been a long-term contributor to Europe's economic takeoff. Coevolutionary change, which produced the Renaissance, the Reformation, the Enlightenment, and industrialization, could start in one part of Europe and attain continent-wide significance. Such events altered the traffic flow, eliminating some nodes while adding others; nevertheless, the surviving hubs could self-organize and reorder the system. The greater resilience of Europe's hypernetwork enabled local institutions of governance and technology diffusion, and ideological adaptation, to evolve at a more accelerated pace, and as a result its economic and social development was able to travel further from its starting point than was China's.[15]

The idea of progress never found a place in traditional Chinese philosophy. As late as the Qing dynasty, the idea of continuous growth in output and productivity was unthinkable. As far back as the Han dynasty, classical Chinese views of history and nature are dominated by notions of the cyclical motion of unity and disunity, and of order and disorder, in which cycles of good fortune turn into decay and immorality. China did indeed experience episodic breakdown, and each collapse remained in the memory of the next dynasty and kept those fears alive. Repeated reminders of a chaotic past and the prospects of a chaotic future could have been behind administrative policy to avoid potentially disruptive innovations. It matters little if the idea of the cycle of fortune was fact or supposition – the fear of collective catastrophe was a persistent theme of Chinese literature and religion.

## 4.6 SOCIAL SYSTEMS AS MULTILEVEL SYSTEMS

Imperial China and a Europe ruled by interconnected royal houses were the longest continuous political systems in history. In hereditary dynastic succession, they shared a common remedy to the dilemma of orderly transition that had been a terminal weakness of historical regimes.[16] Yet after enduring for more than a millennium, both systems vanished during the same decade of the early twentieth century. Differences in their respective hypernetworks account for important later differences in the evolution of China and Europe, up to and including the collapse of dynastic lordship in the period encompassing World War I.

Systems of dynastic succession comprise many inextricably entangled subsystems, and their long-term development is shaped by interdependent bottom-up and top-down dynamics among the system's components. The top nodes are but one part of the network and by themselves do not propel the dynamics of the total system. Familiarity with a system's evolution at the macro level will not enable predictions about its probable future state.

Thus regimes of dynastic succession of Europe and China have enduring qualities embedded in macro *structures* that are distinct from the qualities at the micro *levels*. Even if a subdivision of the whole is subjected to intense observation, the details of the system's parts will not reveal the properties of the whole. Applying the laws that obtain in lower levels will not allow us to reconstruct the hypernetwork level. But observation of that evolution enables us to offer several generalizations for reflection. Historical regimes are likely to be gradual in formation, but sudden in their demise. The source of new structures at the macroscopic level may be hidden in microscopic details. Change at macro levels is likely to spread across micro levels and involve large-scale reorganization at those levels.

This study of the endurance of institutional regimes in China and Europe has considered the trade-offs between dynamical processes of resilience or stability. Although we are still far from establishing the rules that determine a shift from one institutional regime to another, this assessment of dynastic lordship, from a complex systems perspective, allows us to offer an insight about the world of social network architecture that has been relatively unexplored: the manner of assemblage of the various network structures enables spontaneous development of complex behaviors, with important consequences for social evolution. Determining relevant system components, how these components interact, and how local institutional adaptation is nested in system-level variables is an intrinsically complex undertaking. As we progress in representing the multilevel dynamics in the evolution of social institutions, we will be closer to answering the following questions:

- Why did Europe emerge as a system that is more than the sum of its parts, despite its many diverse components evolving separately?
- Why was World War I unavoidable in Europe, despite the high degree of intermarriage among the royal houses?
- How can events in one local network cause a sequence of clustering transitions across the larger system, e.g., the Renaissance, which began in the Italian city states; the Reformation, which began in a small German principality; and the French Revolution and the subsequent spread of nationalism?
- Why do durable regime transitions occur during periods of intermittent hyperactivity followed by long periods of stasis, such as the resurgence of conservatism in France after the worker rebellions of 1848 were crushed? (An outcome not discussed in this volume but that seems to mimic the consequences of 1848 is the Arab Spring uprisings of 2011.)
- Why did intervals of prolonged, intense warfare and extreme disorder, frequently lasting generations, occur between dynastic transitions in China?
- Why might a network structure become maladaptive over the long term, despite the properties of stability and resilience?

This chapter offers evidence that a macroscopic perspective can reveal characteristics that differ from a microscopic perspective. It illustrates how a system's global properties are not readily discernable from or reducible to its micro-level behaviors. No scientific consensus yet exists on the correct way of combining the dynamics at the various levels. Mathematician Jeffery Johnson notes, "Arguably, the need for a formalism to represent multilevel dynamics is this century's greatest obstacle to scientific progress" (2013, 178).[17]

NOTES

1. As was the practice throughout Western Europe, English monarchs held the throne by heredity, but controversy over the right of hereditary kingship continued until the accession of Henry III in 1216. That controversy has never been entirely resolved and has been contested throughout British history. A reason for the unending nature of this dispute stems from the conquest of 1066, which established the claims of a new royal lineage.

2. China is considered the world's longest continuous political system. Europe evolved into a mosaic of nation states, variegated in terms of people, culture, language, and history. As a social, economic, and cultural system, Europe comprises more or less independent parts – subsystems expressed in distinct languages, traditions, and conventions. Yet its historical sources of unity are significant. Because its subsystems constantly and actively interact with one another, it is reasonable to consider Europe itself as a macro system. Most important, Europe enjoyed the continuity of a common system of intermarried dynasties. This system endowed it with the characteristics of what Herbert Simon calls a "nearly decomposable" system (1962), one in which the short-term behavior each component is approximately independent of the short-term behaviors of any of the other components; yet over the long term, the behavior of any component depends in an *aggregate* way upon the behaviors of all the other components. Thus Europe as a collectivity – not any single country within Europe – is the appropriate unit of comparison in this discussion of the Great Divergence.

3. The implications for a system's aggregate resilience of small-world connectivity are discussed in Newman, Barabási, and Watts (2006); Barabási (2003); and Strogatz (2003).

4. Queen Victoria's importance in the network structure of European royalty comes from the fact that her ancestors, most notably King George III, were highly connected. All of Europe's reigning hereditary monarchs since 1939 descend from a common ancestor, Johan Willem Friso, Prince of Orange.

5. For example, a continuous line through the Capetians (987–1328) and Valois, a cadet (younger son) branch of the Capetian dynasty, (1328–1589) to the Bourbons, another cadet branch of the Capetians that ruled until 1792, enabled French monarchs to unify France. Dynastic marriage was a principal means of Hapsburg aggrandizement between 1438 and 1740. The Habsburg monarchy of Charles V, in the sixteenth century, the largest

political entity of its day, was largely the result of dynastic accumulation. The unification of the Low Countries was an accident of dynastic succession. The logic of dynastic accumulation was also behind the Austro-Hungarian monarchy (1867–1918) of the Habsburg dynasty, a multilingual, multicultural empire of more than fifty million inhabitants (Brenner et al. 2003).

6. In one sense, the hypernetwork formation of the papacy is much like the structure of imperial China, being the central hub of a hub-and-spoke system that controlled much of the political competition in Europe, including control of dynastic marriages. It held the essential power to anoint and could therefore legitimize secular power, but it did not exercise that power in its own name. Nor did it control civil administration. The Chinese emperor played both roles; thus, as a concentrator of authority, the Chinese throne far exceeded the power of the pope.

7. Nathaniel Taylor observes, "Ultimately ... in the wake of competition and economic pressure, aristocratic families abandoned co-lordship in favor of a vertical, dynastic structure of succession, restoring the indivisibility of lordship. ... The end result ... was a reorientation of post-Carolingian society under dynasties identified with regional power bases and led by a single (male) heir" (2005, 130).

8. An institution is not a hypernetwork; the relationship between the royals is the network.

9. "Wilson proclaimed that America had intervened not to restore the European balance of power," writes Henry Kissinger, "but to 'make the world safe for democracy' – in other words, to base world order on the compatibility of domestic institutions reflecting the American example. Though this concept ran counter to their tradition, Europe's leaders accepted it as the price of America's entry into the war" (2014, 256).

10. Mayer emphasizes a crisis of legitimacy that "started the final act of the dissolution of Europe's Old Regime." The precipitation occurred when "between 1905 and 1914 the old elites proceeded to reaffirm and tighten their political hold in order to bolster their material, social, and cultural preeminence. In the process they intensified the domestic and international tensions which produced the Great War that started the final act of the dissolution of Europe's Old Regime" (1981, 15).

11. Further discussion of the Song dynasty can be found in Chapter 6.

12. The social rank of the emperors' consorts was less a matter of state policy in China than in Europe, and instances when royal marriage was important for foreign policy, war, or diplomacy were far less prevalent. *Heqin* is the name given to marriage alliances between Chinese emperors, or minor branches of those families, and members of neighboring states. There are hundreds of such marriages recorded in Chinese history. This practice is in sharp contrast with the European tradition, where matches with lines from beyond Europe were rare. The interstate marriages, such as between France and Spain, Scotland and France, England, Scotland, and Wales, might have been considered foreign by the local populations, but they were not "beyond Europe." When stability existed within the Chinese empire, marriages outside the empire were unusual.

13. "The Song had devised so stable a political system that Chao K'uangyin's usurpation was to prove to be the last in Chinese history. In early periods, emperors had repeatedly been robbed of the throne by their great generals, empresses, or civil officials. After 960, this never happened again. Dynasties continued to be snuffed out by foreign conquest or by popular revolution, and members of the imperial family stole the throne from one another, but no subject ever succeeded in usurping the imperial prerogative" (Reischauer and Fairbank 1958, 202).

14. Prior to its destruction the court was "able to appoint capital-based elites to all top-echelon civilian positions in the provincial administration" (Tackett 2014, 240). With the demise of the Tang, "the great medieval families ... vanished entirely from the scene" (3).

15. The conventional view attributes Europe's dynamism to interstate competition. Bloch argues in *Feudal Society* that political fragmentation constrained centralizing monarchs from exercising personal absolutism; because merchants had options for exit, monarchs were prevented from gaining confiscatory powers over the property rights of their subjects (1961, 431). Avner Greif and Guido Tabellini (2010) write that by 1350 Europe's political fragmentation enabled cities to gain self-governance, which facilitated the building of institutions where contractual obligations were enforced via impersonal mechanisms.

   In "Why Europe and the West? Why Not China?," economic historian David Landes (2006) writes that political fragmentation and national rivalries compelled Europe's rulers to pay heed to their citizens, recognize their rights, and promote economic development. In *How the West Grew Rich*, Nathan Rosenberg and Luther Earle Birdzell (1986) claim that the West drew its advantage from institutional arrangements that diffused political power and authority, and which were economically more efficient than the alternatives. In *The Lever of Riches*, Joel Mokyr (1990a) agrees that by fostering political competition between units, political fragmentation created incentives for Europe's technological progress. In contrast, he claims, China's reactionary bureaucracy viewed innovators as troublemakers (231). Other prominent scholars reliant on the "competitive state system vs. unified imperium paradigm" include Max Weber (1927); Jared Diamond (2005); Geoffrey Parker (1996, 2008); and Immanuel Wallerstein (2004).

16. Succession was one area in which Roman jurisprudence conspicuously failed. An emperor could designate a personal heir, but the selection was inherently vulnerable to dispute and frequently provoked commanders to rouse their followers with promises of lavish rewards. From the third century onward, the result was nonstop civil wars that sapped the empire's vitality and opened the door to its destruction by invaders from the north.

17. The central problems for ecology, notes Simon Levin (1992), are pattern and scale.

# 5    Network Formation and the Emergence of Law: From Feudalism to Small-World Connectivity

## with Cameron Harwick

Ties between Germanic chiefdoms started the system of linkages from which the order of European nations arose. We can think of this as a transition from large- to small-world connectivity. We have said that small-world networks are characterized by high clustering coefficients (many nodes connected to a few hubs) and relatively short average path distance. In fact, it only takes a few long-distance links between a few bridge nodes to facilitate communication or information flow across the entire system (see Figure 2.3). Interconnectivity also increases the likelihood of phase transitions in these networks.

By contrast, in a large-world network, there is sparse, even minimal connectivity among nodes, and their path lengths are long. There may be small clusters of nodes (forming communities), but they will be in close proximity to one another; few nodes will bridge the system. Unless they are immediate neighbors, most nodes cannot link. Communication and cooperation are handicapped by language, transport, and physical and cultural barriers that reduce the speed of information flow through a system whose elements exist in isolation. The possibilities for concentration of power are also very weak. There will be no hypernetwork to coordinate the activities of the dispersed nodes and bring order unless a system for the communication of information is established. Change at the system level will occur at infrequent intervals and is likely to be incited exogenously rather than by the system's internal dynamics. We do not possess studies of large-world networks because there is insufficient structure to study.[1] An example is Europe after the fall of the Roman Empire; one could also think of the early tribal cultures of what was to become British North America before 1600, or tribal society more generally.[2]

In this chapter we will explore the role of the legal system in the West, beginning with communal customs, and consider how the laws associated with noble fief holders facilitated the transition toward small-world connectivity. By reducing the number of steps needed to connect one node in the system with another, feudal law increased the system's dynamic stability and augmented its information-processing capabilities, which was supported by the Church's defense of divine right monarchy.

## 5.1   INCREASING RETURNS AND THE WEST'S LEGAL SYSTEM

The previous chapter helped to establish the wider role of institutional dynamics, in particular the legal frameworks for the transmission of landed property and dynastic marriage, in the organic growth of the West's coherence. In this chapter, we observe how the Western legal tradition, and with it the growing autonomy of the legal profession, arose organically, without directionality from a central place, to become a macroscopic historical network, a nexus of institutions, practices, and beliefs that formed a hypernetwork within the wider society. The fusion of Germanic custom and Roman law is an example of structure being shaped by new ways to interconnect within a shared space. That fusion was a mechanism for the invention of new social actors. The emergence of these new actors highlights a key characteristic of European resilience, the capacity for change and stability at the same time.

The evolution of the Western legal tradition is also a story of increasing returns. As legal conceptions were introduced to solve existing dilemmas, new opportunities appeared to extend their use and form new combinations of thinking and practice. Their adaptation and diffusion influenced the design of society, which in turn influenced the legal tradition's subsequent development. Laws selected for further development advanced, while others fell out of favor through negative feedback until they were written out of the tradition or ignored entirely. The more the law was put to work to solve the problems of one group, the more, in turn, it was employed by additional groups, exhibiting increasing returns to scale as a preference coordinator for the entire society.

China's legal tradition, by contrast, emanating from a central place and constructed to serve the imperial dynasty, changed in directions that accorded with the designs and interests of central officials. It was not self-creating, as we shall see, or able to achieve increasing returns to scale.

## 5.2   THE ORIGINS OF STRONG BUT LIMITED GOVERNMENT

Among long-lived civilizations, only Western Europe and East Asia have managed to combine centuries of relative public order with economic dynamism. Even so, the Western political tradition seems to stand apart in its success in maintaining both political order and a high degree of personal freedom, two goals that political economy has long considered to involve trade-offs.

The conundrum of how to avoid creating a state that is too weak to suppress the forces of disorder or too strong to be restrained from becoming a force of disorder itself is not readily resolved. At either of these poles, growth and development will be limited. Indeed, much of the world faces both problems at once: a state that not only fails to protect against, but engages in predatory conduct. Without the protection of property offered by an autonomous legal zone, neither an increase nor a decrease in the state's effective power is likely to expand the opportunities for commerce and economic growth.

The West still benefits from having learned to reconcile two contradictory principles: the unity of the state and constraints on the arbitrary discretion of the state. The core of this practical reconciliation, we argue, originated via a historically unique confluence of two very different types of law: the Germanic tradition of fealty and Roman law, which came together in the medieval feudal order following the breakdown of the Roman political system in the 400s. The former we will call *communitarian*, and the latter, *rationalist*.

Since that time, the Western legal tradition has been the arena of a constant struggle to balance rules and discretion, a struggle that succeeds because of highly effective syncretic institutions and the public ethos that safeguards them. Bloch concludes thus: "The originality of [feudalism] consisted in the emphasis it placed on the idea of an agreement capable of binding the rulers; and in this way . . . it has in truth bequeathed to our Western civilization something with which we still desire to live" (1961, 475). Before moving into the history and establishing its timelines, we will define communitarian and rationalist concepts.[3]

## 5.3 COMMUNITARIAN AND RATIONALIST LAW: FOUR RECONCILIATIONS

Communitarian law is by far the older of the two methods of organizing society. It appears to be a feature of tribal organization originating with the earliest hunter-gatherer bands. In early stages of social organization, the burden of enforcement falls upon the entire community. The people choose the judges, who also have strong personal connections to them. Enforcement evolves experientially on a case-by-case basis and is typically unwritten. Custom is transferred orally, but this does not offer the benefit of ex-post explication since past cases cannot be revisited or their meaning evaluated. Judges and claimants might remember how a similar complaint or query was dealt with for some period of time; but custom transitions to being considered *law* only once it is written.

Communitarian legal orders limit the scale of political organization. First, the enforcement of communitarian law tends to be relatively decentralized, consisting of social pressure in addition to formal punishment. It is legitimated from the bottom up, which enables congruence between law and actual practice. Communitarian law is primarily designed for community preservation. To end the escalation of conflict and allow harmony to be reestablished, it prioritizes restitution for damages or for injury over determinations of individual guilt or culpability. It generally derives its legitimacy from an egalitarian ethos, one that seeks to prevent domination by internal elites or factions. Second, rarely are customs premised on an evaluation of general cases or principles. Norms generally evolve as a response to circumstances in a particular environment and in response to specific disputes. Therefore, altering a customary practice may allow prior disputes to resurface. When different groups come together, their norms of settling disputes will not necessarily harmonize.[4]

Rationalist law, on the other hand, is typically associated with hierarchical political organization and the needs of administering a large and diverse polity. Examples of highly rationalist law are the Napoleonic Code and its predecessor, the Justinian Code, to be considered later. Legitimacy extends from the top political leadership down or from a central source outward. In contrast to communitarian law, rationalist law opens the possibility for incongruity between the content of the law and the actual practice of local communities. Judges are appointed by the state and represent its interests. The law is systematically "imposed." For practical reasons, therefore, the enforcement of rationalist law tends to be the result of conquest and subordination, rather than amalgamation. It is bureaucratic, often lax in practice, and more aspirational, especially in the regions farthest from the central administration. In practice, the king's courts typically relied upon local juries and local officials who were often unpaid.

In an administrative state, organizational enhancements are needed to advance the state's capability for rule enforcement. Literacy must come first; rationalist law is characterized by a written legal code. The elite of a communitarian legal order can be illiterate; the elite of a rationalist legal order cannot. Second, because religion tends to be far more institutionalized in rationalist than in communitarian societies, religious authority will often specifically legitimize the rule of the sovereign over the people (Purzycki et al. 2016).[5] Being recognized by a religious authority, however, does not necessarily constrain the sovereign to abide by limits on their power or to credibly commit to protecting the rights of their subjects. Third, the administration of rationalist law entails the concept of separation between office and officeholder. Functionaries of the state are permitted to execute certain tasks with the imprimatur of the state that they would not be permitted to do in their capacity as private individuals. Such a distinction is alien to the personalist organization of a communitarian legal order.

The advantages and disadvantages of rationalist law are the mirror image of those of communitarian law. Where communitarian law becomes increasingly ineffective as the community grows, rationalist law excels at integrating diverse communities into a cohesive larger unity. The presence of a written code, consciously harmonized among all its parts, makes possible the commercial and political intercourse of far-flung and diverse communities. Empires, for this reason, develop some form of rationalist legal system, although not every rationalist legal system takes part in a political structure of that magnitude.

Because lawbreakers in a communitarian system risk group censure, this can protect against opportunism by group members; rationalist law, coming from afar, leaves its subjects vulnerable to the abuse of power from within the community itself. And because rationalist law is based on top-down legitimacy, it can serve as a vehicle of revolutionary change in a way that communitarian law, which ensures the congruence of law with actual practice, cannot. In principle, the sovereign in a rationalist legal system can upend the entire legal order at once, although practical governance in the wake of such an action will be very difficult.

This holds as well in the area of property rights, where the dilemma is to build a state that is strong enough to employ coercive means to prevent citizens from expropriating the property of other citizens, yet not so strong that it can violate citizens' property rights. Not being able to make credible promises has an economic impact: it will not pay for subjects to make long-term investments or engage in large-scale commerce, if the benefits of such activity can be seized at the ruler's discretion. Legitimation of hierarchically positioned rule enforcers requires a degree of reconciliation with prior distributions of property rights.

In general, there are three outcomes that can result from efforts to rationalize a communitarian legal order. First, the formal law imposed alongside an existing communitarian order may be simply ignored as "dead letter," as a Chinese proverb goes, "the mountains are high and the emperor is far away". Locals may pay lip service to the formal law, but for all intents and purposes, their lives remain governed by the existing communitarian law. There is little disruption, but also little possibility of exploiting the scale advantages of rationalist law.

Second, the formal law may be imposed at a great cost that increases with the variance between it and existing practice. The first priority is often the eradication of previous practices, on the premise that they are not part of the law, although they are often ingrained in codes of conduct. This creates a gap between the behavior that is permitted by law and the expectations and norms of the community. When European colonialists decreed that certain African tribes could privatize their land holdings, headmen, as agents of the colonial state, were able to confiscate and transfer communal land to kin. Latent tribal conflicts over ownership and use resurfaced (Van de Walle 2001). Transformed into agents of the colonial power, the traditional leaders no longer had an incentive to safeguard the community from the opportunistic behavior of powerful group members.

Finally, communitarian law may retain its general shape but be *itself* rationalized rather than replaced by an existing rationalist system. Customs are written down and contradictions are ironed out, with particular customs being justified in light of prevailing values.

This option causes only minimal normative disruption to the community and offers the opportunity to take advantage of heightened political organization. The downside is that the community may have little interest in rationalizing, and even if it does, the process may be slow or fitful. Yet the more leaders impose rationalist templates, the more they risk their efforts being perceived as an unwelcome transgression, as described in the second scenario.

A distinctive process of coalitional bargaining enabled the polities of Western Europe to reconcile their communitarian norms with rationalist lawmaking.

## Synthesis of Communitarian and Rationalist Law

Both external threats (Turchin 2008) and intrastate competition (Zhao 2015) tend to drive political centralization and legal rationalization. Regimes able to organize in a rationalist manner and marshal more resources can prevail against less rationalistically ordered polities. Rome had developed a rationalist legal administration early in its history, but when the empire fell to the Germanic tribal populations, communitarian order resurged. The Western tradition of limited but strong government then grew out of a process somewhere between informal bottom-up norm formation and top-down reconciliation of formal code. The powerful feudal nobility was the force behind the preservation of the contractual character of older Germanic law. The king was the source of top-down imperatives that bolstered political order. A synthesis resulted: extensive borrowing from Roman law enabled a rationalization of Germanic custom. This resulted in the preservation and codification of rights of assembly and norms of consensual decision making, while eliminating election as a condition for eligibility to be head of state and making heredity the sole basis of a rule of succession.

By the twelfth century, the single most distinguishing feature of the Western legal tradition – the notion that law transcends politics and is binding on the state itself – had come to be recognized, and with it the notion that the king may make law, but not arbitrarily; law must be made lawfully, and the lawmaker is bound by it. The rights of citizens are grounded in both communal and state-based codes, and it is this confluence that has given the West its legacy of strong but limited government, which blends public order with a significant degree of personal freedom. The following sections trace how key Germanic contractual traditions pervaded the rationalization of the Middle Ages.

### The First Reconciliation: Kings, Nobles, and the Bond of Fealty

The decline of the Roman Empire took place from the third through the fifth centuries, and brought with it a collapse of the imperium's formal, state-based administration.[6] The organization of the traditional Germanic tribes – the Saxons, Franks, Burgundians, Lombards, Vandals, and Goths – was predominantly based on custom and kinship, as was typical of communitarian legal systems. Families or clans, rather than individuals, held land, and loyalty was owed to particular commanders rather than to the more abstract entities of law or state.

The most persistent characteristic of political authority among the conquering tribes was the notion of fealty, which began as a kinship bond, drawing as it did on the Germanic concept of homage owed by a knight to his lord. On the basis of the bond of fealty, the conquerors were able to reestablish order and legitimacy, and usher in the system we now call feudalism. The lords received land holdings from the king in exchange for military service and fees. They also protected the peasants who toiled on the land. Fealty is at the normative core of feudalism and was both the cause of, and the solution to, the problem of endemic social disorder throughout European society.

On the one hand, legally defined loyalty ties provided not only a hierarchical order in spite of the apparent fragmentation, but also a wider web of bonds than would have been possible under solely kinship bonds. It linked the feudal elites across territorial boundaries into a network of loyalty ties that transcended kinship networks and therefore could be the nucleus for the developing state organizations. Without such a network, the Roman Church would not have been able to exercise the coordinating power across Christendom that it later did. It depended for its defense on royal lineages that in turn attained their legitimacy among the people by having been anointed by the Church. On the other hand, because the kings and feudal lords were a warrior class, Europe remained mired in petty war for centuries. Had feudal bonds been defined only in terms of traditional Germanic law, the West may have been unable to overcome the endemic disorder and continuous warfare between tribes of the post-Roman period.

There is no specific century for the onset of feudalism. In its purest form, feudalism was a conception of social order based upon a unitary command structure descending from the king. When it was imposed by conquest, as was the case with the Norman invasion of Britain in 1066, its actual practice was closest to the idealized form, linking all nobles into a unified command structure and viewing all land as descending from the king as a gift to the nobles in exchange for service. Most of the European population experienced feudalism in an ad hoc manner.

Roman ideals of a unified state never entirely disappeared from the political order imposed by the conquering Germanic tribes who, by the end of the fifth century, occupied much of Italy and controlled parts of Hispania, Gaul, and Britain. Memories of the splendor of imperial Rome were inspiration during the early Middle Ages, and often invoked among its dispossessed people. The new rulers, the Germanic kings, aspired to cloak themselves in symbols of legitimacy derived from remembrances of things Roman, for example, in the issuance of coins to popularize their names and images (Duby 1974). Germanic "kings" in the Gallic wars, for example, had already added Roman suffixes derived from *rex* to their names: Vercingetorix, Orgetorix, Dumnorix, and Ambiorix.

### Consolidation of Germanic Custom and Its Rearticulation As Law

Around the ninth century, the Germanic bond of loyalty began to undergo a transformation from a *kinship* bond to a *legal* bond, which became known as fealty.[7] In this sense, though inspired by Roman practice, it was less an imposition of an existing rationalist order than a partial indigenous "rationalization" of the existing communitarian order.

Bloch notes that by the twelfth century, the classic foundation of feudal liberty and privilege, i.e., the notion of equality in privilege, had achieved recognition as law (1961, 197). A "full-fledged contractual reciprocity that began to be associated with the lord–vassal bond" became a legally enforceable principle of personal loyalty, or fealty, both between the king and the lords, and between lords and their vassals (Berman 1983, 305). It retained the communitarian principle, being based on personal identity rather than more abstract categories. Yet unlike the kinship loyalty from which it derived, the fealty contract could end, with both sides free to seek the services of another.[8] As Bloch (1961, 451) writes, "Vassal homage was a genuine contract and a bilateral one. If the lord failed to fulfil his engagements he lost his rights." By the same token, if the vassal did not provide military services when called upon, or some value that commuted that obligation in terms of money, then the vassal's land could be taken and the vassal removed.

Feudal law emphasized the endowment of autonomous persons as bearers of rights and obligations. And although the particular rights and obligations differed according to social and economic status, they attached to individuals in their capacity as individuals, regardless of rank. This contractual conception of political authority, essential to the Western tradition of limited government, therefore owes its genesis to the mutual character of the bond of fealty.

The West's debt to these legal developments is obvious. Berman (1983, 309) depicts the principle of reciprocity of rights between lords and vassals as the West's first exposure to the notion of mutuality of legal obligations among persons of different rank. The conception of sovereignty eventually came to be viewed in terms of the rights and obligations of fealty that defined the relationship between the knightly aristocracy and the crown. Transferring the concept of mutual responsibility that governed the lord–vassal relationship to the political sphere enabled the Church to defend the right of resistance to a bad prince. This right of resistance was based upon "the universally recognized right of the vassal to abandon the bad lord" (Bloch 1961, 464). That a rationalist theory of rights could be established from out of feudal loyalties contributes a unique character to the Western legal tradition not found in other historical regimes.

Feudalism's legal structure concerned kings and feudal lords, and was, for the most part, only narrowly concerned with lord–vassal relations. It had evolved from Germanic loyalty oaths, especially the law of fiefs, leaving a great gap in secular law. The common people were left out and so too were commercial transactions. This gap in secular law was to be filled with principles derived from the rediscovered Justinian Code.

## Rediscovery of the Justinian Code

Western Europe's model of strong but limited government derives from the confluence of rationalistic Roman law and the older, communitarian Germanic law (Kelly 1992, 92), which began to cross-pollinate after the rediscovery in the eleventh century of the *Codex Justinianus*, a multi-volume codex of Rome's civil laws commissioned by the Emperor Justinian (482–565), including laws incorporated during his reign. By 1130, the Justinian Code had spread across Europe in the curriculums used by the newly forming law schools. Its study over the ensuing centuries made a significant ingress into the feudal order. A melding of rationalist and communitarian elements occurred that featured the advantages of both types of legal order: latitude for personal freedom combined with the capacity for sophisticated hierarchical organization. Political expropriation was curbed, as was the hazard of redistributing wealth according to an egalitarian ethos. Communitarian law was rationalized, but we shall see that key compromises, rather than farsighted design, strengthened the central government while constraining arbitrary exercises of power. Had state power depended only upon rationalist law, it could have been instrumental to the aggrandizement of the personal power of the rulers, but its fusion in Western Europe with the traditions of the Germanic tribes prevented the administrative law of the state from becoming entirely subservient to the wishes of the ruler.

Roman law jurists had made serious efforts to reconcile statutory legislation with customs based upon the consent of the people and established by usage. They created law where existing custom was incomplete.[9] This included new activities developing from the expansion of trade and commerce, such as land transfers out of the family trade; marriage and female inheritance not covered by customary law; and eventually statecraft.

At the time the code was discovered, the property arrangements of early feudal Europe were still recognizably Germanic.[10] The tribal system of *Gewere*, for example, governed landholding, although *Gewere* failed to clearly distinguish between legal title and physical control. The Germanic tribes recognized various forms of limited ownership, but unlike movables, such as cattle or sheep, land belonged to each family collectively. Family ownership gradually developed into the private ownership by the family head, but for a long time that head could transfer ownership only with the consent of the nearest heirs. Such an arrangement stymied commerce not only in land, but also in the commodities that might be produced on the land if it were alienable. As trade and commerce began to pick up in the eleventh century, *Gewere* was felt to be increasingly restrictive. A modern economy required more formal systems of land transfer. Again, Germanic law was largely unwritten, varied from place to place, and assigned rights and obligations based on personal identity – all features that impeded commerce.[11]

The usefulness of the Justinian Code was immediately apparent, and Roman ideas became integral to the development of a general European legal tradition. It now offered a store of legal principles and rules that were invested with the authority of ancient Rome and centuries of distinguished jurists; it held out the possibility of a comprehensive legal code, providing substantive and procedural law for a wide range of situations; and it included mechanisms to amend law in ways that were consistent with underlying communitarian principles. It distinguished, for example, between ownership and possession, and between the different obligations resulting from contracts and torts, distinctions that became increasingly necessary as the volume of commerce increased.

The code's rediscovery left the inhabitants of Europe with a dual legal tradition to address particular matters and resolve conflicting interests. It significantly reduced the role of the feudal lords as the fonts of justice and administration. The interests of a great number of groups could now be served by a formal legal tradition. Merchants and city dwellers were eager to adopt the code because of its predictability and uniformity, and indeed the code's first post-Roman usage is reputed to be its voluntary adoption by Spanish merchant fairs in the twelfth century. By codifying the necessary and sufficient conditions under which a property owner was entitled to redress, Roman law enabled individuals to extricate their property from communal control. This liberty, previously enjoyed by all Roman citizens, was reclaimed first by urban dwellers across Europe but later extended to all inhabitants and subjects of kings, as Roman law enabled jurists to override communal practices like *Gewere*.

## *The Second Reconciliation: Merging Germanic and Roman Law in the Definition of Sovereignty*

The kings throughout Europe had grand plans for the application of Roman law to statecraft. They envisioned the possibility of robust public law with which to reconstruct a centralized state whose legitimacy resided in statute, rather than custom. Kings employed jurists from as early as the 1200s to augment their own legitimacy via efforts to codify and harmonize previously unwritten elements of the legal order. These jurists compiled and revived Roman law, aided by canon (Church) law, to assert royal prerogatives in diplomacy, defense, legislation, taxation, and justice. The powers of monarchy were strengthened during the eleventh century, when kings across the continent took the initiative to consolidate political power and to separate secular authority from that of the Church. The nobles of the realm, we will see, responded quickly with their own efforts to reassert their particular liberties and privileges through the creation of parliaments in the eleventh and twelfth centuries.

As Roman law became the standard platform for legal discourse across the continent, kings and their apologists found in Roman texts a basis for expanding their own mandates. They tried to eliminate seigneurial courts administered by feudal lords on the premise that the right to administer justice had been appropriated from the king. The French kings, in particular, adopted elements of Roman law during the late medieval and early modern periods to codify the spheres of the law that were "alienated" from the king, who was its true source, and to inculcate universal obedience to the state. To further bolster the monarch above the feudal lords, kings used a Roman law precept, *legibus solutus* ("released from the laws"), which was applicable only to the emperor, to argue that the king was above the law, based upon the notion that the king is just as absolute in his rights as is the *dominus* over his estate.

However, the wave of assertive monarchical rights gave rise in the sixteenth century to a countercurrent. Monarchomachs, Huguenot lawyers of an anti-monarchical persuasion, also scoured the ancient texts for precepts to constrain the French crown from seizing more and more authority, and to justify the legal permissibility of resistance. This right of resistance derived from the idea that the populace taken together, in its corporate body, was sole owner of the kingdom. The king was delegated the authority to rule the people, and with this came a tutorial function as guardian, or curator, of public affairs and administrator of the people's estate, but proprietorship remained with the people and could not be alienated or squandered.

In the Monarchomach theory of constituent power, the people hold collective dominion, and kings are merely occupants appointed to exercise power that was fully recoverable and revocable by popular mandate. People could not have been constituted by kings; there had to have been people before there were kings to rule over them. Kings, then, were constituted by the people. Thus, the Monarchomachs claimed, the people were the sources, not the subjects, of royal power, laying the foundation of constitutional republicanism. By extension of *lex regia* (the hypothetical right of the people of Rome to confer authority on the emperor), resistance could be thus justified as a legally valid act of recovering the rights delegated to the king by the people against a ruler's unlawful seizure of power, or as response to a breach of the ruler's contractual obligations.[12]

Having a doctrinal basis for limiting sovereignty would have meant very little without a social context in which to carry it out. A social or coalitional context was essential to the West's relative success in achieving limited government. Legal doctrine derived from Roman law supplied basic conceptual material for arguments limiting sovereignty, but the defense by the nobility of its corporate rights underpinned this constraint. If Europe's royal lineages had not coevolved within a web of ties to feudal society, whose customs and obligations they were bound to uphold in order to maintain their own power and legitimacy, they would have had little interest in restraining the growth of the state's statutory authority.

## The Third Reconciliation: The Fiscal Role of Parliament and Urban Enfranchisement

A history of the Western legal tradition would not be complete without considering the essential role played by parliaments, shaping agreements between the sovereigns and their peoples or estates, and expanding the contractual nature of sovereignty; and in this development we can see the genesis of the unique capacity of Western sovereigns to make credible commitments.

Parliaments (*Cortes Generales*) appeared first in Spain and scattered across the Iberian Peninsula; meetings that resembled parliament first occurred in Catalonia in 1027 and were formalized in 1192. The practice spread: Castile 1216; Aragon 1218–1236; Navarre 1253 and Valencia 1261. The Model Parliament in England was held in 1295. The French Estates-General came later, meeting first in 1302. The impetus for the creation of the parliaments came from the nobles, who, as power consolidated around the kings, had seen their own powers and capacity for resistance diluted.[13] As early as the eleventh century, and with increasing regularity during the twelfth century, the nobles began to reassert their own rights and privileges.

Kings could have systematically withdrawn noble privileges, but at great political cost. Economist Roger Myerson (2008) explains that kings who tampered with noble privileges, whether those of an individual or a group, stood to lose the esteem of the entire nobility. A king could try to bypass the nobles by recruiting new members, but the new supporters, of course, would have little reason to trust him, and he likewise could expect little loyalty. Lack of commitment power, Myerson reasons, presents an opportunity for a challenger to unite factions that do not expect equal treatment under the incumbent. The creation of a formal written constitution, such as the *Magna Carta*, prevented the ruler from arbitrarily displacing supporters who had provided past service.

Nevertheless, parliaments were not an inevitable upshot of feudal order; a simple proof of this rests in the evolution of feudalism in Japan. It did not result in a parliamentary system, not for lack of nobles but because of the absence of independent townships. In Europe, the commercial wealth of the towns rendered the parliaments particularly useful to the monarchs.[14] Enfranchisement of the towns enabled the crown to expand its fiscal capacity. Offering the towns a role in the levying of taxes, in turn, enabled them to gain leverage with the crown to see that their interests were attended to.[15] Compliance with the sovereign's requests for taxation was exchanged for promises by the crown of greater fairness in assessments and levies, and rendered urban property less susceptible to the dangers of expropriation via confiscation, repudiation of debts, or currency devaluation. From the increasing returns to cooperation, both the towns and the sovereign reaped benefits. Enhancing the creditworthiness of towns facilitated the crown's ability to borrow, enabling town merchants to support exceptional levies to the crown for the purposes of warfare.

The requirement for parliamentary consent for taxation could be used to punish the king for expropriating the rights of his subjects, making the temptation to violate contracts with creditors less appealing. Paradoxically, by limiting the discretion of the king, enfranchisement built collective confidence that promises would be carried out, and this helped to build trust, thereby enabling kings to pursue plans of their own and strengthening the monarchy over the long term. Without a mechanism to prevent abuses, a king stood to lose the trust of the wider community and thereby the ability to exercise power; but when monarchs stayed within the limits set by parliament, they gained the cooperation of the corporate bodies of the realm, thus acquiring a mechanism that could be used to gain consent, cooperation, and revenues from the nobles, towns, guilds, lawyers, and bishops to carry out their plans reliably.[16] By binding the sovereign to fulfill their promises to protect commercial property, enfranchisement expanded the contractual notion of government while giving kings access to the towns' expanding commercial wealth.

Between the fifteenth and eighteenth centuries, the relative importance of national assemblies expanded in northwestern Europe, while it declined in southern and central Europe.[17] This occurred because kings who used parliaments as sources of revenue lost momentum in pushing the cause of royal absolutism forward. With the power to bargain over taxes, parliaments, especially in the northwest, were able with widely varying success to push back against concentration of power by the monarchy and safeguard their own privileges. In Spain and France, where the crown was able to secure an independent source of revenue (in Spain from the colonies and in France from direct taxation of the peasantry) without depending on a consensual mechanism, rationalization under royal auspices could proceed relatively unchecked. But where fiscal necessity required consultation, as in England and the Netherlands, the nobles were able to effectively preserve their political leadership as representatives of the rural population. Thus there was a further reconciliation of feudalism with the needs of the modern state in northern Europe.

While the rise of the towns had a critical role in forging the Western legal tradition of limited but strong government, their role is consistent with the narrative that emphasizes the foundational role of contractual obligations between the lords and the crown. The crown's relationship with the feudal nobility set the tone for integrating towns as corporate entities with distinctive rights into the polity. Legal historian Antonio Marongiu reflects that, even against strong countercurrents, "in the age of absolutism the assemblies found the strength to survive through the deep-rooted belief in the contractual nature of agreements between sovereigns and their people or estates" (1968, 233). The legal precedent of parliamentary pacts resides in the feudal contract, reinterpreted to meet current and future conditions (92).[18] Again we see increasing returns at work.

### The Fourth Reconciliation: People and the King

As noted, feudalism's structures concerned the kings and the feudal lords, and was only about them. Serfs were not protected by feudal law. But as early as the eleventh century, the Church started to promulgate the notion that the relationship between the king and his subjects was also governed by the duty of fealty.[19] The contractual basis of political sovereignty, inherited from Germanic custom, thus gained a dual character: in addition to the ties of mutual obligation between the nobles and the king, Roman law also provided the scaffolding for a similar mutual obligation between the crown and the people. One aspect of this duty was the establishment of kings' courts to hear the grievances of the common people and adjudicate these on the basis of the law developed along Roman lines by the medieval jurists. From this notion came the right of the king to extend his power by expanding the sway of his own judicial institutions, often at the expense of the rights formally exercised by local lords. In England the king's court was where common law was created after the Norman Conquest. In principle, all the king's subjects, no matter how humble, were entitled to their day in court to defend their honor, their person, and their property.

Nevertheless, in contrast to the nobility, the people, meaning the serfs under the manorial system, had little recourse for punishing a king for malfeasance. The barriers were very high for dispersed rural communities to collectively organize a challenge to a monarch, who ruled as the pinnacle of the feudal hierarchy. It was partly in recognition of this inherent problem of political mobilization (collective action) that in *The Old Regime and the French Revolution* Tocqueville argued that without the nobility there would be no true constraint on the ruler, and thus no real freedom ([1856] 1955). Tocqueville seems to have appreciated the Germanic (communitarian) origins of Western liberty, but not the Roman (rationalist) origins, which were what eventually extended to non-nobles the same right to a trial by one's equals that originally only belonged to the lords. To the nobility, the monarch was *primus inter pares*, and his status was legally constrained. But to the people, the king's status was steeped in magic and extraordinary power. From the eighth century, Frankish kings were anointed with sacred oils that gave their spirit a sacred quality they shared only with the bishops. In *The Royal Touch*, Bloch links the political history of Europe with religious or magical ideas of kingship. He suggests that supernatural expressions of the king's power were also expressions of the king's political mission as head of the people (1973). The sacred and secular responsibilities of kingship were both inspired by the same font of communitarian idealism. But especially from the fifteenth century onward, European kings used Roman law to establish their domination on the basis of a direct connection with the people, again reconciling Germanic and Roman notions of lordship. Roman law helped to formalize the king's responsibility to protect the politically weak.

The kings used Roman law to establish their powers on the basis of a direct connection with the people.[20] However, that enlargement of the monarch's responsibility carried with it the danger, inherent to rationalist law, of an unconstrained sovereign, unable to credibly bind himself and make commitments. On the basis of popular legitimacy, a king could rule as an absolutist because if the people tried to constrain him, they would face large barriers to collective action. Over time this final reconciliation of the kingship with the populace spurred the nascent demands of groups with little prior access to rights and protections under feudalism.

## 5.4   WHAT THE WEST STILL HAS TO OFFER

During the first two decades of the twenty-first century, numerous books and articles have highlighted threats to the Western conception of liberalism, from both within and without. Those concerned with preserving the West's unique political legacy should remember that constitutional controls over political power, not democracy alone, separate Western law from the laws of China and the rest of the world. In the West, limited government has a long historical pedigree grounded in a living legal tradition. Rome as much as Greece was a source of this unique political tradition. Without the principle that law is supreme over the state and that the ruler is, to paraphrase the twelfth-century English jurist-cleric Henry de Bracton ([c.1235] 1968) "under God and the Law," democratic control can transform into arbitrary power. "It is not the source, but the limitation of power," wrote Hayek, "which prevents it from being arbitrary" (1944, 71).

The powers and responsibilities of European kings evolved from the magical to the contractual, but their powers were never as sweeping as those belonging to Chinese monarchs. As a practical matter, kings in medieval Europe lacked the administrative machinery to either collect sufficient revenues or to undertake extensive everyday management of the polity.[21] The governance of commerce belonged to the towns; irrigation was typically under the jurisdiction of the lord; and education fell within the jurisdiction of Church leaders.[22] To attain durable power, kings had to motivate the corporate groups of the realm, i.e., the nobles, guilds, towns, lawyers, and bishops, as captains of society to cooperate with kingly directives. Thus they found it necessary to bind themselves, to make credible commitments, to these corporate bodies and to rule via a coalition of civil society leaders.

As early as the thirteenth century, legal scholarship articulated the separation of law from political power as such: "The king must not be under man but under God and under the law, because law makes the king" (Bracton ([c.1235] 1968, 33)). This restraint, established by fixed rules and a shared ethos on the arbitrary use of power, is the legacy that undergirds the prosperity and liberties that citizens of the West enjoy. Even when monarchies claimed absolute power, the law transcended politics. The basis of US constitutionalism is that the lawmakers are themselves bound by the law. That tradition of government constrained by law originated in the first reconciliation of the oath of fealty with the rationalist notions of the state articulated in Roman law.

## Lessons from Europe's Reconciliation of Germanic and Roman Law

In this section we explore what lessons developing countries can take from the West's evolving legal infrastructure. A sound legal system is critical for strengthening commitment power in governments, which in turn are critical to the success of economic policy. If a government has only weak incentives to carry out such promises as keeping the value of the currency stable, economic actors who recognize this will respond opportunistically, selecting short-term payoffs over longer-term investments – behaviors that produce lower levels of investment across society.

The Western legal tradition derives from layers of practice built up over the course of centuries. Within the larger decentralized structure of Europe's network organization, the legal profession arose with its own specialized forms of learned discourse and a nexus of institutions. It was not just a body of knowledge recorded in texts; it was also a tradition of praxis. It had an institutional body comprised of courts and law schools that were self-governing, in which lawyers could gather and develop ways to think about and practice the law.[23] As such, it is self-creating and difficult to replicate and transfer.

With its study of the West's legal formation, the first lesson that this chapter carries for political-legal reform in general, and for efforts to transplant existing legal forms and theories to the rest of the world more specifically, is that *an institution's legitimacy depends more on the process by which it was formed and developed over time than on the ends it served at any single point in time.* As a network of relationships that could continuously adapt to the needs of the society, the Western legal tradition is best understood as something organic, a living system, not a mechanism managed from a central place. Its very nature as an open system enabled it to evolve in tandem with other cultural transformations, such as the Renaissance, the Reformation, the Enlightenment, and industrialization, that characterized European society.

The evolution of the Western legal tradition provides some clues about how to engage with the complexity of governance in fragile regions, where the framework for an organized state is either absent or has dissolved. We've traced Europe's unique governmental trajectory to the confluence of Roman and Germanic law, from the fall of Rome, through the feudal institutions and the parliaments, and to the establishment of institutions that protected private property from the sovereign's grasp. The broadest lesson from this historical approach is that institutional and legal frameworks must take into account existing "tacit" knowledge, i.e., the knowledge embedded in practice (Polanyi 1958), in an iterative and empirical process. Whether top down or bottom up, it must balance an interplay of formal and informal rules.[24] If the Roman law of Justinian aspired to regulate morality and eliminate tribal customs, Roman legions would have been required to impose it uniformly across Europe. Berman tells us that instead, "It was the twelfth-century scholastic technique of reconciling contradictions and deriving general concepts from rules and cases that first made it possible to coordinate and integrate the Roman law of Justinian" (1983, 9). If custom is at too great a variance with formal law, the result will be, at best, that the law is highly costly to administer or, at worst, that old patterns of conflict are revived.

A second lesson is the *importance of preventing the occurrence of a legal "vacuum" when transitioning from one set of rules to another.* During the gradual emergence of the West's legal institutions and the centuries-long transition to a state-based system of rule making, most activities of the population were safeguarded either through seigneurial or Church courts. For example, in France, community decision making once took place in traditional village assemblies before a seigneurial official. Over time, these were increasingly held before an official of the crown, but without a gap in the transition from one regime to another. The strategies that traditionally enabled the community to manage the moral complexity of their daily lives did not disappear until after the state had acquired the ability to coordinate a new, comprehensive legal regime.

The spread of Roman law succeeded because it provided communities with solutions for actual, existing problems. It spread by filling in gaps in existing custom as social relations became commercialized. It was sought after as a way to address useful objectives. Roman law gained increased utility as more groups turned to the law to remedy potential conflicts or to anticipate contingencies that might arise as the web of social relations expanded via commercialization. Thus we observe the usefulness of law spreading from kings, nobles, and bishops to merchants, guilds, and townspeople, and eventually to peasants. This expansion, or democratization, of law as a preference coordinator for the entire society exhibits increasing returns to scale, like the spread of social media on the Internet. The more a particular platform like Twitter or Facebook is used, the more useful it becomes. This well-established network effect applies to the use of law and had consequences for Europe's economy. It created a contractual framework for privately invested enterprise to accumulate capital, enabling credit to pass from savers to merchants and eventually to industrialists. There was a political effect as well, eventually enabling rights to spread from the privileged orders to the common people. The decentralization of networks fostered the independent status of law and its use by many distributed actors, from the humblest peasants and government officials to aristocrats by birth.

By contrast, many independent states, especially former European colonies, have struggled. The colonizing rulers in these states manufactured new legal regimes patterned and/or transported from the home country to replace the older customs that governed traditional community relations. Communal customs were uprooted before a viable alternative could come into play, leaving many aspects of community activity without legal safeguards at independence. This vacuum enabled the proverbial local "big man" to expropriate many of the rights of the population, using personal connections with central authorities to protect those usurpations. The imposition of national law thereby enables those with access to power to act with limited responsiveness to local populations, rendering the new institutions of the state into tools of oppression.

Third, *legal changes are more likely to be legitimated when they address existing problems.* Medieval kings established Roman law courts in response to the unsatisfactory provision of justice by manorial courts. To exercise justice effectively, kings employed jurists to write law that enabled the royal courts to attend to many activities that Germanic law or the feudal custom did not address in a consistent way. Cities adopted the *Codex Justinianus* in whole or in part to remedy the commercial weaknesses of Germanic law. Germanic kings adopted Roman ingredients to administer vastly expanded territories. There was a popular basis to the initial rationalization of Rome's legal system. It met the demands of the unrepresented population for written rules, encouraged by a desire of fairness, and it developed over the next millennium through jurists' discussions of contemporary legal problems (Stein 1999).

These are all examples of how directed legal change enjoys a greater chance of success if it can address specific dissatisfactions with the existing legal system and offer superior alternatives. On account of its relevance to actual needs, the demand for law in the West followed the logic of increasing returns in which at each stage of economic and political complexity the demand for law grew. The network structure accommodated this growth by allowing institutions and practitioners of the law to join the continent's hub-based structure of power without rupturing the connectivity among existing centers of power. Eventually, legal antecedents established in the premodern period allowed private firms in the West to mobilize capital on a massive scale without state intervention, further reinforcing the role of law and augmenting its nonpolitical character.

At a time when four billion people have inadequate access to legal services or protection from abuse by the powerful, it is useful to reconsider how law is the basis of Western democracy, and to rebalance the emphasis on the reform of elections and political parties in global development policy. Democracy alone is not the hallmark of the West's liberal heritage. Rather, the unique character of the West's democratic heritage derives from its political and judicial institutions, which are supported by a body of legal scholarship that reconciled Germanic and Roman law, and which emerged from feudalism to "tie the King's hands" and constrain kingly discretion. The foundation of the West's political development is the constitutional restraint on political authority. Its legitimacy resides in binding those who govern to the same laws as other citizens. This legitimacy of an apolitical legal tradition is the bedrock of liberalism and has enabled the Western legal tradition to support a state powerful enough to be effective in maintaining order, but in which political power is constrained.[25] The law's emergence, both as an institution and practice, within the larger network structure of society was critical in the development of limited government.

## 5.5 CHINA'S LEGAL TRADITION: LEGALIST VERSUS CONFUCIAN

In China's history it is very difficult to identify periods or circumstances that could have given rise to a tradition of fealty akin to Germanic law, one that could offer systemic protection to individuals and communities from an overbearing state.

The birth of China's state traditions is associated with the extermination of the warrior aristocracy early in Chinese history. It was a critical feature of subsequent state-building strategy to block the formation of any group with sufficient resources to field armies or with leadership responsibilities to local constituents that could acquire primacy over the prerogatives of the central state. The imperial officialdom did not intend to negotiate with a corporate body in possession of its own resources and rights. The bureaucratic clans of the Han and Tang dynasties filled the local leadership gaps left by the elimination of the landed, warrior clans, and they had no incentive to stem the centralization of authority and demand institutional constraints on the sovereign. They acted as representatives of the state's interests, not the interests of civil society. Local efforts to attain autonomy were treated as dangerous precedents, and no legally constituted corporate representation emerged with the capability to foil the development of an all-powerful central state. When contestation for local autonomy occurred, it generally took the form of an armed rebellion, rather than demands for charters of legally established rights.

China had two main philosophical and legal traditions, legalist and Confucian, both of which were statist. The former is a tradition of comprehensive administrative and criminal law that empowered the state to mobilize people and resources. Developed during the Warring States period (453–221 BCE), "legalism" was an alternative to the older Confucianism. It enabled rival states to expand revenues, repress dissent, and enlarge their armies, and is widely considered to be the ideological basis of the successful unification of the Warring States in the third century BCE by the Qin dynasty (221–206 BCE).[26] Legalism also rejected the *laissez-faire* of the minimalist state associated with Daoist ideas. Legalists were scholars in the court who strove to eliminate impediments to effective top-down governance and viewed the privilege and protocol associated with tradition as unnecessary. They rejected the Confucian ideal of creating social order through virtue and ethical examples, and held that a state required absolute power to realize its potential for wealth extraction. Under legalist guidance, the positions of command and control were placed directly under the Qin rulers. Officers of state were appointed by the ruler on the basis of their qualifications, talent, and accomplishment. To ensure the stability of the state, the legalists championed a highly mechanistic model in which the only hereditary office should be that of the emperor.

Qin rulers mobilized society along military lines and registered the entire population into household units responsible for taxes, military service, and public works. Local officials who failed to meet quotas were harshly punished. Scrupulous records were kept, according to an equalitarian ideal; the registration of households, commoner and gentry alike, made the people equal (Von Glahn 2016). Similarly, in the command structure of the army, bureaucratic institutions replaced the hereditary military elites. The Qin did not eliminate all the hereditary patrician clans, but they did greatly diminish the role of the nobles. Aristocratic fiefs were avoided in favor of direct control of the administration by the emperor, through the appointment of officers supported by taxes on peasant landholdings. Subsequent Chinese dynasties followed this model of resource mobilization, in spirit if not in fact.

Thus China's aristocratic clans never gained sufficient military, political, or ideological strength to demand rights that could institutionally constrain the sovereign. No legal document or pact like the *Magna Carta* exists in China to hold that there can be no levy by the monarch without the consent of council, that common pleas shall be held in a fixed place, or that one must be judged by one's peers, or to ensure merchants safe passage in and out of the realm.

Whereas legalist intervals often occurred at the beginning of new dynasties that were undergoing rapid change, political Confucianism was employed throughout Chinese history to maintain harmony via obedience to tradition. In Confucian tradition, the political rule of government is established by "Heaven" for the benefit of the people, and rulers should aim to exhibit exemplary conduct by protecting the livelihoods and well-being of the population from adversity.[27] Confucian thought idealizes power that is constrained via moral virtue as personified by the Confucian gentleman, rather than by legal codes or a written constitution.[28] An empire-wide Confucian ethos is an ideological means to harmonize diverse interests by unifying a governing elite around an established curriculum of great texts. It is communitarian in the sense that these texts are revered as a time-honored tradition, but it is not communitarian in the sense of being "of the people." The interpretation of the great texts is part of an oral legacy handed down from teacher to teacher over the generations, but it is the prerogative of a literary elite chosen by examination.

Both legalist and Confucian approaches to public administration are highly rationalistic and supportive of a strong, centralized state. They both seek an all-encompassing source of political and moral order, and this quest continues to animate the underlying unity of Chinese culture and political life (Pines 2012). The legalist–Confucian state exercised authority over economic resources to an extent that no European monarch could ever hope to accomplish. It also represented a check on that power by counterbalancing it with a code of ethical responsibilities to use the power of the state to meet the basic needs of the population. But institutional forms of credible commitment, derived from coalitional limits on the monarch's power, have not been within China's institutional probability frontier.

Putting the period of China's socialist revolution in the context of the legalist–Confucian dynamic, we can interpret it as a "legalist" effort to remobilize the state's access to the resources of the society. Under Xi Jinping, party leadership has called for a return to Confucian principles, to seek stability through harmony as a foundation for longevity. But in doing so, an old weakness of Chinese economic development is reappearing in a new form. Transactions in China's nascent private sector often depend on personal trust among company managers. If there is not enough trust in market transactions to sustain a technologically and globally competitive economy and to channel long-term capital investments via privately invested firms, then China's path toward economic development will continue to depend upon top-down directives from the state.

Western firms, by contrast, matured in an environment where property rights enjoyed protection in a culture that linked innovation with freedom. This economic freedom is maintained by civic arrangements in a diversity of institutions balanced with functioning markets. Together, they empower the self-organization of ordinary people and, from time to time, enable a revolt against arbitrary and elite power. Institutions of civil society such as the Church or the corporation arose to provide for the welfare of communities, and helped to create an advantageous nexus that enabled freedoms of science, education, speech, and communication to flourish in the West.

The Western legal tradition, and its reconciliation of freedom and law grounded in civic responsibility, advanced via increasing returns. Its connection with the market was but one part of the support it attained, enabling it to take precedence over the will of the sovereign and become the universal preference coordinator for society. China's growing global role, with its different civic traditions, challenges Western theories of progress that link political and economic liberalism.

NOTES

1. A large-world network would be very large and sparse but can still be random. The test for whether a network is large-world or small-world would probably be how the path length scales with size: if it's small-world, it should scale logarithmically and if it was large-world, exponentially.

2. These examples are very different from the world in which Stanley Milgram did the pioneering experiment on small-world connectivity. The world it depicted, the United States in the 1960s, already had extensive infrastructure and a shared language, and transport and legal systems. His experiment employed one of these technologies, the postal service system, to communicate and trace relationship chains. The environment that we call large-world has none of these institutional capabilities (Travers and Milgram 1969).

3. There is a long history of legal scholarship using various terms to distinguish Germanic from Roman roots, but no generally agreed-upon category. We provide our own definition of "communitarian law," which differs slightly from the established ones, and which distinguishes it from communitarian political philosophy.

4. Intermarriage among noble families extended the organization of early medieval Europe beyond the maximum scale of communal social organization. Matthew Bandy (2004) and Robin Dunbar and Richard Sosis (2018) write about the maximum size of communal organization.

5. Purzycki et al. (2016, 327) test impartial rule-following and find that their results "support the hypothesis that beliefs in moralistic, punitive and knowing gods increase impartial behaviour towards distant co-religionists, and therefore can contribute to the expansion of prosociality." Organized religion, they conclude, can serve as a mechanism "to sanction violators of interpersonal social norms, [and] foster and sustain the expansion of cooperation, trust and fairness towards co-religionist strangers."

6. The Germanic tribes overran Rome on several occasions after having been dominated by the empire for a number of centuries.

7. A full-fledged feudal system had not yet developed during the reign of Charlemagne (768–814), but the practice of holding land in fealty, or in fee,

was widely practiced. Vassals of the king became the core of Charlemagne's army, with each vassal granted property in exchange for service. Vassals were expected to provision their own weapons, horses, and equipment in times of war. In fact, the true system of vassalage of the late Middle Ages is only found in regions with Carolingian roots (Fried 2016). Thus Charlemagne's empire was the precursor of and laid the foundation for the feudalism of the high Middle Ages. Charlemagne's servant and biographer, Einhard (775–840), affirms that throughout his reign Charlemagne was keen "to reestablish the ancient authority of the City of Rome under his care and influence, and to defend and protect the Church of St. Peter" (Fried 2016, 525). During his lifetime, the unity of his empire was continuously at risk of breakdown. His institutional resources were meager, and he had limited surplus to train and pay for legions of troops. His claim to be supreme ruler was therefore not unassailable but depended on his special relationship with the Church. The spread of monasteries and clergy across his Holy Roman Empire is perhaps his most enduring institutional legacy.

8. By contrast, Japanese feudalism, which shares many features with that of the West, differs in two ways, according to Bloch (1961, 452): "the vassal's submission was much more unilateral," and "the divine power of the Emperor remained outside the structure of vassal engagements."

9. The *Digest* of Justinian identifies custom, based upon usage, as having the force of statutory legislation. However, the precise boundaries of custom were a topic of intense legal debate during the Middle Ages.

10. North of the Alps, literacy and knowledge of Latin among the elites expanded greatly during the reign of Charlemagne in the eighth century, thanks in large part to the spread of schools established by the Church. These schools trained scribes, chaplains, and administrators, and became essential to the exercise of royal power. South of the Alps, and in Italy in particular, a system of lay education, with an emphasis on teaching the law, had existed since classical antiquity. Accordingly, during the Carolingian epoch, Roman law operated only in the south of France and Italy. Elsewhere, the enforcement and promulgation of law was unstable and depended on local custom and oral dissemination. Frankish law was unwritten, relying upon oral tradition and ad hoc verdicts that treated every decision as a new instance (Fried 2016). One of Charlemagne's central aims was to

establish order throughout the realm in an evenhanded way, and his influence can be found in Frankish, Bavarian, and Alemannic regions, despite the prevalence of oral legal traditions. But among the Saxons, Thuringians, Frisians, and Angles, few enduring signs of Charlemagne's influence are perceptible.

11. During the high Middle Ages, even customs were recorded and written down, e.g., the French jurist Philippe Beaumanoir's (1247–1296) *Coutumes de Beauvaisis.*

12. According to one tradition of research on medieval Europe, domestic political interests fractured along the lines of economic class, in part due to the Roman legal heritage. The enabling of corporate orders, such as the landed nobility or the urban guilds, to define their liberties as distinct from those of other social groups set up a basis for class conflict. Another tradition, represented by the historian Rodney Hilton (1985), sees the origins of class conflict in the emergence of capitalism from feudalism.

13. Parliaments, consultations between the king and the great magnates of the realm, have their institutional antecedents in the *curias* of ancient Rome, and the *colloquia* of the early Scottish councils.

14. In the twelfth century, the rural aristocracy and the kings competed to gain access to the resources of the townspeople. The landed elites sought urban cooperation to enhance their own independence from the crown, a tendency the crown wanted to curtail.

15. In England a steady link exists between trade, local self-government, and enfranchisement in parliament. Beginning in the thirteenth century, boroughs (self-governing entities smaller than a city) that were willing to pay for the right to manage their own tax collection were also more likely to be enfranchised. Charles Angelucci, Simone Meraglia, and Nico Voigtländer (2017) find that boroughs that petitioned the crown to be self-governing tended to be commercially important in medieval times and therefore had incentives to remove inefficient and extortive royal administrators. They note as well that many of these same towns later joined the parliamentary side in the Civil War (1642–1651) and strongly supported the Great Reform Act of 1832, which gave them greater electoral representation in the House of Commons.

16. This was the essence of the king's *time-inconsistency* problem. The problem of time-inconsistency occurs when a decision maker states

a preference for one position but acts according to a different preference once the time for implementation arrives (Kydland and Prescott 1977).

17. Economic historians Jan Luiten van Zanden, Eltjo Buringh, and Maarten Bosker (2012) claim that these differences in institutional development help to explain the economic divergence between northwestern and southern and central Europe.

18. Pacts that favor a dominant group in one period set a precedent for arguments that can be the basis for expanding citizen engagement in ensuing periods. For example, rights won by nobles to participate in lawmaking and/or trial by their peers were eventually also obtained by the merchant or craft guilds. These rights became more inclusive over time.

19. It is difficult to disentangle the effects of Christianity and those of Roman law because the Church articulated and promulgated its rule using the protocol of Roman law, as Berman documents in *Law and Revolution* (1983). By the later Middle Ages, "the Germanic peoples adopted the theory inherent in Christian doctrine – which was almost wholly of a Latin-Roman complexion – and the ascending theme [i.e. bottom-up legitimacy] was, so to speak, driven underground" (Kelly 1992). The Justinian compilation of Roman law was rediscovered and made the basis for legal instruction in eleventh-century Italy and, in the sixteenth century, came to be known as part of the *Corpus Juris Civilis*. Successive generations of legal scholars throughout Europe adapted its ancient principles to contemporary needs. Medieval scholars of canon law were also influenced by Roman law scholarship as they compiled existing religious legal sources into their own comprehensive system of Church law and governance. The clergy were central to medieval culture, politics, and higher learning. By the late Middle Ages, these two systems of law – civil and canon, both derived from Roman law – were taught at most universities and formed the basis of a shared body of legal thought common to most of Europe.

20. The Bourbon monarchs of France continued the tradition of subordinating the administrative functions of the feudal lords and supplanted seigneurial with royal jurisdiction. In the eighteenth century, kings protected peasant rights against the nobility, thereby supplanting the ties to their lords, and making the dues owed by peasants to their feudal

master's residual. According to Tocqueville, this fueled peasant hostility to feudal lordship and led to the overthrow of the entire edifice of the old regime.

21. In the Holy Roman Empire begun under Charlemagne, the emperor enjoyed greater financial independence than other royal houses.

22. Compared to China's emperor, the kings of Europe had limited power to engage in public administration. European towns as autonomous communities managed their own schools, hospitals, and markets. Towns had their own governments that levied their own taxes.

23. Medievalist Magnus Ryan (2014) charts the growth of a professional culture of legal practice and education that spanned several centuries from the twelfth century onward.

24. Economist Svetozar Pejovich (1999, 171) writes, "If changes in formal rules are in harmony with the prevailing informal rules, the interaction of their incentives will tend to reduce transaction costs in the community (that is, the cost of making an exchange and the cost of maintaining and protecting the institutional structure) and clear up resources for the production of wealth. When new formal rules conflict with the prevailing informal rules, the interaction of their incentives will tend to raise transaction costs and reduce the production of wealth in the community."

25. Strengthening government while protecting individual property was an aspiration for James Madison and other framers of the US Constitution.

26. Internal conflict peaked during the Warring States period; against this background, the competing states laid the institutional foundations for the unification of China under a single empire. The victors in intrastate competition embraced a highly rationalist, top-down means of imposing central authority, stifling dissent and imposing strict discipline.

27. The notion of Heaven in Chinese philosophy is not that of the seat of God; Heaven exists in the cosmological sense as part of nature.

28. Without an independent civil society to counterbalance state power, China's growth depends on state-led development to a far greater extent than its high-performing neighbors. The institutional history of East Asia does not feature an autonomous legal infrastructure to protect assets from political authority. Jose Edgardo Campos and Hilton L. Root (1996) argue that during the high growth period of 1960–1990, in order to compete in the global economy, industrial and commercial interests had to find a substitute source of legal infrastructure to promote economic growth,

and this necessity had a direct bearing on the structure of the regional economies on two levels. At the policy/institutional level, without an established framework of private-sector contracts for coordinating mass manufacturing, the high-performing East Asian economies depended on state bureaucracy and state planning to achieve economies of scale. Investment strategies and often the capital for keystone investments were coordinated from above. There was often a central ministry that had budgetary and supervisory jurisdiction over all others. Japan's economy evolved a sophisticated mix of state- and firm-based coordination, with the state bureaucracy playing an essential role in organizing sector-level coordination.

At the transaction level, East Asia's high-performing economies rely on balancing organized state power with informal enforcement. Relational contracts play a critical role in economic transactions; informal codes of conduct and reliance on informal trust prevail. Commercial actors rarely litigate, lawyers are relatively few, and dependence on the cultural tradition of *guanxi*, or relationship-based trade, substitutes for a weak system of contract law.

# 6   The Network Foundations of the Great Divergence

## with Qing Tian

This chapter builds upon the competition theory of European states and Confucian state theory, and uses a complex systems approach and network analytics to enrich our understanding of innovation and the Great Divergence.

The traditional interpretation of the Great Divergence depicts the West as a collection of numerous small states engaged in competition, with the ultimate goal of increasing their economic advantage or protecting themselves against more powerful states. This intense competition provided incentives for the states to explore and adopt whatever innovations would provide a competitive advantage. This is, in general, a valid argument. However, the European states were not only engaged in military and economic competition; they also used social and diplomatic means to strengthen security and expand their power. Marriage was important, and through it the royal dynasties in Europe forged strong connections (see Figure 4.1).

The marriage network of premodern Europe, as noted in Chapter 4, exhibits mixed features of small-world and scale-free networks. Although its degree distribution doesn't follow a perfect power law, the communication channels to larger nodes or hubs are highly skewed, meaning that a few highly connected hubs link the smaller nodes with one another. The network also shows small-world characteristics because it has an average shortest path that is comparable to random networks, but with a much higher clustering coefficient.

This chapter will show that these features of the European network not only facilitated the spread of innovation across the continent but also provided niches in which to harbor early innovations. Decentralization also weakened the monarchs, which allowed the powerful merchant classes to form alliances with them and become important actors in the system. The merchants rise in stature and influence laid the foundations for other social and institutional innovations, and the eventual economic takeoff in Europe. We further show that major "power clusters" existed in the network, and that they were not independent, but interconnected. The connections between those power clusters constrained the monarchs' ambitions, as well as the possibility for continent-wide unification, and provided strong motivation for making full use of technology to undertake outward expansion from the shores of Europe into new trade routes and colonialism. That expansion created additional incentives for the development of ever-newer technologies, further empowering the expansion, creating a tremendous momentum, fueling industrialization, and launching Europe onto a fast growth path.

By contrast, from the Qin dynasty (221–206 BCE) onward, and throughout much of China's history, China was a unified state, and Confucianism was elevated as the state philosophy. Scholars have traditionally pointed to Confucian officialdom as the root cause behind the stifling of innovation, leading to the Great Divergence. With a well-defined bureaucratic governance system, the emperor had formal channels through which to collect revenues to finance his army and build a powerful empire. As a large empire, the major challenge was to maintain domestic stability rather than engage in external conflicts; China had no great need or motivation to advance its technologies for competition or expansion. Its centralized hub-and-spoke governance structure allowed officials to effectively disseminate useful ideas and promote their adoption, but also to filter out innovations that could be harmful to imperial rule. Its highly centralized system also prevented other groups, such as rich merchants, from becoming powerful actors in the system and developing an independent private sector.

The network characteristics of the European states and China represent two different development paths and outcomes that continue to shape how the actors in the two systems act and interact.[1] Network analysis can provide additional insights about how these distinctive patterns arose, the patterns of coalitional stability with which they are coupled, and why disruptive technologies like those associated with industrialization could occur in Europe but did not take place in China. It cannot be used to claim that a population in one geopolitical environment had a greater tendency for invention than another, or to describe the cultural-scientific relationship that drives technology invention in the first place. But it can link China's economic growth prior to the eighteenth century to the steady but incremental spread of useful innovations across the empire. Periods of relative political stability over the vast region enabled China to amass a great range of both cultural and technological achievements. In contrast, Europe's greater receptivity to innovation lay in its own network structure of multiple hubs that encouraged lateral connectivity, enabling numerous information cascades. In pre-eighteenth-century Europe, the long links between multiple independent hubs served as connectors that could create, transmit, and exploit disruptive innovation as an engine for growth, and enabled Europe to make a great leap.

## 6.1   NETWORK STRUCTURE AND INNOVATION IN EUROPE

Marriages among the elites, a Europe-wide phenomenon, was a key feature of Europe's authority network. The most eminent royal houses accumulated more marriage connections than others over time and became hubs in the network. The existence of multiple hubs would prevent any one from acting as a central filtering mechanism or cut-off point. The features of small-world networks also allow breakthroughs to arise from different points in the system and spread contagiously. One such category of important vertexes would have been the royal academies of science and higher learning that facilitated communication and innovation, linking communities of inventors with important outside groups.

As we further examine the European marriage network to identify several major clusters, our analysis will provide additional insight about the landscape of power, which shows a system-level constraint that provides a strong motivation for outward expansion. It also allows us to expand the ideas of niche construction, discussed at length in Chapter 3, and introduce the concept of near-decomposability to extrapolate key points of comparison in the divergence of the European and Chinese systems of innovation.

## Power Clusters in the European Network and Motivation for Outward Expansion

In Chapter 4, we looked at Europe's network of 239 houses created through dynastic marriage (Figure 4.1) from the fourteenth through the twentieth centuries. Now we look at the clustering of royal houses (Figure 6.1). We also look at the most powerful players in these clusters (represented in Figure 6.2) to understand the nature of their power. Chapter 2 identified three measures that can be used to depict the power of an actor: betweenness centrality, which represents how often a given node falls along the shortest path between any two other nodes; eigenvector centrality, which means having few direct connections, but many indirect connections; and simple degree centrality, i.e., the number of connections a node has.

The European marriage network encompasses six major power clusters, represented in Figure 6.1 by different shades of gray. The power of cluster 3 (light gray) is associated with its large size and many powerful lineages, particularly in terms of eigenvector centrality. These lineages could wield "global" influence through strategic marriages. The Hohenzollern is one of the most powerful in this cluster, with high eigenvector and betweenness centrality, and therefore could serve to bridge royal houses. Cluster 1 (white) is not very large but contains another powerful clan, the Wittelsbach, which ranks high in all three centrality measures, meaning it could have substantial local and global influence as well as be a broker. Cluster 2 (light gray) contains one of the most powerful families, the Bourbons, in terms of betweenness centrality and degree centrality; it could have great local influence and also serve as a broker. Cluster 4 (dark gray)

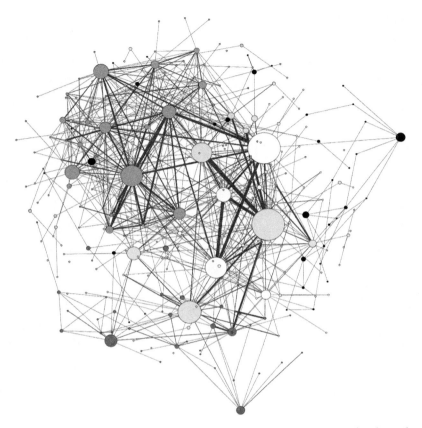

FIGURE 6.1 Major clusters in the European marriage network. The node size represents betweenness centrality, or how often a given node falls along the shortest path between any two other nodes. We focus on betweenness centrality because we are interested in understanding the connectivity of the network. The modularity method in Gephi finds a total of sixty-two clusters, but the majority of these clusters are tiny. Only six clusters have more than five royal linkages, shown in shades of gray: 1 (white), 2 (light gray), 3 (gray), 4 (dark gray), 5 (black), and 6 (also black). Other clusters rarely include more than two members.

derives its power mainly from its size. Its three most powerful members are the houses of Tudor, Trastamara, and Capet, but their centrality measures are not as high as the powerful lineages in clusters 1,

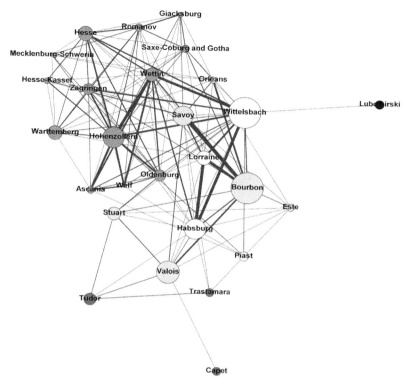

FIGURE 6.2 The most "powerful" royal houses that have at least one measure of centrality (degree, betweenness, or eigenvector) among the top 20 lineages. As in Figure 6.1, the node size represents betweenness centrality; and line thickness is proportional to the number of marriages between two clusters.

2, and 3. The lineages comprising clusters 5 (black) and 6 (also black) are relatively few in number.

A simplified picture of the relationships also shows that clusters of different shades of gray are themselves interconnected, with clusters 1 (white), 2 (light gray), and 3 (gray) forming a tightly knit power triangle at the center (Figure 6.3). Clusters 1 and 2 have the strongest connections, followed by connections between clusters 1 and 3, then connections between clusters 2 and 3. Cluster 4 (dark gray) integrates the powerful triangle mainly through connections

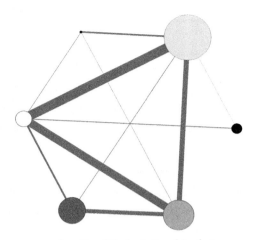

FIGURE 6.3 Simplified relationships between power clusters. Node size is proportional to the number of houses in a cluster. Line thickness is proportional to the number of marriages between two clusters. As in Figure 6.1, the clusters are shown in shades of gray: 1 (white), 2 (light gray), 3 (gray), 4 (dark gray), 5 (black), and 6 (also black). Cluster 5 is the smallest in size.

with clusters 1 and 3, with stronger connections to cluster 3. The smallest, cluster 5, (black) maintains linkages to the power triangle, but with stronger connections to cluster 3. Cluster 6 (also black) connects mainly to cluster 1.

This hypernetwork of marriages created by the powerful monarchies for the purpose of strengthening their power had the unintended consequence of constraining their ambition for power. While wars were a constant feature of the landscape, no single monarchy could annihilate all the others to bring about the unification of the whole of Europe. Embedded in the large web of family connections, some European monarchies found a measure of security in achieving a balance of power, while throughout history, in other parts of the world, empires grew through wars and conquest. This constraint of network structure, together with limited national or regional resources, also propelled European elites to amass power through outward expansion. Beginning in the fourteenth century, when missionaries and traders brought technologies from the East to Europe, Europeans broke through their constraint with the establishment of new trade routes and settlements.

## Near-Decomposability, Niche Innovation, and the Rise of the Merchant Classes

The power clusters and their interconnections demonstrate *near-decomposable* features in Europe's sociopolitical landscape that allowed innovation to thrive in certain societal sectors and regions, namely the rising merchant classes and emerging city states. Herbert Simon's insights concerning near-decomposability illustrate why we can treat Europe as a complex macro system; they are a basis for some of the logic that is applied here to distinguish Europe's innovation environment from China's. Simon observes that both the autonomy and interdependence of processes associated with different functions are central to the formation of complex systems. "The property of near-decomposability," he writes, "has important consequences for the behavior of a system that possesses it" (2000, 8). In other words, the way a system is subdivided determines its long-term dynamic behavior. If a system is perfectly decomposable, the parts will have no effect on one another. But by being "nearly" so, they are not totally independent. Europe is composed of mainly independent parts, with subsystems expressed in distinct languages, traditions, and conventions. Yet because these subsystems constantly and actively interact with one another, it is reasonable to consider Europe as a macro system – despite the economic, social, legal, and cultural variation within it – and as highly adapted to local changes in a way consistent with Simon's notion of near-decomposability.

These insights on near-decomposability apply when we consider how the merchant classes were able to evolve relatively independently from other social groups, away from the estates and villages of bishops, kings, and nobles. Their relative independence from feudal lordship enabled them to form traditions of civic responsibility radically different from those of Europe's earlier agrarian civilization. Simon's insights can be applied to the emergence of these new nodes – the merchant elites, as well as the friars, the universities, the craft guilds, the Inns of Court in London, the *Parlements* of France – which fostered relative administrative autonomy and a self-sustaining ethos, and had great impact throughout Europe, from the south of Spain all the way to the Baltic towns, as ideas spread from the new city states until they affected nation states. Merchant communities in Europe's cities acquired the social capital and knowledge to manage risk, and their emergence over several centuries matches the model of innovation in which change begins in niches – in this case, niches provided by the decentralized network in Europe – until it attains a critical mass and spreads.[2] The establishment of rules and contracting rights that protected gains from trade allowed for the growth of private enterprise, reshaped business and commerce, and forced the ruling classes to adapt or forgo opportunities to expand their wealth. As the volume of social contracts and trade grew, a class of legal and financial professionals specializing in spreading risk and settling disputes formed a web of private enterprises that spanned the entire economy and eventually spread to many parts of the globe. The European sociotechnical and cultural advances of the past millennium – including an independent merchant class with considerable mobile assets; the separation of Church and state institutionalized by events of the eleventh century; a continent-wide system of universities (Bologna in 1088; Oxford 1096; Cambridge 1209; Padua 1222; Salamanca 1288) guilds that by the thirteenth century controlled entry into manufacturing in many European towns; and competing states after the Treaty of Westphalia in 1648 – ultimately made sovereignty the basis of international law.

Each advancement illustrates the adaptive properties of Simon's near-decomposable systems,[3] in which the costs of undertaking an innovation are confined to that unit (such as a merchant class), diminishing the costs of coordination. Near-decomposability also makes it possible to avoid the greater cost of altering other subunits, or the whole structure of which it is a part, until the innovation has proved its worth.[4] The capacity for coordination among the independent subunits makes adaptive change to the environment easier. This idea is compatible with the notion that competitive states set up the dynamic of growth.

As trade and commerce grew and became increasingly sophisticated, parallel changes occurred in social values. Cities, which were the main centers of trade by the sixteenth century, became the focal points of such change. They fostered competing notions of morality; as cities each had their own needs, they developed their particular moral codes to match and were "impervious to outside criticism" (Rosenberg and Birdzell 1986). Moral differentiation was reinforced by the Reformation, which furnished a template of ethics adapted to the fulfillment of economic obligations and in line with concepts of economically derived social status, linking business success and the worldly acquisition of wealth with virtue.

## Decentralization, Weakness of Kings, and Evolution from City States to Nation States

In Europe's city states, rich families also engaged in intense competition, and it was not only advantageous to acquire political power, but even necessary for security. The kings also needed merchants for revenue to support military activities. The decentralized network allowed opportunities for the rich merchant class to become a power player though pacts with the king.

Contracting rights allowed trade to flourish across Europe, despite the centralizing instincts of strong monarchs. If kings in one jurisdiction decided to repress merchant rights, those merchants would leave for more favorable contracting rules elsewhere.[5] When Spanish troops sacked Antwerp in 1576, its merchant community fled to safe havens in the northern Netherlands.[6] In 1685, when Louis XIV revoked an edict promising religious tolerance of the Huguenots, many of whom were merchants, they fled to London, Berlin, and Geneva, as well as cities in the Dutch Republic.

The autonomous status of cities is essential to the argument that attributes European growth to the division of authority among a number of national polities. It helps us ascertain why political barriers to innovation were fairly easily and rapidly overcome. A decentralized Europe of thriving private markets, flourishing civic traditions, and responsive state polities is well documented and well understood. Nevertheless, for a complete picture of how innovation transformed European society, one must understand how cultural and informational transitions spread laterally across the continent, transforming institutions, beliefs, and values. This entails understanding the consequences of adding or removing connections in a network. Change was facilitated by coalitions formed between the powerful royal families and powerful merchant elites, with the sprawling network of many royal houses serving as bridge nodes that enabled innovation in one part of Europe to have catalytic effects on another. The freedom that powerful communities of European merchants had to link with other merchant communities with numerous connections could reshape diffusion patterns of the network. Moreover, the openness of European merchant communities enabled adaptations to changing environments, whereas the Chinese system inhibited responsiveness and mobility, and was more prone to calcification. Chinese merchant communities tended to grow by consolidation, European ones by outreach.

Since Europe lacked political unity, the merchants whose wealth, skills, and connections could transform their cities into great centers of commerce played competing municipal hubs against one another in their search for protection of their property rights. Should one European power try to suppress technological and financial innovation, other hubs could offer safe zones. Those states that supported the merchant classes gained an economic advantage, and this forced recalcitrant monarchies to adapt.

The progress of private enterprise continued even after many of Europe's autonomous city states eventually lost their independence during the early period of modern state consolidation (1600–1800); by then, a symbiotic relationship existed between royal authority and independent merchant activity. Kings advanced the financial interests of wealthy merchants, protecting their property rights, while the merchant classes were crucial for providing monarchs with access to low-cost credit to finance their armies.[7] It would not have mattered much whether that dynasty descended from England, France, or Spain; no matter how it tried, no European monarchy could absorb the property rights of merchant elites into the state without limiting its own access to their credit markets.

## 6.2 THE CONFUCIAN STATE AND THE STIFLING OF INNOVATION

To understand the development history of China and its differences from Europe, it is important to recognize that China was unified from the time of the Qin (221–206 BCE), and that the paramount challenge for the emperor was always to sustain the unity of a large territory. As early as the Qin dynasty, forms of administrative management were introduced that became a framework for later generations of imperial courts to rule the vast empire. An interlocking system composed of four elements was created, with the emperor at the apex; a small number of palace chamberlains, who oversaw the compartments of the palace bureaucracy; civil ministers at court, with well-staffed bureaus, which managed a nationwide civil and military bureaucracy; and at the district level, low-level civil officials who selected officers and clerks from the local populace. The emperor was the central node through which decisions and information flowed. Communication was channeled through this bureaucratic system of Confucian-educated men that extended across China.

Legitimacy stemmed from a tradition of moral rule via personage rather than institution. It was a moral authority personified by the Confucian gentleman, as we shall see, which highlights the difference to the authority of Western rulers. To understand the idea of the moral authority that permeates China even to this day, we must return to the Confucian–legalist foundations, first mentioned in Chapter 5, of political authority in imperial China. Chinese dynasties, regardless of their ethnic or ideological origin, became Confucian in their maturity; once they achieved stability, they institutionalized Confucian ideologies to secure normative consensus, broaden societal cooperation, and legitimize the functions of the imperial state (Fung 1948; Gernet 1996). A mature dynasty needed to establish a broadly accepted, yet ideologically hegemonic, political philosophy. Legalism was too destabilizing; it lacked sufficient respect for tradition. The short-lived Yuan dynasty (1279–1368) stands out for failing to recognize the value of having a merit-based bureaucracy to support the emperor.

It was through this bureaucracy of educated men that communication was transmitted out across the empire and then back to the emperor, enabling successive dynasties to overcome great distances and ethnic diversity and unify distant regions. This administrative proficiency allowed imperial China to accomplish what few nations have: political stability over long periods; a tolerance for ethnic diversity; an economy capable of supporting large metropolitan centers; competing philosophical approaches to the role of government and the morality of administrators; and a meritocratic system of recruitment of officials (Finer 1997).

From the Song dynasty (960–1279) onward, imperial officialdom generally strove to be representative and inclusive to prevent localism and fragmentation. Recruitment and appointments were made according to provincial quotas, in proportion to each province's population, to ensure that the officialdom represented the whole country. As a source of legitimacy, the combination of meritocracy and inclusivity enhanced the prestige of the emperor. A Confucian curriculum standardized outlooks and procedures, enabling the bureaucracy to grow more regionally heterogeneous while remaining ideologically homogenous. Yet this bureaucracy of mandarins, the very centerpiece of China's stability and prosperity, and a force for social mobility, hampered innovation in several ways.

A widely held scholarly consensus presents bureaucratic pervasiveness as the reason China was finally overtaken by the West in the nineteenth century. Sociologist Dingxin Zhao, for example, claims that the failure to industrialize was a result of the Confucian–legalistic social order, and that China could not have experienced industrial transformation endogenously, i.e., it needed the arrival of the West to challenge the dead weight of the Confucian code. "The Confucian-Legalist political ideological framework, which functioned as a 'capstone,' was not seriously undermined until the nineteenth century," he writes, "preventing any real Chinese breakthrough and development of industrial capitalism until change was forced by Western and Japanese imperialism." The problem was that "in late imperial China, no matter whether the inventors were gentry or hands-on artisans, the nature of the Confucian-Legalistic state determined that neither inventions nor scientific discoveries would yield wealth, prestige, or authority" (Zhao 2015, 363).

Economist Justin Yifu Lin (1995) has argued that the bureaucratic meritocracy system drew the brightest Chinese to the imperial government, stifling the prospects of modern science. The bureaucratic elites in general enjoyed not only dominant political power over all other parties, but also economic status. Since anyone could become part of the bureaucratic elites by passing the exams, it was said that "a gold house can be found in books." The Confucian education, however, enforced the normalization of ideas and discouraged competition for novelty. To prepare for the exams, notes Lin, candidates spent years studying and memorizing the Confucian classics through which doctrine was internalized. Because a unified ideology of Confucius was essential to successful imperial rule, subjects such as mathematics were left out of the exams, reducing the potential for producing scientists and advancing science.

It is well established that the practice of controlling innovation from the top down was natural for a government whose every decision came from a central hub. The mandarins, particularly from the Ming dynasty (1368–1644) onward, had a primary role in containing potentially disruptive homegrown technologies, such as long-distance shipping (which only lasted from 1405 to 1430) that could reach ports in East Africa or the printing press, the use of which came to an end in the 1720s. These technologies were treated as subversive, not unlike sectarian cults with rebellious tendencies.[8] The mandarins, acting as system managers, focused inward when considering technological progress because their overarching goal was to maintain social harmony (Pines 2012). Their zeal to reduce any streak of independence within one sector of the economy or within any one region, the unrelenting lookout for any potential heresies that could foment deviations in opinion, and their efforts to control potential dissidents, nonconformist thinkers, and nonconformist cults such as Buddhism or Daoism likely deprived the empire of many potential sources of innovation, novelty, and renewal, making change far more turbulent when it finally did arrive.

The scholar-bureaucracy evolved as a cut-off point, or circuit breaker of sorts, in China's hub-and-spoke network structure over many centuries of disintegration and reorganization. This stabilized the administrative state, ensuring that rapid innovation was unlikely unless it initiated from within the mandarinate, and that communal values were not subjected to pluralistic sources of preference formation. But it meant that periods of traditionalism were generally followed by decline, instead of reform and renewal. The common doctrine that defined the responsibilities of officialdom and formed the basis of its long and continuous tradition of governance left little space for innovators to gain recognition as socially valued actors. The cultural ethos was such that the merchant and gentry classes didn't challenge these bureaucratic elites and sought instead to become members of, or associated with, that class, rather than gamble on sociotechnical disruption.

The formation of new social nodes was greatly feared, and throughout much of Chinese history a technology with the potential to create new nodes represented a political threat rather than an opportunity. In fact, during the twilight of the Qing dynasty in the late nineteenth century, this is exactly what transpired: merchants and industrialists became increasingly hostile to the imperium. The notion that independent enterprises could become agents of disorder became self-fulfilling. The development of private commerce opened the empire to strong demands for reform, and the emerging industrialists, along with their workers and professionals, began to question the orthodox principles of Confucian rule. Their ties to new methods of production and to global production networks placed them on an inevitable collision course with the dynasty. Their rejection of the precepts of imperial order became an impetus for rebellion.

Economist Timur Kuran, in *Private Truths, Public Lies: The Social Consequences of Preference Falsification* (1997), demonstrates that "preference falsification" is pervasive in social relationships, shaping actions, biasing knowledge, and inhibiting change, yet also sparking revolution. (In preference falsification, the articulation of preferences is constrained by expectation of the consequences.) This would be especially true among members of a tightly interconnected governmental bureaucracy. The opinions of a self-selected elite ruling cohort are more susceptible to manipulation than those diffused through an entire society. The speed with which a politically expedient consensus unravels in a highly centralized hub-and-spoke system, and with which a new one can be substituted, subjects a regime to dual consequences: It can help leadership shape collective decisions, as with the shift from the Cultural Revolution to the market-oriented policies of Deng Xiaoping, but it can also fuel revolution against the incumbent orthodoxy, as occurred in the last decade of the Qing dynasty and resulted in its precipitous decline. The diffusion of contrary opinions within an elite set of critical actors was dramatic, and the unraveling of the previously long-lived elite consensus occurred quickly.

## State Control of Keystone Technologies and Underdevelopment of a "Private Sector"

The challenge of sustaining the unity of a large country led the emperor to seek control over key technologies and strategically important industries, and this control also provided another important source of revenue. For example, the production and sale of commodities required by the court – carriages, wagons, weapons, ceramics, sophisticated textiles – took place in state-controlled workshops that also sold their wares to the well-to-do gentry (unlike Europe, where craft guilds serviced the demands of the court for luxury goods). Sales of primary commodities, such as salt and iron, were also under the grip of the state, or at times conducted through a franchise monopoly bestowed by the emperor. The state also established standards for the training and certification of architects, civil engineers, managers, and builders of critical infrastructure, such as roads, bridges, canals, and dams. By contrast, European monarchs were rarely as intrusive and had limited independent access to disruptive technologies before civil elites could claim them.

Most important, the state also maintained control of essential natural resources. State monopolies in salt and iron were introduced by the ancient Qi dynasty (685–643 BCE) and, throughout imperial times, most mines remained under government control with assigned minimum production quotas. With its monopoly of metallurgy, the state controlled the manufacture of cannon and artillery (Lin 1995; Needham 1956, 1969), and thus the development and dissemination of gunpowder weapons. This monopoly contained the diffusion of military technologies that might have endangered state unity.[9] The capacity to limit the spread of arms and metallurgy contrasted sharply with that of European governments, which imposed limits within their borders but could not impose continent-wide limits on the exploitation of metal for new military technologies.

Wealthy merchants are found throughout Chinese history, but their ability to control certain manufacturing sectors or develop new technologies, for example in printing, munitions, or shipbuilding, was limited, especially from the Ming dynasty onward. Merchant elites and state-organized urban guilds could not attain control of enclaves within the wider polity, or sway over keystone technologies, as their European counterparts did.[10] "Towns and villages were an integrated system," notes Fairbank, "and merchants remained under the control of the gentry class, instead of setting up an independent trade and economy" (1948, 181).[11] Nor did they obtain protection of their movable assets, having no credit to use as leverage with the emperor, since the imperial state depended upon peasant taxation, not merchant credit, as its primary source of revenue.

A notable exception was during the Song dynasty, when relatively high levels of political liberty coincided with urban expansion, and commercial and industrial growth, and the state's largest revenue came from commercial or industrial sources. Also in the Ming era from about 1520 onward, following a period of withdrawal and defense after its initial military expansion, there was a revival of commerce and urban development. An urban middle class and rich businessmen collaborated with the state economy in ways that resembled the early development of capitalism in Europe. These periods of promise, however, eventually ended with the fall of the dynasty – the Song due to constant barbarian threats and finally the Mogul invasion; the Ming due to a variety of financial and political crises, from the local to the court level, typical of the end of a dynasty.

The Confucian state in general had a tradition of honoring land husbandry over commerce. Merchants were thought to be "sly" and therefore less likely to be loyal. In late imperial times, the roles of merchant and gentry were increasingly blended as rich landlords also participated in trade and commerce, and merchants invested in land. Nevertheless, the strong top-down control of the system would not allow rich merchants or gentry to become powerful political players. The emperor did not need to make pacts with them either, although at times the state tapped leading merchants or gentry to regulate local markets and govern commercial taxation when the bureaucratic system lacked resources for tax collection (Mann 1987). Even after the First Opium War in 1840, when the Qing government was forced to open the door and develop national industries, it preferred state enterprises and maintained an ambivalent attitude toward private enterprises, hampering development of the private sector, diminishing overall economic growth, and contributing to the failure of industrialization (Wang, Yanhao, and Yi 1997).

Yet the important landlords and rich merchants did not operate independently from the hierarchical government structure; they sought out social and other relations with local government officials, and some of them engaged with higher-level officials. Not only were they able to secure bureaucratic exam spots for their sons and other relatives to become part of the government elites, but they also purchased degrees and official titles. Their interests and security were thus protected by the government officials, and they were often important local power players. In this way, political leadership created support for the regime among a broad coalition within the society. At the same time, the selectivity of the examination system enabled control of recruitment to remain with a small cohort of court officials to whom the provincial office holders reported. This small group of palace insiders decided which examination finalists to recruit.

It was because of these connections, particularly at the lower levels of government, that corruption became entrenched, especially in matters of tax exemptions. The empire's reliance on local gentry and merchants to self-govern commercial taxation also created ample opportunities for corruption. For example, merchant organizations often had many monopoly privileges in local markets and abused them for personal gain. Wealthy landlords could bribe tax collectors to remove their land from the tax rolls. As hard times caused indebted peasants to transfer their land to wealthier landlords who had the means to gain tax exemptions, this also increased the pressure on the remaining taxpayers, increasing their burden. All this put greater fiscal pressure on the peasants, leading to further impoverishment. Local corruption, interlaced with that at the court, could spell the end of a dynasty when exacerbated by natural disasters, peasant uprisings, the defections of local notables, and support for local warlords.

Although the imperial clan, the ancient nobility, and all officials were tax exempt, nobody was exempt from obligatory labor duties and a household levy in cash. Nevertheless, the system was prone to corruption because it enabled elites, such as the gentry and merchants, to exploit informal linkages and family ties to obtain privileges and exemptions from taxation, and from obligatory labor to work on large government projects, as well as military conscription. Bribes to avoid these obligations were commonplace and diminished the capacity of the governor to maintain the local militia and post office. Corruption inherent in the relationship between the bureaucratic system and the wealthy members of the population may have been more significant than the stifling of innovation in contributing to the cycles of decline and destruction. Forces of decay that arose internally eventually made the empire vulnerable to conquest.

Brutal episodes of collapse were always lurking in the background of great periods of expansion and stability. Periodic systemic disintegration was the by-product of this highly integrated structure. Warfare and violence often originated from the periphery; but once the capital fell, rebellion spread across the empire. The periodic collapse of the central government severely damaged social infrastructure and national defense, undoing previous periods of growth and causing reversion to a prior level of social complexity. It would generally mark the end of the mandarins, both as a social class and as an institution. A new dynasty would have to reestablish the system and train a new cohort of administrators.

## The Puzzle of China's Unexploited Inventions

One of the great mysteries of Chinese economic history, long debated by scholars, is why some of the greatest innovations that developed and flourished there eventually fell into disuse and were ignored, or even forgotten, causing the empire to lose its significant lead in technological development. Following Joseph Needham, the most cited student of China's innovation systems, historians are still fascinated by the "puzzle" of China's failure to fully exploit its technologies, the same ones that were later taken up by the West to establish global superiority. "The implications of this failure for world history," writes Mokyr, "are awesome to contemplate" (1990a, 218–19). Had China been the first great nation to industrialize, its cultural norms would have been the ones to spread across the globe. The following is just a small list of Chinese innovations.

**Maritime Innovations** China's maritime reach in the fourteenth century extended the farthest in the world. Its shipyards were also building the world's largest merchant ships, and the first ships engineered with watertight bulkheads. It had long before devised the first magnetic compass (second century BCE, with modifications for navigation in the tenth and eleventh centuries) and the first stern-mounted rudders (first century). The immense cargo junks of the Ming dynasty, having nine masts and multiple decks, could displace between 2,000 and 3,000 tons at a time when the largest English ships displaced at most 400 tons. Between 1405 and 1433, the Ming emperor sent off scores of these "treasure ships," accompanied by hundreds of other ships of the fleet, on expeditions to ports in the Indian Ocean and up the Arabian Peninsula. At its peak, the Chinese navy was reported to have numbered more than 3,500 ships. By 1500, however, a new emperor had decreed an end to sea voyages and, in 1525, the destruction of all oceangoing ships.[12]

**Printing Press** It was a Chinese peasant who invented movable type printing in ceramic in 1041, and in wood in 1049; experiments in tin and bronze movable type were also recorded, along with the printing of paper money. Printing, however, was generally limited to the emperor's court and officialdom, as classical texts were reprinted for the preparation of exam takers. By the sixteenth century, European missionaries in China were printing not only hundreds of their own Christian book and tracts, but translations of Western technical and medical works. Still, the use of the printing press for non-imperial works came to an end in the 1720s, when the third Qing emperor placed a ban on the practice of Catholicism and the priests' printing presses.

**Gunpowder** Gunpowder was used in fireworks as early as the ninth century. By the tenth and eleventh centuries, the Chinese were using it in weaponry, such as "fire lances" and "thunder crash bombs," and had built cannons by the thirteenth century.[13] Although the Chinese embraced the military uses of gunpowder long before the Europeans, by 1642 Ming fighters had to rely on Portuguese cannons against those of the Manchu invaders – China no longer made them; the victorious Manchu Qing reportedly cast their own cannons from European models with the help of Jesuit priests.

Much later than China, and with vastly different results, Europe embraced the full innovative potential of all these technologies, as well as many others, the knowledge of which (with the exception of the printing press, invented independently in the mid-1440s) came from the East via reports from traders, missionaries, seafarers, merchants, and military officials. As a socially transformative agent, the printing press alone is linked to three disruptive movements in European history: the Renaissance, the Reformation, and the Scientific Revolution. Europe took the technologies of the Far East and accelerated the pace of its industrial development, appetite for trade, and empire building (Eisenstein 1979; Dittmar 2011).

Why then did Europe, not China, push the boundaries of innovation forward? The elaborate bureaucratic system allowed for effective rule of a large territory, which gave the emperor immense economic and political power. There was generally no great need or motivation for outward expansion except that a new dynasty often had to go through an initial period of military expansion to consolidate the empire. Rather, the maintenance of domestic order within the confines of its far-flung borders was always the first priority and a continuous challenge. In contrast, a major challenge for small European states was dealing with neighbors; even an outbreak of civil war was an invitation for conflict with rival dynasties. The aristocratic families maintained a string of ties across the continent, which transformed domestic conflicts into occasions for new dynastic coalitions to form.

At times the empire did have to face and deal with military conflicts with neighboring states, especially on the northern and western borders. But in its relations with its smaller neighbors, China often sought to "buy" influence and bring the local leadership into its orbit without war (Kissinger 2014). This, too, reflected the Confucian idea of harmony that was applied to relations between nations beyond members in a family and actors in the state. For example, although at the time of Zheng He in the early the Ming dynasty the royal fleets were better equipped than the European ships, the emperor did not use the missions for conquest or to amass wealth (Gang 1997). Frequently, generous gifts were disbursed to manifest the beneficence of the emperor and to enhance China's influence by heralding its wealth, culture, and technical accomplishments (Roderich 1993, 1998).

## 6.3   DISRUPTIVE INNOVATION, NETWORK STRUCTURE, AND THE GREAT DIVERGENCE

Much is written about how Europeans came to view nature as a potential resource to organize and exploit. Economic historians Sidney Pollard (1973) and Clive Trebilcock (1981) emphasize that this was not a national so much as a European phenomenon that took hold during the nineteenth century. Each region played a role in the entire process. Once a technology became established in one region, a new but related set of skills arose in another region, and industrialization spread quickly, albeit unevenly, throughout Europe and North America.[14] What theory best explains how these worldly values spread with revolutionary impact so rapidly across the continent?[15] What made it possible for inventions and ideas to proliferate from their national origins to be absorbed into the national cultures of rival states?

This chapter has argued that channels for innovation diffusion are determined by the global network structure. Each network system had its own strengths and weaknesses. However, once it had taken shape, the ensuing network topology governed the possibilities for transformation, and this had evolutionary consequences, including path dependence, at the system level.

Europe's topology enabled the development and self-organization of innovative ideas and inventions within a mosaic of semiautonomous niches organized around cultural and religious affinities, as well as private and communal economic and business interests. The distributed connectivity of the large hubs presented multiple pathways through which information could flow from local units through the whole system and back. In imperial China, a uniform Confucian ideology stifled innovation and the network topology imposed numerous cut-off points.

The networks of political authority in Europe and China served parochial purposes, with motivations related to their specific challenges: in China, to rule a large territory, and in Europe, to enhance the competitive power of small states in a fragmented landscape. The highly centralized authority network in imperial China enabled periods of unmatched stability and prosperity over a large territory, creating a powerful empire. However, the examination-based bureaucratic system, as the central piece of imperial rule, stifled innovation by enforcing a uniform Confucian ideology. Centralization also prevented the rise of an independent merchant class and consequently the development of a thriving private sector, both of which were associated with industrialization in Europe. And the system was prone to corruption because it ensured paramount political power of the bureaucratic elites and other actors, such as eunuchs, gentry, and merchants who sought personal gain through social relations with royals and government officials.[16] This corruption at both the court and local levels would grow extensively over time, impoverishing the peasantry and eventually causing revolts and revolutions that destroyed the system. Chaos and conflict would follow until a new dynasty gained a foothold. This process repeated itself throughout China's history.

In Europe the alliances among dynasties provided each royal house with some level of security in a highly competitive system. The decentralized network also enabled the creation of niches that harbored early innovation and allowed a merchant class to develop its own ethos, governance systems, and legal frameworks; but decentralization that allowed technologies to germinate also weakened the monarchs, who were compelled to make pacts with merchant elites so as to draw on them as sources of credit to finance war efforts. The same small-world network also constrained ambition for inward conquest of rival houses. Additionally, economic growth was constrained by geography and limitations in natural resources (even today this is a factor acutely affecting the mind-set of Europeans in dealing, for example, with climate change and environmental sustainability), providing further motivation for outward expansion. When advanced technologies from the East became known to the Europeans through missionaries and other channels, they saw a way out of their constraints by exploiting these technologies to full advantage through an outward expansion. That expansion created incentives for technological innovation, heightening rivalries among the states. The development of new technologies was a catalyst that further empowered expansion, and this in turn raised the stakes for acquiring technological proficiency.[17]

By contrast, traditional empires were "fenced-in territories" in which trade could occur and to which the population belonged. The leadership controlled the main trade routes in and out, and utilized that control to enhance its sway over the population. Access to the outside world was generally restricted to subjects the emperor could keep in check. No power in Europe was hegemonic in the way the Ottomans were in the Middle East, the Mughals were in India, or the imperial dynasties were in China. Europe's sovereign states competed aggressively for a larger share of the trade that crossed its borders, and this competition was to transform how the states were governed and by whom.

By the end of the eighteenth century, signs of overseas expansion were everywhere, creating a collision of divergent domains in Europe, altering what was acceptable abroad and what was to be tolerated at home. The export–import trade was a conduit for ideas in science, finance, and commerce, which were to be highly disruptive to the status quo. Outward expansion unlocked a new era of creativity, with opportunities for individuals and groups to trespass across geographic and cognitive boundaries, and create new types of social organizations and new notions of risk, reward, and responsibility. In the commercial sphere, there were new forms of agreements between trading partners, and new ways to manage risk. Joint stock companies, the stock exchange, short trading, option trading, merchant banking, insurance, and commercial law spread both internationally and within countries.

The overseas settler communities and the codes of conduct they endorsed were unsettling and transformative at home. Heretical cults, such as the Puritans, Quakers, Anabaptists, and Mennonites, that took root overseas sprouted new forms of social organization. In their community organization, the settlers experimented with new models of self-governance. New forms of social covenants were institutionalized that violated conventions but which were nevertheless to influence the intellectual climate at home. These offered space to loosen existing social bonds and create new expectations that were then reexported to the country of origin.

Outward conquest allowed proactive European dynasties and merchant elites to amass resources that changed the balance of power among states and between competing social groups within states, leading to new wars and renewed attempts to consolidate power. It was in this new round of wars, initiated by the unification and modernization of Germany in the late nineteenth century, that many social and institutional innovations were introduced, such as mandatory free public education, primary health care, merit-based civil and military administration, mass transport, and comprehensive conscription. Powerful empires that were unable to make the necessary institutional reforms, such as the Austro-Hungarians, fell behind smaller powers such as Prussia, which mobilized its entire population to acquire technical proficiency (Root 2013).

The small-world royal network was an important part of this evolutionary process. It played a critical role in facilitating the flow of information and the diffusion of social and technological innovations across Europe. And it eventually succumbed to a process it had initiated. The innovations that monarchs had initially adopted to help ensure their power enabled the kind of mass mobilization for war that eventually led to demands for expanded suffrage and national self-determination, whose spread resulted in the destruction of the Old Regime.

## 6.4   A MODERN ROLE REVERSAL IN GLOBAL INNOVATION

Traditional arguments for the Great Divergence emphasize the differences in institutions (centralized versus decentralized), incentives (competition and property rights versus mercantilist policies), and social organization (the influence of feudalism on the growth of cities and relations between rulers and merchant elites) in seeking to understand the social and ideational sources of European industrialization. But an approach that utilizes complex systems and network analysis places the divergence of East and West within their specific geopolitical contexts and their long-term evolution. We build upon the conventional debate of centralization versus decentralization, then move beyond it to probe the sources of higher-order connectivity, and establish a direction for empirical research to provide richer insights about differences in innovation and the Great Divergence.

We also show that in each region, although the ruling class was motivated to strengthen its own power, its actions had unintended consequences that ultimately led to the destruction of the system. Europe and China experienced massive system change to arrive at their current situation, but it is important to remember that many of the old challenges, inherent in the geopolitical context and the system, remain embedded in their structures.

If we look back at the whole of human development, there are many examples of regions, regimes, and economies that borrowed technologies and then developed them further. Doubtless, the upsurge of Europe from the fourteenth century onward and the advent of the modern era of the West were facilitated by inventions, of greater and lesser importance, from the East (Gernet 1996). China's current leadership sees going outward and the adoption of Western technology as a way to escape its own constraints and the "trap" of falling behind Western development. It remains to be seen, however, whether China can avoid the pitfalls associated with its past. Particularly, can its centralized system become sufficiently adaptive to propagate the necessary incentives for firms and the private sector to make research and technology commercially viable without the disruptive "structural" consequences?

No single nation or collection of states is uniquely responsible for the forward advance of humanity. Progress is made by mutual influences and a relay of technological innovation. Has the baton been passed to China, and if so, will China succeed in its new role? In the next chapter we'll tackle the puzzle of what regime leaders know about the strengths and weaknesses that reside in China's model of rapid economic growth, and explore the possible reversal of roles, with China's managerial elite embracing cutting-edge technology as they aspire to make China a pacesetter for the world.

NOTES

1. Loren Brandt, Debin Ma, and Thomas Rawski (2014) argue that the institutions of imperial China revolved around a unitary regime and state control. This promoted stability and prevented economic and institutional reforms that could have threatened the status quo.

2. The process of sociotechnical transition has several stages in the niche model of innovation proposed by Frank Geels (Geels 2004; Schot and Geels 2008). First, the beliefs and activities of actors are embedded into rules and institutions. Once the actors share a set of rules, a new basis for regime legitimacy forms. The transformation is complete when the newly established innovation reshapes the landscape, and having gained prevalence, it gains further advantage from use. Change always begins below the surface, in niches that offer innovators protected spaces, like an infant industry shielded from mainstream market selection. Most innovations remain at the niche level for a long time or even die out there; breakouts to the sociotechnical regime level rarely occur. For the rare success whose utility becomes apparent, wider diffusion occurs, and its broader adoption leads to a new sociotechnical context. The positive feedback occurs via increasing returns to scale. Once established, an innovation's benefactors then seek to obstruct further innovations that pose a challenge.

3. The idea of system near-decomposability has some similarities in consumer theory to weak separability, where the marginal rate of substitution between any two goods in the group is independent of the quantities consumed of any good outside this group.

4. In biology, a central problem in development is the assignment of different tasks so that the proliferation of cells conforms to function, such that patterns for limbs or eyes, for example, are replicated. Differentiation in the replication of form is necessary for a functioning physiology to develop.

5. Economic historian Eric Jones (1981) argues that merchants built up independent power in Europe by playing rulers against one another; in China, dynasties that came to power after the Song dynasty (960–1279), which Jones views as a golden age for innovation, exemplified by the coke smelting of iron ore and the great ceramic innovations of the northern Song dynasties, hindered merchant independence.

6. The Hapsburg monarchy in Spain rose at the expense of Spain's flourishing urban culture. The bounty of gold and silver from the

New World that flowed into the coffers of the Spanish throne relieved the crown of the need to support secure property rights. Elsewhere in Europe, however, kings competing for the resources with which to build states had to turn to the merchants. This meant that merchant interests in property rights, as well as their mobile assets, had to be protected.

7. At the outset of the Age of Discovery, in the fifteenth and sixteenth centuries, China possessed larger, more technologically capable ships. Their construction was due to the comparative advantage that ship-builders derived from the strong central state. Yet bigger and better ships were not what enabled European merchants to eventually operate across the globe; institutions that protected property rights were critical to how the West grew rich – its monarchs felt pressed to ensure property rights (North 1968).

8. In Chinese history, religious sects, such as the White Lotus, Wang Lun, or Eight Trigrams, were connected with political rebellion. There also were historical rebellions, such as the Panthay Rebellion by Muslims.

9. Throughout China's history, profiteering individuals evaded these controls (Hartwell 1966, 1967).

10. Craft-worker guilds had been established since the eighth century in order to facilitate the recruitment of artisans for public works and to coordinate the taxes that artisans and merchants owed the government. The guilds attained a certain degree of autonomy in some regions during the Ming dynasty, but never to the same extent as the guilds of medieval Europe.

11. In feudal Europe, the landed ruling class settled in manors, and European towns could expand outside the feudal system, instead of being integrated into it. Medieval burghers gained their independence by having separate habitats in new towns, and a new political authority to protect themselves from the kings of national states. The gentry of China became the dominant class in the towns which were primarily administrative centers. The essential connection of the gentry with officialdom drew them into these centers. The gentry family's best security, in short, lay not in a sole reliance upon landowning but by combining their landowning wealth with official prerogatives. "Family property, in itself was no security, but officials who were family members could give it protection" (Fairbank 1948, 41).

12. The fleets of Chinese admiral and court eunuch Zheng He (1371–1435) reached Eastern Africa and included 317 ships and crews totaling 28,000.

13. Historian Tonio Andrade (2016) attributes the failure to develop artillery to the density of the walls that surrounded Chinese cities. China built walled cities so well that they could withstand artillery, which made them impervious to direct attack.

14. Trebilcock observes that industrial growth is often a regional, not a national phenomenon: "Some allowance must be made for the fact that economic advance may be highly regionalized, and that an industrial region in one country may compare, and may co-operate, more closely with an industrial area in a foreign country than it does with its own agricultural hinterland. Thus, industrialization, in this sense, may be more a European experience than a national one, though still by no means a uniform experience" (1981, 3).

15. By the middle of the eighteenth century, parts of France and Germany had attained manufacturing successes that resembled British capabilities (Crouzet 1967). French thinkers were leaders in Europe's scientific and technological advance. Their search for practical application of scientific investigations led to major improvements in machine development, from lathes to looms, and in the application of steam power to transport. Although relatively slow to industrialize, France led England in the systemization and institutionalization of the study of science.

16. Even when corruption was declared to be the number one problem, the government attributed it to the business sector and to the greed of merchants and landlords.

17. European outward expansion was also fueled by a missionary zeal to spread the Christian faith. This zeal was first conveyed with the Crusades, continued to the New World, and then later to China. There has been no equivalent motivation in China's outward ambitions.

PART III  **The Coming Instability**

# 7    Has the Baton Passed to China?

with Liu Baocheng

The powerful royal houses and imperial dynasties may have passed into history, but vestiges remain in the modern regimes of Europe and China. European nations are still seeking functional integration of their economic and social systems in a way that preserves their respective fundamental rights and grants each an equal role in determining aggregate change.

China does not have to find a consensus that recognizes the constitutional equality of subnational units. But it too faces issues that can be traced to its past. The strength of China's hub-and-spoke system is the capacity to control its massive population over a vast land mass – a design conceived by the Qin dynasty (221–206 BCE) – to carry out long-term planning and attain grand goals.[1] Indeed, modern China has embarked on a massive campaign of overseas expansion to acquire resources, technology, and distribution channels for its goods.[2] The campaign has created incentives for innovation with an intensity that is unique in Chinese history. Yet the governance structure may contain the same weaknesses that felled dynasties – multitudinous layers and siloes of bureaucracy under central control, with admission to the ranks of the party's elite promising privilege, determined via rigorous examination and proof of loyalty, and susceptible to corruption and the appropriation of government decision making by the officials to benefit their own families.

China's trajectory, the path that led to it becoming a market-oriented economy, is one that no other developed nation has followed, and has resulted in structural characteristics that have no counterpart elsewhere. However, its unique market economy construction has it at loggerheads with the West and has produced one of the principle sources of uncertainty in the global economy.

## 7.1 CHINA'S UNIQUE DEVELOPMENT PATH

In this section we review the important events that characterize China's reforms and look at an important question: Is China's economic transition incomplete, is it faltering, or will China transition into a market economy that is distinctive from others, even as it shares some fundamental properties?

China has not approached its transition by applying Western principles. Its commercial practices and trade and technology goals reflect its ambition to be a globally successful socialist economy.[3] As economists Ronald Coase and Ning Wang note, "China's economic reform was never intended to dismantle socialism and move to capitalism"; it "had been intended to save socialism" (2012, 154, 156). Not until the 14th Chinese Communist Congress, held in 1992, and reinforced in the 15th Chinese Communist Congress in 1997, did China decide to give a name to its brand of economics, adopting the phrase "socialist market economy." Market values are not intended to take priority over socialist ones. When China escaped a direct hit from the 1997 East Asian financial crisis, faith that "only socialism with Chinese characteristics can advance China" was strengthened; in 2004 this was reinforced by formal resolution during the party's 16th National Congress (Jiang 2002).

### China Defies Global Change Experts

If China were doing poorly, an incomplete economic transition might explain why. The structures responsible for China's high growth deviate from the two conventional Western approaches, neoliberalism and institutionalism.

A neoliberal macroeconomic approach to transition requires a developing country to privatize, liberalize market access, and open the national account. It counsels a dual approach: stabilization that entails reduced government borrowing, fiscal tightening, and enhanced revenue collection; and structural adjustment that eliminates state-led sectoral planning, state-owned industries, and state-directed investment. Clearly, China didn't view these lessons as being applicable and has integrated into the world economy on its own terms.

For the institutionalists, specialists in governance and institution building, reform is an exercise that identifies the gaps between current practice and best practice, and then adds the missing particulars, such as company, labor, and environmental laws. The goal is to replicate known technologies, institutions, rules, and practices; if the proper blueprints are followed, markets in transition will settle to the same steady state that characterizes established economies.

## Building a Market Economy, the Chinese Way

China's market reforms have been a process of discovering dynamic synergies of its history, resources, and social capacity.[4] The opening of one opportunity created room for others to follow, some blending familiar patterns, others creating fresh combinations, and all reflecting a blend of pragmatism and hybrid institutional selection based upon dual-track strategies of creating market openings while preserving socialist responsibilities.

Corruption and political factionalism both took new forms after 1976 once the Cultural Revolution had ended. During the 1970s the scarcity of goods compelled reliance on personal relationships with commune members, causing a proliferation of clientelistic vertical relationships with regime officials. Extensive embezzlement and extortion was reported as rival factions within the same work unit competed for prerogatives. These prerogatives included access to priority housing, feasting, and the appropriation of public goods (Liu 1983). Reform shifted the focus of political rivalry outward, away from the work group and away from an accumulation of internal prerogatives and toward the acquisition of wealth from the market. This made the reform process a springboard for economic and social mobility.

From 1978 to 1989, Deng Xiaoping (1904–1997) served as paramount leader of the People's Republic of China. Many observers credit Deng as being the mastermind of Chinese economic reforms, believing he must have known the results he wanted; but initially he, along with his comrades, had no strategic plan in mind. In fact, a pragmatic approach to economic opening, known as Deng Xiaoping Theory, was adopted in the Chinese constitution in 1997. A key to putting this theory into practice was that Deng allowed many local initiatives to be tested and then studied them as prototypes for national policy. A large variety of local experiments, many of them encroaching on incumbent regulations, were tolerated, and successful practices were recognized and scaled up. This receptiveness toward bottom-up experimentation transformed the national market. It encouraged local initiative to attract investment and expanded opportunities for private businesses in activities not dominated by state-owned enterprises (SOEs).

Who could have expected an annualized 7.48 percent GDP growth over thirty-eight consecutive years? One twist in the reform process led to another. The national economy veered, often drastically, from the predictions of central leadership as bottom-up initiatives altered the aggregate Chinese global economy and triggered new sets of reactions. The SOEs, for example, had to adapt to patterns co-created with private-sector firms, ushering in new trains of change.

Deng's policymakers had to answer questions that institutionalists in the West tend to overlook. For example, how can industrialization take place, and a poor economy experience structural transformation, in the presence of low fundamental capabilities when skills and institutions are weak? The instinct of early leadership was not to wait for institutional development, but to proceed with market development. With their penchant to think in terms of outcomes rather than legal processes, they allowed growth to drive both the form and function of rules and regulations.

Each solution prompted another round of compositional changes to the structure of China's economic institutions. In this regard, the population of China behaves the way all people in a market environment do, proactively filling in niches of opportunity. China's pathfinders were embodying their own version of a utilitarian ideal, finding the greatest sum of individual happiness at the least cost to the collectivity.

Coase and Wang write that "[the] Chinese leadership ... fully recognized their inexperience in building a market economy" (2012, 152). The first generation of reformers didn't have a preconceived notion of where they should end up and didn't possess a roadmap for the journey. They simply wanted to get a stagnant economy moving. As the Chinese saying goes, "You don't risk falling when you stand at the foot of the mountain." Their greatest advantage was their pragmatism; "rejecting class struggle and embracing socialist modernization, China finally broke the spell of a negative sum game of economic development. ... Their bitter disappointment with Mao's grandiose but disastrous socialist experiment had clearly taught the Chinese to be skeptical of any grand blueprint for reform" (153).

The introduction of market principles began in late 1978 with Deng's announcement of an open-door policy, permitting foreign businesses to set up shop in China. Then came the decollectivization of agriculture and the granting of permission to local entrepreneurs to start businesses. The reform approach was a tentative probing, "looking around while treading ahead ... crossing the river by feeling the stones."[5] Deng was also known for "catism," his famous idea that it matters not whether the cat is black or white so long as it catches mice.

The early reformers weren't held hostage to Marxist stereotypes or to old expectations, metrics, or rewards. They had no past successes, and no habits, practices, or familiar behaviors to overcome. Ideology had failed them once. So dogmatism was avoided, as was acceptance of what could not be tested. This attitude was promoted in Deng's speech at the closing of the 1978 CCP annual Central Work Conference, which set the tone for launching the grand reform program of opening the economy to market forces; the program had the cumbersome title "Emancipate the Mind, Seek Truth from Facts, and Unite as One in Looking to the Future," and was widely interpreted to mean that nothing was off-limits and that development had no endpoint.

Deng's administration resolved not to get modernization wrong a second time by following some new dogma. As they proceeded, they learned to perceive a market economy as something that is fixed in neither form nor structure: not inherently virtuous, but useful; a problem-solving mechanism comprising both institutions and technology that must be continually tinkered with. Accordingly, after an initial reform was promulgated, its structural deepening continued and experimental improvements followed until better solutions were developed.

Yet at the same time, China's market reformers were acting in a way consistent with Mao's influential 1937 essay "On Practice," in which he wrote, "Discover the truth through practice, and again through practice verify and develop the truth. . . . Practice, knowledge, again practice, and again knowledge. This form repeats itself in endless cycles, and with each cycle the content of practice and knowledge rises to a higher level" (Mao 1965, 380). Policymakers were engaging in what researchers today would call a positive feedback process, their central concern being to use existing capacity to fit new tasks. For example, rather than introducing a fully formed and comprehensive legal code, China built its commercial laws as markets and contracts came into existence and required them. Its policymakers didn't view the creation of a rule-of-law environment for economic transactions, such as that which governed Western economies, as a realistic goal in the span of a single generation or two. Lawmakers often copied templates from the International Rules for the Interpretation of Trade Terms and the Uniform Customs and Practice for Documentary Credits, developed by the International Chamber of Commerce. But even when the templates were copied, the capacity to monitor their enforcement was deficient.

Once the leadership identified a set of purposes to fulfill, such as feeding the population through market-based allocations or engaging the rural workforce in commercial manufacturing, they devised solutions based on China's actual social capacity. The point of reference was always China's own preexisting capabilities. This caused its transition process to diverge from both capitalist and socialist notions of sequencing. The authorities opted for hybrid institutions and strategies, in large part because they were seeking opportunities presented by an existing global trading system. And contrary to most Western counsel, the Chinese failed to see a clear distinction between market and state, assuming that an economy could be controlled by the state's preferences rather than by market forces.

While moving away from the closed model of Soviet socialism, China had no existing system to emulate. Instead of engaging in a futile debate over whether the country should follow the capitalist or the socialist road, Deng proposed a practical criterion for action during his famous Southern Tour in early 1992. He called it the "three conducives" (*san you li*): Action should be conducive to social productivity, to the integrated strength of the nation, and to the elevation of people's livelihood (Deng 1993, 372).

The rural population had been organized into cooperatives, called work units, since the 1950s, but instead of abolishing their collective quotas, in 1979 the authorities allowed households to keep and market whatever they produced above their quotas, thus harnessing individual incentives while keeping the cooperatives in place to continue to supply their array of social services. Within two years of the introduction of this "household responsibility system," agricultural productivity surged, and fruits and vegetables reappeared for sale at the roadside in baskets and barrels throughout the countryside, a phenomenon not seen since the introduction of the commune system.

Development along dual public and private tracks allowed the expanding private sector to grow without the need to liquidate public-sector firms. This process, undertaken in the 1980s, made it possible to introduce new practices without eliminating older ones, moving the economy along both tracks at once, with the faster track consisting of privately invested, for-profit operations. Rather than risk wholesale disruptions in a society that had just experienced, within two generations, a long-running civil war followed by the wrenching social change of collectivization and the Cultural Revolution, Deng strove to ease further transition. Instead of abruptly overhauling SOEs via privatization, according to the disruptive principle of shock therapy, Deng accepted their eventual replacement by a newer, for-profit (although not necessarily private) sector according to the principle of "whoever caught more mice." The dual structure of reform diminished political risk and minimized implementation costs since it was carried out by the preexisting network of CCP bureaucrats throughout the country.

Another contribution of the dual-track policy was job creation. Allowing for self-employment via entrepreneurship offered a way to resettle the millions of youth subjected to Mao's "Up to the Mountains, Down to the Countryside" (UMDC) campaign, which lasted, despite a few suspensions, from 1956 to 1978 (Wu and Fan 2016). UMDC changed the fate of an entire generation of Chinese, of which more than seventeen million "educated" (*Zhiqing*) and urban young people were dispatched to live in rural areas. The overwhelming majority of them were graduates from junior and senior high schools, and many were from the Red Guards, sent off to "unlearn" their Cultural Revolution zealotry. Its objective was to have the youths reeducated by peasants while contributing to rural development. In anticipation of their return, university entrance exams were reopened in 1977, and the following year the Second National Conference on the UMDC Work resulted in plans to end the reeducation program, resettle the young people, and offer them employment options, primarily in the same kinds of small-scale retail startups that had been offered to redundant workforces from the ailing state-run factories that had once provided the proverbial cradle-to-grave security of the "iron rice bowl" (Wu 2016). Ratification of the Company Law of the People's Republic of China in 1994 came later and allowed for the creation of limited liability companies.

Just as rural householders gained consent to sell for profit whatever they produced over their allotted quotas, town and village governments were permitted to retain controlling shares in commercial enterprises that they could set up as legal entities known as Town and Village Enterprises (TVEs).[6] According to Article 17 of Law on Township Enterprises, which went into effect on January 1, 1997, a fixed percentage out of the TVE proceeds would be withheld to replenish social expenditure for community welfare, and the rest reinvested back into the business or going toward other necessary expenses. This was a hybrid form of a commercial entity, which relieved the central government of the need to regulate and tax the nascent private sector or the TVEs directly in order to provide revenues for public goods, such as schools and hospitals. The TVEs remained under the stewardship of the local mayors, but now they could engage in commercial activities with other for-profit, privately invested partners, often via management buyouts. In a span of two or three decades, some grew into multinational firms, such as Haier and Lenovo.[7]

The TVEs proved to be a sound idea; during the early market reforms of the 1980s, the privatizing of socialist assets caused the central government to suffer a decline in its revenue base, which fell below that of market economies in the West. By keeping social service functions with the TVEs, the central government didn't have to shoulder additional responsibilities at a time of contracting local public budgets but could gradually build a new national revenue system. Unfortunately, this has also meant that the rural areas with fewer for-profit businesses received fewer social services, causing income disparities and social inequalities to grow.

In rural areas where the business climate was not conducive for TVEs, surplus workers migrated to cities, joining assembly lines, serving as housemaids, working at construction sites, or delivering parcels. Nevertheless, the free movement of labor did not result in the free movement of people. Due to the household registration system, migrant workers were not allowed to take their social entitlements with them, which created a gap between rural and urban dwellers in terms of social welfare and income.[8] The Chinese Bureau of Statistics' *Survey Report on Peasant Workers 2017* reports that nearly 28.7 million peasants had migrated from the countryside to cities for jobs paying monthly salaries of RMB 3,275, or less than US$500. This demographic windfall is likely to disappear by 2025 as the effects of the one child policy set in and the labor pool contracts (Das and N'Diaye 2013).

Another deviation from the standard playbook has helped speed China's transition: its land ownership policy. All land belongs to the state, a tradition also inherited from its dynastic past. Farmers, developers, and industrialists alike rent land from a sole landlord, the central government, for a fixed period.[9] This allows flexibility for the government to eventually reclaim the land for strategic purposes, such as building industrial parks, dams, or highways. Uncertainty over property rights, however, has encouraged farmers to use fertilizers and pesticides excessively, and to over-dredge local rivers for the sand essential to making concrete (Tian 2017). The government is deliberately ambiguous in stating the terms and conditions for lease renewal upon expiration. Still, the rapid development of infrastructure can be traced to the ownership flexibility possessed by the government; being the sole landlord frees it from lengthy negotiations with tenants.

In the financial sector, the state also allowed no-name, numbered bank accounts, a practice that had been common in Korea (after April 1, 2000, Chinese banks did not create new accounts, but old ones have not been systematically phased out). From one perspective, this is an invitation to help corrupt operators hide their ill-gotten gains; but it also encourages people to channel money into state-owned banks. If the state were to insist on knowing depositors' names, fewer deposits would be made, the black market would flourish, and the state-owned banks would have less access to private savings. We can appreciate the practicality of this approach by comparing it with that of India. After independence, India's central bank established much stricter, more legalistic criteria for accessing the banking sector and ended up with a thriving black market not just for goods and services but also for the management of capital. Overzealous regulation has prevented India's formal banking sector from attaining the scale, as a percentage of GDP, of the Chinese formal banking system (Root 2005).

## Competition among Local Governments Reduces Interest-Group Capture

Because China's governance is so centralized, at first glance it might seem that competition, the key driver of economic performance, is weak. In fact, most of the time the central government only issues policy guidelines. Local governments compete with one another by offering incentives to attract investments. Many of China's billion-dollar private enterprises, for example that of Liu Yongxing's East Hope Group, built their business conglomerates with help from a local government (in his case, the City of Sanmenxia). The East Hope Group, founded in the early 1980s with interests in agribusiness and metals, eventually eclipsed an SOE that had an exclusive right to purchase bauxite (Barboza 2009). Similarly, in 2015 the Cangzhou City government of Hebei province competed with Chongqing to win the relocation of Hyundai auto assembly from Beijing by offering land concessions and a substantial subsidy of RMB 1,800 per square meter floor space for the plant. Chong-En Bai, Chang-Tai Hsieh, and Zheng (Michael) Song (2014, 7) conclude that "competition between local governments may have played a central role in allowing new [private] firms to emerge and challenge incumbent firms."

Effective public-sector management is a crucial variable needed to attract investment in private enterprise. It is this competition that has created what Yingyi Qian and Barry Weingast (1997) call federalism with Chinese characteristics. "Tournaments" among local government jurisdictions encourage the commercial management of SOEs alongside efforts to attract private-sector firms and stimulate local growth and local employment. Many have become shareholding companies, although the government is usually the largest share-holder. The party leadership, at various subnational levels, entered into contracts with the central government about what could be regarded as local surplus, to be consumed and reinvested locally. Local actors, including governments, SOEs, and rural production teams, gained various exemptions on a particularistic basis. Local leaders who met or surpassed the growth targets set for them by central administrators could advance their own administrative careers, and this enhanced market competition. Hundreds of "tournaments" are conducted locally and successful ones are scaled up, reducing dependence upon top-down global formulas.

By giving the state sector, especially local leadership, latitude to adapt to market demand, party leaders could see that the experimentation with private investment and consumer demand was beneficial to the larger goal of modernizing the country; and this later served to open SOE reform to some market forces. Over time, the private sector's adaptive responses to the market, and the failure of the state-owned sectors to keep pace, gave party leaders ample justification to demand higher levels of performance from SOEs. David Li and Francis Lui (2004) argue that so long as the private sector continuously outperforms the state sector, pressures will increase on the latter to adapt, reform, improve productivity, and seek access to new markets. Subjected to the increasing discipline of the market economy, laggard performers can be winnowed out. Policy makers adapted to the position that what matters most, company performance, is a matter of market competition, not the form of ownership. This competition has been a key to slowly but surely applying a market yardstick to state-sector performance.[10] During the eight-year negotiation for accession into the World Trade Organization (WTO), the catchphrase among Chinese industries was to prepare to "dance with the wolves" of the West. Unfortunately, this was often a justification for excessive protection of China's industries from WTO members; but overall, entering the WTO did reduce regulatory capture and rent seeking by domestic elites.

Maintaining the pace of institutional and regulatory reforms seemed to be a method to prevent them from being locked in at unsatisfactory levels. Each sequence in the reform process was followed by another wave of reforms, preventing incumbents from locking in their gains. When the first-generation internal reforms ran into barriers, a second generation of reforms, those that brought in outside investment, was promptly introduced to encourage further market evolution. Then came third-generation reforms: the global outward push. Company managers who weren't ready for the next wave could lose whatever they had gained in the previous one. The process of continuous reforms allowed policy to remain within a virtuous cycle, inhibiting interest-group entrenchment. Local government officials were evaluated on the commercial performance of enterprises or regions under their authority, and they were eager to embrace innovations that could produce growth even if opportunities to acquire wealth via corruption burgeoned.

## Adverse Terms of Global Integration

The international environment is another reason China's economic transition deviated from Western expectations. The geopolitical environment in which it had to seek resources to fuel its development differed in important ways from the international environment faced by nations that had developed prior to it. After its rupture with the Soviet Union in 1958, China was shunned by both camps until January 1979, when the United States reestablished full diplomatic relations.

An inadequate per capita resource base made access to resources, especially energy security, China's early and paramount global policy goal. The West had first-mover advantages with regard to access to global resources. Western-based firms, for example, already dominated the purchasing market for oil. China didn't meet the eligibility criteria to join the International Energy Agency (IEA), a consortium that includes about half of the world's oil consumers and helps its members develop strategies to meet their energy needs. To meet its growing domestic demand, China had to seek out "rogue" suppliers, regimes shunned by the West.[11] The relations China established with its trade partners – Sudan, Pakistan, Angola, Cuba, Bolivia, Venezuela, Ecuador, Sri Lanka, Zimbabwe, and Libya – gave those countries the opportunity to participate in globalization that the West, for one reason or another, had fully or partially denied them. Many of these governments had little interest in the democratic community or sharing sovereignty with the international community on domestic human rights issues. And China was not about to let economic boycotts disrupt the flow of resources to its ports. To the contrary, China learned to use trade sanctions to its own advantage. For example, on May 25, 2014, China settled protracted negotiations for Russian gas at a time when Western sanctions had made Russia desperate for foreign exchange. Since 2006, China has committed billions of dollars in loans to Venezuela, a major supplier of its oil, despite animosity between its two most recent presidents, Hugo Chávez and then Nicolás Maduro, and the United States. China tries to claim the moral high ground, arguing that sanctions penalize innocent citizens under bad rulers. It is also China's traditional belief that the "winds blow in different directions in different seasons," meaning that permanent friends or foes don't exist over a long historical perspective. If a future relationship is uncertain, why give up an immediate gain?

Geopolitical tensions increased when the West refused to recognize China's territorial claims over Tibet, Taiwan, and various South China Sea islands. Among the permanent UN Security Council members, China alone had not been granted complete recognition of its territorial claims. Russia, with its seizure of the Crimea, has since joined China in this regard.

Finally, China's system of government has always been out of alignment with the spread of global democracy. Its identity clashes with key aspects of international liberalism: the emphasis on the democratic community; on shared sovereignty with the WTO, the UN Security Council, the World Court, and other organizations; and on the right of the international community to protect populations oppressed by their leaders.

## 7.2 A GREAT LESSON OF ECONOMIC HISTORY, NOT LEARNED

To date, the Chinese approach to transition has assumed the inevitability of an uneven and gradual transformation, dependent on how the actors perceive the opportunities they obtain at each step along the way. But this has left China's development as a market economy with a structural impediment. According to a number of independently compiled indexes, the quality of China's rule-of-law environment, contract enforcement, and informational transparency are on par with many of the poorest performers in the world. Its market access is the most restrictive of the G-20 economies and property rights are not secure. The government engages in Internet surveillance and censorship. Civil society organizations, and an investment and risk culture, built as they are upon a framework of the independent rule of law, have shallow roots in China.

One of the consequences is that China faces a crisis of public trust, and this is partly to blame for the current trade strife with its foreign investors and trade partners. One side of this deficit is illustrated by the many stories dominating the headlines of deception by firms and public officials. Tax evasion arrests, formerly unheard of, are on the rise. Hundreds of peer-to-peer lending platforms have vanished, along with their clients' funds; household products are often reported tainted; faulty vaccines, fake data, and knockoff labels persist, despite new standards and penalties. Yet when crackdowns do occur, their effectiveness can be compromised by high-profile "disappearances" and opaque police and judicial proceedings.

What is behind this scourge of malfeasance? Is it only because now there is some openness to reporting on it, more social media, and the government lets tension vent by publicizing these matters? The economic reforms have turned China into a massive, urbanized market economy, yet one that is still largely built on personal ties, local reputations, and moral sanctions that are communal in origin. Yet traditional use of reputation as an effective form of social control – the sense of shame cultivated by Confucius – has been rendered hollow by scandal after scandal involving corporate, consumer, and political bribery and fraud. These norms function best in an environment of dense social networks, consisting of small, tightly knit groups of relatives, friends, and acquaintances. As China urbanizes, however, it is transitioning from a villager culture into a stranger culture. More often than not, exchanges are conducted outside of one's small, trusted circle, transactions are rarely repeated, and local knowledge of past behavior is not effectively monitored. And the communal approach, dependent as it is on informal constraints, limits the complex exchanges among unrelated, unknown partners that fuel growth.

The institutional evolution of any modern economy requires more than voluntary arrangements among related parties. A legal framework is needed for an independent civil society, including the enforcement of property rights and an independent judiciary to protect the public from fraud and malfeasance – and, at the very least, to counterbalance the consolidation of state power. Without these, uncertainty will continue to constrain healthy risk taking or the appetite to engage in multi-period transactions.

To compensate for underperforming insurance and capital markets, state lenders step in as the primary providers of long-term investment but consume capital that could be allocated toward private-sector investments in research and development. The underlying problem is that, short of checks and balances, the CCP lacks the capacity to credibly commit to safeguarding the intellectual property rights of players within these markets.

The party has acknowledged that there is not enough credit information to assess the risk profiles of market players. By 2020, the government hopes to establish a centrally managed "social credit" big-data system to monitor the business and social reputations of China's 1.4 billion citizens. The party has made some progress    toward    creating    internal    accountability.    But accountability systems and self-monitoring among civic associations are virtually nonexistent. Instead, the state has chosen to monopolize the dissemination of information and often acts alone as the reputation enforcer in society. This central control over information and communication weakens civil society, leaving no independent institutions to serve as a buffer to monitor either the state or private actors.

The same trust deficit that affects China's relationships domestically impairs trust with its most important trading partners: those that develop the technology China needs to become a high-income country. So far, technological advances have mostly come as free rides on institutions developed elsewhere, from economies whose institutions better protect developers' property rights and safeguard incentives to invest time, resources, and energy into ideas and products.

China has yet to transition into a society in which good laws are the backbone of mutual trust. It still needs rule enforcement that is not strictly moral but is also encased in the institutional activism of a wide range of organizations and interests. Archaic, informal "social trust" systems whose legitimacy resides in the personal virtue of government officials are poor substitutes. One of the great lessons of economic history is that independent institutions that are protective of property rights become more essential at each successive stage of development.

Yet, and despite the structural impediments that China experienced during its economic transition, it is fully poised to become a global player. The impact of its economy on the global political economy has the potential to disrupt that economy in a number of ways.

## NOTES

1. The Qin dynasty was the first to unify China, eliminating the feudal classes and setting up the hub-and-spoke structure that has perpetuated imperial rule throughout subsequent Chinese history.

2. On December 18, 2018, to celebrate the fortieth anniversary of China's reform and opening-up, Chairman Xi Jinping delivered a speech in Beijing, proclaiming that the nation is in a position to shape the world without a desire to dominate, and is strong enough that no one can dictate to it (*China Daily* 2018).

3. According to World Bank Development Indicators (World Bank 2016), China increased its GDP from US$149.54 billion in 1978 to US$11.20 trillion, in 2016, an increase of 7.48 percent that exceeds the growth of all other countries during the same period.

4. Key steps in the modernization drive have been Mao Zedong's Great Leap Forward for steel production; Deng Xiaoping's Four Modernizations, assimilating foreign technology; Jiang Zemin's globalization, marked by accession to the WTO in 2001; and Xi's China Dream and Community of Shared Future in Xi's discourses 2018.

5. These words, attributed to Deng, are actually from Chen Yun (1905–1995), a vehement opponent of capitalism who was Deng's political rival and opposed most of his modernization policies. See *Selected Works of Chen Yun* (1988, 279).

6. In rural areas today, these work units are called people's communes and production brigades; in urban areas, they are called street offices. Both are examples of collective ownership. The word "capitalist" was generally avoided in official declarations that described and authorized their activities.

7. Haier, for example, began as a TVE at the end of 1984 in Qingdao, Shandong province, with one assembly line for the production of refrigerators, saddled with a debt of RMB 1.47 million, and with 800 workers facing unemployment (*People's Daily* 2000). By the end of 2016, Haier was a global giant in the household appliance industry, with around 80,000 employees, and had acquired General Electric's appliance division for US$5.4 billion.

8. So long as the household registration or *hukou* system persists, China earns a demographic dividend that endows it with competitive advantage as a manufacturing powerhouse in the global marketplace. Arthur Lewis (1954) described this manner of primitive accumulation in which a "capitalist" sector develops by expropriating labor from a non capitalist, "backward," "subsistence" sector.

9. Farmland is subject to strict zoning by central government, with leases running from three to thirty years. This incentivizes farmers to over-

fertilize and use potentially dangerous pesticides since they have no way of knowing if their children will inherit the land. Urban land is leased as follows: seventy years for residential housing; fifty for industrial development; fifty for education, science and technology, culture, health care and sports; forty for commerce (such as a shopping mall or office building), tourism, and recreation; and fifty for other multi purpose use (Tian 2017).

10. Oleh Havrylyshyn, Xiaofan Meng, and Marian Tupy (2016) argue that in twenty-five years of reform in formerly communist countries, the gradual reformers tended to get "stuck" in transition because delays allowed elites to capture state institutions and resist subsequent liberalization. Rapid reformers generally ended up with better results by reducing the risk of elite capture. Applying this yardstick to China is problematic. Chinese reformers did not abruptly overhaul SOEs via privatization; nevertheless, a conducive environment for the market allocations was created.

11. China is one of eight IEA "association" countries, having acquired that status in 2015 (IEA 2019). See the IEA website, https://iea.org/countries/China.

# 8  China's Ambitions and the Future of the Global Economy

## with Liu Baocheng

A persistent assumption of Western policymakers has been that global integration would engender structural changes within China and relax its pattern of top-down interventionism. Related to the West's optimism is the idea that China's business leaders would gain more say in the overall policies of the CCP. Going outward and consolidating power at home by shoring up state control over the economy seem like conflicting priorities to Western observers. However, this overlooks an entire set of community values that the CCP is committed to upholding. The agenda for going outward is made viable politically because of populist policies at home, including government efforts to reduce poverty and regional disparities, particularly in the agriculture sector, improve the *hukou* (household registration) and the plight of migrant workers, and rein in official corruption.

Since the launching of Chairman Hu Jintao's "harmonious society" initiative in 2005, the party has sought ways to reconcile an open economy with social stability at home. Essential to Hu's harmonious society initiative is a dual goal: to strengthen the state sector and expand central planning while encouraging private businesses to flourish in the market – and to do this while not allowing business leaders to reach the commanding heights of the policymaking machinery. The policies of Chairman Xi do not seem to be changing in the direction that the US policy community has been hoping for. To the contrary, the party has been strengthening its control over outward expansion, which favors activities that are state-dependent such as the energy grid, mineral extraction, and large-scale infrastructure.

Table 8.1 *From complacency to urgency: China reluctantly opens to the outside.*

| | |
|---|---|
| Two opium wars present a wakeup call to China's leadership | 1840–1860 |
| Westernization movement | 1861–1895 |
| Defeat in the Sino-Japanese War | 1894–1895 |
| Restoration movement to create constitutional monarchy (analogous to the English Magna Carta) | June 11–12, 1898 |
| Boxer Rebellion | 1889–1900 |
| The revolution of 1911 and end of dynastic rule | 1911–1912 |
| A war-torn state: civil wars, anti-Japanese war, Korean War | 1912–1953 |
| Independence and member of the socialist bloc | 1949–1989 |
| Socialism and closed economy | 1949–1978 |
| Reform and open-door socialist market economy with Chinese characteristics | 1978–2015 |
| Going global, investing outward | 2001–present |

China's Ministry of Foreign Affairs uses the term New Democratic Revolution Period to describe the years 1919–1949.

China's opening to the outside world was gradual up until the early 2000s, as Table 8.1 suggests.[1] Through the eighteenth century, it was an economic powerhouse; but reliant as it was on the incremental spread of useful innovations, it could no longer compete with or defend itself from the West, which had taken a great leap in its economic productivity. China was finally overtaken by the West in the nineteenth century.

## 8.1  CHINA'S SEARCH FOR SOFT POWER

China's global ambitions suddenly accelerated after 2005. The new strategy of seeking greater engagement with overseas markets and finding outbound investment opportunities had three principal components. The first was continuing China's traditional strategy of

Table 8.2 *The number of Chinese outward investors, 2006–2016 (Ministry of Commerce 2017).*

| Year | Number of Chinese outward investors (thousands) | Number of Chinese enterprises established overseas (thousands) | Number of China's ODI recipients |
|------|------|------|------|
| 2006 | 5.0 | 10.0 | 172 |
| 2007 | 7.0 | 10.0 | 173 |
| 2008 | 8.5 | 12.00 | 174 |
| 2009 | 12.0 | 13.0 | 177 |
| 2010 | 13.0 | 16.0 | 178 |
| 2011 | 13.5 | 18.0 | 177 |
| 2012 | 16.0 | 22.0 | 179 |
| 2013 | 15.3 | 25.4 | 184 |
| 2014 | 18.5 | 29.7 | 186 |
| 2015 | 20.2 | 30.8 | 188 |
| 2016 | 24.4 | 37.2 | 190 |

securing its resource supply; as such, the initial wave of outward investment focused on commodity and extraction industries. The second was concerned with supporting developing economies by shifting excess capacity abroad, including through contracting international projects and reviving the "Silk Road Spirit" in the Belt and Road Initiative (also known as One Belt One Road) that would connect China with Central Asia, South Asia, the Middle East, and Europe. The third component comprised direct investment in overseas production, especially to promote innovation-driven production.

The Belt and Road Initiative, proclaimed with much fanfare in 2013, combines roads, railways, fiber optic channels, and power transmission lines across the continents with sea lanes and ports. Other global initiatives that China has engaged with include the Paris Treaty on Climate Change in 2016, and the Special Drawing Right (SDR) basket, also in 2016. As a supplementary foreign exchange reserve held by the International Monetary Fund (IMF), the SDR is a unit of account, not a currency, and represents a claim to currency held by member countries; the Chinese considered joining it to be a milestone in the internationalization of its currency and global recognition of its financial stability. Additional initiatives include cosponsoring, with 56 member countries, the BRICS (Brazil, Russia, India, China, and South Africa) Development Bank (established in 2014, later renamed the New Development Bank) and underwriting the Asian Infrastructure Investment Bank (established in 2015). China also pursues regional integration in the Shanghai Cooperation Organization (established in 1996), an international alliance of Eurasian states consisting of eight members and four observers, and in the China led China-CEEC (established in 2012) with 17+1, comprising China, eleven EU members, and five Balkan countries. There are initiatives in Africa, such as the Forum on China–Africa Cooperation (established in 2000), with fifty-three African countries and the African Union, to advance the Collaborative Blueprint for Economic and Social Development between China and Africa. Chairman Xi has also proposed the establishment of an alliance on corporate social responsibility among Chinese companies.

The third initiative is to seek opportunities that improve China's position along the value chain through the acquisition of firms overseas. High-profile acquisitions, including Smithfield Foods (2013), Motorola Mobility (2014), Hoover (2018), and Starwood Hotels (2016), are a means by which both state-owned and private Chinese companies aspire to increase their global footprint. By acquiring name brands, they hope to bypass import agents and penetrate into local distribution channels in the developed markets. The drive to build, through mergers and acquisitions, global R&D firms has pushed Chinese investment in US firms up 843 percent from 2011 to 2016, from US$4.9 billion to US$45.2 billion (USTR 2018, 104).

The overseas direct investment (ODI) drive is complemented by other trends among China's private investors, such as acquiring overseas real estate; for example, real estate purchases in the United States by Chinese citizens peaked at US$31.7 billion in 2017, and were US$27.3 billion in 2016 and US$28.6 billion in 2015 (National Association of Realtors 2017, 12). Both state-owned and private companies are buying farms overseas to stock the home market, and private firms are pooling resources to take advantage of opportunities opened up by the Belt and Road Initiative.

From 2012 to 2016, China's global investments doubled, and from 2004 to 2016, ODI grew for thirteen consecutive years, with an average annual increase of US$15.9 billion (a median rate of increase of US$12.28 billion). ODI flows hit a historic high of US$196.2 billion in 2016, ranking second in the world. Moreover, 2016 was also the second year that ODI exceeded China's foreign investment inflows (Ministry of Commerce 2017).

Since 2006 the number of Chinese enterprises going global has increased rapidly. By the end of 2015, some 20,200 investors had established 30,800 enterprises overseas, spreading across 188 countries and regions, with net foreign assets totaling nearly US$4.4 trillion. At the end of 2016, that total had increased to

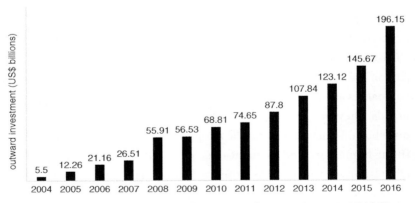

FIGURE 8.1 China's outward investment flow, 2004–2016, in US$ billions. The data for 2004–2005 include China's nonfinancial ODI only, and data for 2006–2016 include China's ODI across all industries (Ministry of Commerce 2017).

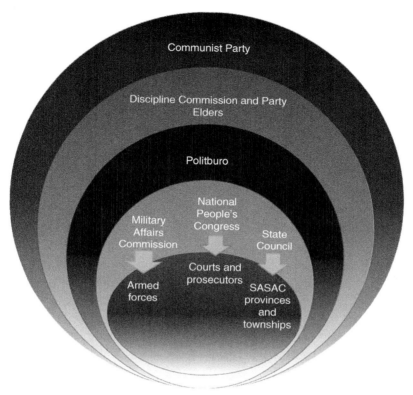

FIGURE 8.2 An approximate illustration of China's national-level political power structure under CCP leadership.

US$5.0 trillion. In 2016 alone, ODI registered explosive growth, in spite of domestic slowdown: net foreign direct investment was US$196.2 billion. All told, 24,400 local entities across 190 countries received Chinese investments in 2016.

This outward investment drive will enable China to supplant the United States as the largest global investor. China's contribution to world economic growth since 2007 has noticeably topped that of the US, reaching 32.2 percent in 2016.[2] Its emergence as a global actor has transpired with an intensity that neither critics nor backers could have predicted. Inevitably, as China's engagement expands, it will take globalization into new territories. This will include an effort to exert ideological leadership among its trading partners and within the international community.

China's transition into a global actor is consistent with one supreme rule observed in the previous three cases of regime change: structure determines how ideas and behavior spread on a network. The structure of the Chinese economy accords the state a foundational role in policy and administration. Whereas Western states had to enter into compacts with powerful merchant elites, in China the banking sector is largely state owned or controlled. Managers are recruited from within the CCP cadre system. The number of SOEs, including both the central and local level, is estimated to be 150,000. Petroleum, mining, telecommunications, utilities, transportation, and several industrial sectors are dominated by SOEs. There were 103 Chinese firms on Fortune's 2016 list of the world's largest companies; and in 75 of these the government owns more than 50 percent.

### Creating a Community of Shared Interests, Shared Responsibilities, and Shared Destiny

While China has considerable experience and capacity for infrastructure-led economic development, its new mission is far more profound than just financing buildings, railways, and roads. Chairman Xi fully appreciates that if China's far-reaching market reforms make it the world's largest economy, then another momentous shift in global dynamics may at last be under way – a change in the very structure of global capitalism – making the system of global trade and investment more compatible with the Chinese model. In this vein China will seek to build coalitions with countries that increasingly depend on it for prosperity, and this could change voting patterns in, and eventually the structure of, international organizations.

In October 2017, China's global objective, to be a rule giver and no longer just a rule taker, was announced at the 19th National Congress. Xi affirmed that China would use its growing stake in international investment and cooperation to shape global politics and institutions to better suit its own interests. And he articulated China's plan to roll out a body of thought for the betterment of the world. China wants to bring the global periphery, and then the wider world, to its view of global order (Xi 2017). This raises some very particular questions: How will China's version of state capitalism affect its trading partners? And will other countries be likely to adopt and adapt some of China's policy innovations, making its experience a source of new variations in global governance?

Anticipating this, Xi exhorted his countrymen to "hold high the banner of socialism with Chinese characteristics" and show the world that China "offers a new option for other countries and nations who want to speed up their development while preserving their independence; and [that] it offers Chinese wisdom and a Chinese approach to solving the problems facing mankind" (Xi 2017). Xi's address referred to ancient classics and visions of former imperial grandeur, as well as "the darkness of domestic turmoil and foreign aggressions," and promoted the combined study of Confucianism and Marxism to create a new Chinese nationalist sentiment. This, he said, would shape China's efforts to counterbalance the US strategy of promoting democracy as a global norm. China's model would be more inclusive, demonstrating to the world that elections and privatization are not prerequisites of development. Proper governance matters more than the mechanism by which leadership is selected.

Xi declared that China's model of socialism is not just about economic structure; it is an alternative to Western democracy. "We respect the right of the people of all countries to choose their own development path," he said. "We endeavor to uphold international fairness and justice, and oppose acts that impose one's will on others or interfere in the internal affairs of others, as well as the practice of the strong bullying the weak" (Xi 2017). If the gains of adapting market economics can accrue to a fundamentally non-Western society such as China, then why not to India or Vietnam? By following the channel

China has created, other emerging nations can aspire to increase their voice and influence in global governance.

## 8.2   THE HUB-AND-SPOKE RESURFACES, AS IT HAS FOR MILLENNIA

Under CCP leadership, China reinvented itself along lines distinctively new and distinctively Chinese at the same time. As a global actor, it pursues a systemwide ethos that is in accordance with its own habits and conventions, institutions and belief systems, rather than those of the West's academics and planners. One underlying idea in particular continues to carry the imprint of ancient norms. To ensure there is no challenge to regime stability, mechanisms have been created to prevent those with an independent power base, one derived from the control of independent economic resources, from ever being in a position to challenge political leadership.

This can be seen in the manner by which all layers of government bureaucracy, including SOEs, are managed, i.e., in conjunction with the guardianship of a CCP committee that supervises its performance. Such dual-track management is also subject to periodic inspection by the task force of the CCP Disciplinary Committee, dispatched to monitor political correctness and operational efficacy. The Ministry of Organization, unlike other ministries, has a special function that is vested directly by the CCP Central Committee, instead of the executive line of the State Council. It is in charge of all cadres (party-selected managers and officials) and has oversight of personnel recruitment for virtually all ranks.

After joining the WTO in 2001, at the end of Jiang Zemin's and Zhu Rongji's terms as party leaders, a set of reforms was introduced that demonstrates how the CCP intends to maintain control over both technological innovation and outward expansion. In 2003, the CCP established a troika of organizations – the State-owned Assets Supervision and Administration Commission (SASAC), Central Huijin Investment Ltd., and the National Development and Reform Commission (NDRC) – through which it maintains control of all facets of the economy as an integrated multilevel system. These organizations have the authority to intervene in corporate business activity, to ensure that not only economic growth, but also performance, is in line with the overall party objectives. Together the troika illustrates a feature of what legal scholar Mark Wu calls "China Inc.," organized to "exploit complementarities to further advance state interests" by integrating the polity and the economy (2016, 278). This represents the Chinese notion of checks and balances.

The SASAC was established by the State Council (to whom it reports directly) and according to its charter has managerial oversight of all of China's SOEs. It is responsible for monitoring SOE executives' performance and ensuring that they operate in accordance with CCP and socialist market economy principles. The executives are official party cadres, selected by the Central Committee's Organization Department, who have usually achieved ranks in the state bureaucracy as vice ministers or bureau directors (a different ministry oversees performance and ideological inculcation of rank-and-file workers). The Organization Department also decides leadership appointments for the provinces, municipalities, and autonomous regions.

The second arm of the troika, the state-owned investment company Central Huijin Investment Ltd., was also founded by the State Council, with initial capitalization of RMB 372.5 billion. The State Council exercises shareholder responsibilities and appoints the investment company's board members. Central Huijin's mandate is to hold government stakes in the country's state-owned banks and financial enterprises. In 2007 the Ministry of Finance bought all Central Huijin's shares and moved the company into a newly established sovereign wealth fund, China Investment Corporation (CIC), as a wholly owned subsidiary, responsible for the management of CIC's foreign exchange reserves through investment in global financial markets. A colossal sovereign wealth management vehicle, its scope now extends to both domestic and international markets. Like SASAC, Central Huijin reportedly does not interfere in the daily operations of the firms in which it invests; nor, reportedly, does it involve itself with CIC operations or investments; it does not trade. The third member of the troika, the NDRC, grew out of the much older state commissions, and sets commodity prices for electricity, oil, natural gas, and water. It is also responsible for creating, coordinating, and implementing China's Five-Year Plans for the state's economy (Wu 2016, 276).

The party's ability to influence Chinese business entities is not limited to SOEs; most key business leaders in private firms have also attained membership either with the CCP or with eight other non-ruling parties under CCP leadership.[3] But SOE executives have not been invited to join the twenty-five-person Politburo, from which the seven members of the keystone Politburo Standing Committee are selected. Thus, the elite cadres of the CCP maintain a controlling presence not unlike the imperial bureaucracy. While SOEs retain oligarchical control over the pillar economic sectors, private sectors are allowed to thrive alongside them.

To ensure that managers receive uniform ideological training, the Party School of the Central Committee of the CCP, sometimes translated as the National Academy of Governance, with branches across the country, is responsible for the education of the party's 90 million members.[4] It trains and enables the accelerated indoctrination of public servants in CCP ideology.[5] China promised to organize its economy with Chinese characteristics, and it has done just that. It has created a market economy governed by an organizational design based upon its own history, traditions, and values.

## 8.3   DIFFERENT OUTLOOKS ON MARKETS, AND WHY IT MATTERS FOR GLOBALIZATION

China's global interventions are fashioned to accommodate deep social mores and cultural roots. It has a far longer record of continuous governance than other nations, and has produced a large body of literature, some of it nearly 2,000 years old, on the moral obligations of leaders and the role of officialdom. This history provides the country with a legacy of guiding precepts, encoded within its social institutions, to form a template for the future and from which to draw when facing situations of uncertainty.

Confucianism is being melded with Chinese socialist ideals by Chairman Xi's administration to create a new version of "socialist market economy with Chinese characteristics," engaging a wide range of popular and academic sources. The new Confucians assert that China's recent developmental experience constitutes a moral, ethical, and social counterexample to the Western model, an assertion that comes from such diverse writers as Chinese philosopher and bioethicist Ruiping Fan; Confucian scholar Jiang Qing; political theorist Daniel Bell (Qing 2012); Wang Jisi, the dean of the School of International Studies of Peking University; and Justin Yifu Lin (1995), economist and former senior vice president of the World Bank. Yudan Chen (2016) of Fudan University studies how traditions shape Chinese foreign policy; Jae Ho Chung (2016) of Seoul National University writes about China's unique blend of central control and local discretion; and Toronto University's Mingjun Lu (2016) identifies Chinese cosmopolitanism with an embrace of diversity and a desire to share one's abundance with others. Drawing on a Chinese value survey, the Dutch social psychologist Geert Hofstede has coined the phrase *Confucian dynamism* to identify cultural traits, such as persistence, thrift, and a sense of shame, that contribute toward economic growth (Hofstede and Bond 1988). A growing number of contemporary scholars worldwide have drawn attention to the expanding role of indigenous philosophical considerations and moral values in discussions among Chinese policymakers about a uniquely Chinese approach to the proper relationship of state and market.[6]

The Confucians stress that China must not deviate from the mainstream of its national cultural heritage, that modernization must not break the historical continuity of the nation, and that a government's political legitimacy must be defined by its results, not by process; in other words, they ask: Does it provide good governance, competent leadership, and success in satisfying its citizens?

They question the universality of the advantages of small government, decentralization, and free markets, all of which are stressed in Western developmental discourse, and herald instead the application of hybrid solutions to local problems. Less concerned with identifying the ideal institutions than with moving from Point A to Point B, China's message to other emerging nations is to first find the stepping stones in the waters they must cross and then to adapt their indigenous capacities to that part of the global economy they want to join.

Chinese thinkers have begun to claim that their own Confucian traditions offer more for the long-term interests of populations in the periphery of globalization. Outward policy was long an instrument to keep the tribal clans who inhabited the desert steppes of Central Asia from crossing into China. "The steppe nomads ... gave China her background in foreign and international relations before the advent of the modern West," wrote Fairbank (1948, 80) of the origin of Chinese foreign policy. Fairbank's observations seventy years ago were consistent with the idea that a Confucian gentleman seeks world pacification.

Today as well, there is no evidence that China's overseas ventures will ensure return on investment. Is China once again thinking about "pacification" of the pastoral steppe populations who might otherwise stir unrest on its periphery?[7] China's risk-taking calculus in the Belt and Road Initiative reveals a willingness to lose money in the short term to obtain long-term stability on its borders. The initiative is intended to revive the glory of both the Han dynasty's Silk Road, a land route that operated from 130 BCE to 1453 CE, and the Ming dynasty's sea route, the significance of which was highlighted by the fifteenth-century expeditions (eighty-seven years before Columbus) commanded by Zheng He. Unlike the journeys undertaken by early Western seafarers, China's maritime expeditions were not intended for Chinese merchants – and likewise the construction of the Silk Road. The Persians, not the Chinese, conducted much of the known world's commerce and reaped the profits. The Ming dynasty's investments in its navy and in road maintenance, historians now claim, were not profitable according to standard cost/benefit accounting.

Pines explains China's global vision by referring to China's philosophical past, "Confucius and his followers actively promulgated the vision of a superior man who cultivates himself with the ultimate goal of 'bringing peace to the hundred clans [all the people]'" (2012, 79–80). Summarizing the moral implications of Confucian cosmopolitanism, Fan remarks that the "the moral virtue of benevolence is central to the kingly way of Confucian politics" (2011, 8). This concept of foreign aid and development assistance contrasts with the West's emphasis on political transformation and structural reform.

China's remarkable success in poverty alleviation at home is put forward as a better way to incorporate needed change into the global system. In the four decades after market reforms began, according to UN standards, 740 million Chinese were lifted out of poverty; and since 2013, an additional 68.53 million have been helped. Under the "Blueprint on Poverty Alleviation Development in China's Countryside 2011–2020" issued by the Central Committee and State Council, SOEs and other government agencies, such as national universities and military police forces, must actively participate in meeting poverty alleviation targets, and many have received quotas for poverty reduction.[8]

The Chinese see humiliation as the end result for countries upon whom the United States has tried to impose its version of the "enlightenment" of globalization. The rationale given by Chinese thinkers is that transplanting democratic institutions among populations that lack the necessary social norms and institutions to support them will lead to dissatisfaction and unrest. The real issue is that China opposes rules of the game that can reinforce the West's positional or moral advantage and reduce China's own legitimacy as an international actor.

Chinese commentators like to depict their country as having been more successful than India at combating corruption. Democracies can only hope to combat corruption effectively if they have a legal system that is efficient and accessible, a free media, and an educated and economically secure population; without these, anti-corruption efforts are likely to produce meager results. But developing countries rarely have these capabilities. India meets only one of the conditions, a relatively free media. Singapore, the Chinese commentary goes, was particularly successful at reining in corruption during the early stages of economic growth, without a free media and without a fully democratic political system. This success is greatly admired in China. Moreover, a successful anti-corruption campaign is a way that leadership with low scores on the democracy index can bolster legitimacy and gain public support; this makes China's model particularly appealing to leaders in places such as Vietnam and Saudi Arabia.

Chinese officials are forbidden from accumulating significant wealth, but there is nothing to prevent members of their families from doing so, and those assets acquired by family insiders are hidden from public scrutiny. This type of elite capture, in which private interests influence government rulings to their own advantage, tends to be a systemic property of the China model. Without a free press this is readily hidden. Chinese media avoids reporting about the wealth of prominent official families.

China doesn't promote a particular methodology to determine universal best or second-best practices. In this vein, Lin (2009) makes the case for "effective government and efficient market," based on China's experience. China rejects the greater emphasis the West places on proper legal procedures and elections in favor of obtaining a particular desirable outcome, such as GDP growth, the creation of new industrial capacity, the attraction of investment, and the creation of greater income-generating opportunity for the population.

The conceit among Western thinkers, explains Fan, is the belief "that their moral intuitions reflect a global moral and political theoretical common ground. ... The universality of these assumptions is radically falsified by China, which constitutes a moral, social, and political counter-example" (2011, 1). Thus, a major part of China's narrative about its role in the global order places China in conflict with the United States with respect to leading non-Western regions toward peace and prosperity, and dashes the West's hope of bringing China into conformity with the imperatives of Western historical and political models.

When China uses its resources to position itself in a way that can have transformative consequences for the larger system, it sets the stage for a possible challenge from the United States. It matters little whether the underlying source of the tensions is a philosophical difference or that the market structure of the Chinese economy differs from the institutions of the West. In reclaiming great power status by presenting itself as a buttress against Western liberalism, China will exacerbate differences over security issues while giving US policymakers grounds to depict it as a revisionist power, setting up a contest that veers far beyond philosophical issues about what constitutes a market economy.

## Disillusion and Conflict with the West

In the early 1990s, US policymakers were willing to disregard China's publicly stated commitment to make socialism the medium for global economic progress. The prevailing view at the time was that keeping China out of the international economic architecture was more dangerous than letting it in, and that China would seek to adapt, rather than to try to change the system from which it drew benefits.

The assumption that guided the Western policy approach was that eventually private firms would outperform state-invested firms, which would lead the Chinese economy toward greater compatibility with the norms of the West's privately invested companies. US policymakers across the political spectrum also presumed that China's transition to a market economy would create a constituency in favor of domestic political reforms, producing a middle class, as had occurred in the United States during its progressive era of the late nineteenth and early twentieth centuries, when demand for democratic reforms emanated from the educated classes.[9] Policymakers hoped that, with internal democratic reforms reshaping the polity,

China would redefine its global role and see the benefits of sustaining the liberal world order as the status quo, and then seek inclusion as a coalition member. As incomes rose, so the narrative went, a clash between the middle classes and the authoritarian nature of the regime would be inevitable.

When China joined the WTO in 2001, the size of its economy wasn't a particularly relevant concern. Western supporters hoped that a growing stake in global prosperity would serve as an incentive to align its behaviors with the rules that served to bolster the wider "democratic" stability of the liberal international order. China would become, in the policy vernacular, a "responsible stakeholder" and converge to liberal principles in both its economic and political organization and values.

That perception is changing. China's global ambitions have caused disappointment, alarm, and consternation. China's announcement of its global ambitions in various policy statements since 2015 has had the effect of a lightning rod on its trading partners in the West and has driven objections to its deviation from normal market economy practices up several notches.

After years of negotiation, progress on a bilateral US–China investment treaty came to a standstill in 2016 amid frustration with China's state-run management of its market economy. US officials consistently criticize China for failing to follow through on reforms to reduce excess capacity, open the political system, reduce subsidies of SOEs, and eliminate forced technology transfers for foreign firms seeking to operate in China. In its 2016 report, the US–China Economic and Security Review Commission, established by Congress in 2000 to monitor trade and national security issues, notes "This year marks the 15th anniversary of China's World Trade Organization accession. While China's transformation has accelerated over the past decade and a half, its economic liberalization has fallen far short of global expectations. The reality of the US–China economic relationship, too, has turned out to be much different than many had hoped" (USCC 2016). The commission did not consider China to be a market economy, or even on the path toward becoming one. China, it claimed, deviates from accepted practices by the extent of the state's influence on the output decisions of enterprises, the absence of collective bargaining, the unequal treatment of foreign investments, and the extent of sectors closed to foreign investment, along with the failure to embrace the principle of democratic participation. The commission concluded that the sheer size of China's economy has already begun to influence the dynamics of the global system, and this has given rise to fear that its investment rules harm Western firms.

The commission also found that "the state exerts excessive control over resource allocation, and that China's domestic reform agenda is aimed at strengthening the hand of the state and not promoting economic liberalization" (USCC 2016, vii). China, it said, must be prepared "to relinquish a substantial degree of state control, overcome entrenched interests, and endure the short-term and medium-term economic pain that structural reform creates" (2016, 3). It claims that China was reverting to an earlier, state-led development paradigm. "Despite Chinese officials' repeated promises to cut production in industries such as steel, aluminum, and coal, reforms have taken a backseat to policies aimed at maintaining employment and economic growth" (USCC 2016, 3). The 2018 report went much further, drawing attention to Chinese military expansion and declaring China to be a revisionist power and strategic competitor seeking world domination.

The commission's views toward China are widely advocated by both Republican and Democratic leaders, and based on the perception that Beijing has been a free rider on the stability of the political order that it treats with skepticism and that it is now trying to change to fit its own interests. Both political parties accuse China of employing mercantilist policies, including currency manipulation and protectionism, by subsidizing and protecting its own industries and artificially debasing its currency. Thus China is held accountable for exploiting the stability of the liberal international system that enables it to prosper at an unprecedented rate, while irresponsibly discounting the reciprocity and protocol that make the system sustainable. Politicians of both parties point out that it purposefully reduces consumption at home. So long as its system encourages excess capacity, China will be exporting subsidized goods at below market prices and impairing free enterprise. They claim as well that China has not developed into a fair, reciprocal, and market-oriented partner for trade and investment, and that its subsidies to help exporters and discourage imports harm the interests of Western firms. Once considered an outdated, radical position, it is now common for commentators in the West to say that allowing China into the WTO and giving China preferred nation status were among the great mistakes of the previous century. US trade representative Robert Lighthizer has claimed that international organizations such as the WTO are not designed to deal with "mercantilism on this scale" (CSIS 2017).[10] He wants China to move faster and further with market reforms so that it becomes more like the predominately privately invested economies of the West.

More than a decade earlier, then US trade representative Robert Zoellick had an optimistic message when he told an audience in New York that "closed politics cannot be a permanent feature of Chinese society. ... It is simply not sustainable" (2005). Again, the conviction is that the relationship of the state to the economy can only move in one direction, toward liberal ideals. This belief has been the bedrock of US engagement with China and underscores the extensive influence of ideas of social development derived solely from Western economic history. It reflects neither China's history nor its current ambitions.

We are learning that the nexus between open markets, open polities, and economic prosperity is far more dependent on historical context. The clock cannot be set back, and China is creating its own role as a global actor.

## Is China's Rise Attuned with Market Economics?

We opened this chapter asking whether China's transition experience calls for greater flexibility in defining a market economy. Coase and

Wang (2012) see many essential characteristics of a market economy in China, most notably that the reforms have created a global information-processing system that exhibits elements of a self-correcting, spontaneous order. They are referring to the emergence of coherence through the independent actions of large numbers of individuals with limited local knowledge, and to a system in which prices play a predominant role in coordinating decision making by individuals, firms, and the government. China has accomplished this in the context of a substantially regulated market system; and, if Coase and Wang are right, its economy is qualitatively, not substantively, different from other market economies. Thus China's economic transition in effect raises the broader question: What is it that subjects human behavior to the rules of economics?

The Chinese, by solid consensus, agree that their current economic structure can propel them to greater global economic prominence, and that their SOEs, even more than the private sector, have the endowments necessary to augment China's standing. The risks of a global technology war only strengthen their resolve to increase the reach of the state industrial complex. China will not alter its fundamental development path without conclusive evidence that its model is destined for failure. If constructive synergies are to be mobilized to the benefit of both China and its Western trading partners, it will require a greater understanding of what types of provisions key constituencies in China are willing accept, and which issues the Chinese leadership views as foundational to core economic philosophies that they are not willing to abandon.

## 8.4  POSSIBLE SCENARIOS OF CHINA'S ROLE IN THE GLOBAL ECONOMY

If we look at the major economic events of the past twenty-five years that are promoting change in how policy is conducted, including the East Asian financial crisis and the 2007–2008 global recession, none represents a transition point more so than the rise of China. Centralization is a tendency with a long past in China, but the "going global" campaign sets China on an unprecedented journey. It may change China fundamentally, just as an earlier transition point transformed the web of royal houses that once crisscrossed Europe. There are many scenarios to ponder for how this transition will unfold.

1. **Path Dependence Prevails** China reverts to the underlying components, or base laws, of its former grandeur and seeks its future by rediscovering the key institutional formula of its past Confucianism: obedience and state rule. Although current institutional frameworks show strong similarities with those of the past, going global creates momentum that cannot be entirely anticipated or controlled from a central place.

2. **China Stagnates in a Middle-Income Trap** Chinese political leadership increasingly expresses confidence that growth is unstoppable, and that what has worked in the past, i.e., technological upgrades attained via SOEs, is applicable to the challenge of achieving high-income status in the future. This may not work out as planned. Trumpeted by both macro- and microeconomists alike is a scenario of Chinese growth succumbing to its many contradictions, unable to surmount the middle-income trap, unable to rise higher, and finding high-quality growth unattainable. The insurmountables include: the feebleness of China's institutional foundations, resulting in inadequate organizational capacity and property rights protection; resources that are not optimized because entrenched interest groups block reform; a weak culture of innovation, in particular, a weak connection between fundamental and operational research; and too much emphasis on trophy projects, such as the Three Gorges Dam or landing a spacecraft on the moon, while everyday technology is underfunded.

3. **Poor Policies That Prioritize Political Control Expand the State-Run Economic Sector** In this scenario the developmental priorities of the state squeeze out private firms. A diversion of capital to SOEs enables them to grow more rapidly than the private sector, but their returns on assets are lower than the private sector. Over 44 percent of SOEs lose money, and their misallocated assets are not reallocated to more productive private operators. A resurgence of SOE control over key sectors could reduce incentives for innovation and productivity, and, by increasing related-party transactions, expand the opportunities for corruption. Thus,

dependence upon state-centric development strategies causes China to become mired in a middle-income trap of its own making (Lardy 2019).

4. **China Moves toward Institutional and Cultural Convergence with Western Liberalism** Chinese growth will eventually produce institutional and cultural convergence with Western liberalism. In this scenario and the previous one, the West has little to worry about; in the long run, its lead will be preserved and it can continue to diffuse its economic model of private investment and its cultural values of personal freedom around the world. Is it just too soon for the momentum of international liberalism to have swept up China, since easing the poverty of 700 million people is not the same as producing 700 million middle-class Chinese?

5. **Western Economies Converge toward China's System** In this scenario, privately invested Western economies seek industrial policies and trade protection from their own governments in order to compete with China. Since China will not change, the argument runs, the United States will adapt state-led industrial policy itself; in effect, the United States must become more like China to cope with the large upfront costs and long gestation of research and development, and to coordinate overlapping investments from various sectors. This replicates solutions offered to counter "Japan Inc." that were common during the 1980s.

6. **Global Capitalism Bifurcates into Separate Camps** As a market economy with unique structural characteristics, China decouples its economy from the West. China becomes the focal point of a giant cluster of interconnected emerging economies, an attractor for those that seek to emulate its success. Through the loans and development projects that China has forged with Europe, Africa, Latin America, and the rest of Asia – the rest of the world, in fact – a giant cluster of linkages with other nodes in the global economy gives the global economy a new structure. This could bifurcate the global economy into separate camps of state capitalism versus privately invested firms, perhaps inciting a global trade war that goes far beyond US–China trade disputes.

7. **A New Cold War Looms** Claiming the two systems cannot coexist, US government officials deem China to be a rising adversary to Western liberalism, a revisionist power, and a champion of an alternative global order. A white paper on China's economic aggression, from the White House Office of Trade and Manufacturing Policy, has already asserted that "China's acts, policies, and practices ... threaten not only the US

economy but also the global innovation system as a whole" (OTMP 2018, 20). It calls for immediate remedies to a longstanding problem. The unease is not so much about the feasibility of China's model, but about the harm that model might do to Western economic interests, whether or not it succeeds. As China's economy grows, it may reshape the landscape for future global innovation by altering the profit-to-risk ratio upon which capitalism has thrived. It could do this, first, because the deep pockets of state-owned banks remain a source of funding for Chinese firms that enables them to better withstand the vicissitudes of the business cycle; and second, because, propped up by the state, Chinese firms can unload excess supply on international markets, so that even if they lose money, they can stay in business and drive out firms that depend on market sources of funding. Finally, with its growing supply of skilled engineers, China can copy, replicate, and produce new products so quickly that private Western firms don't have time to recover the R&D costs of innovation. Chinese firms are better situated to pursue profitable opportunities in developing regions. They can offer cheaper (but often lower-quality) versions of Western products that are affordable to nascent consumers, both governments and households.

8.  **China Leapfrogs the Western World** China is able to overtake the West on the strength of its "efficient market supplemented by effective government." With its highly integrated decision-making structures, China can mobilize resources, both domestically and internationally, more effectively than Western counterparts.

9.  **Preventative Chaos Brings Resilience through Variation** As described in the closing of Chapter 3, a variation of arrangements could help stabilize the global economy. Complex systems converge to local, not global optima, and to resilience through variation; and a variation of arrangements could help stabilize the global economy. China's different types of economic structures might under some circumstances offer the world economy useful tools to deal with recession and more capacity overall, as well as more diversity to combat common issues such as global warming and global downturns.

10. **Interconnectivities Define the Future in a World of Multiple Feedbacks in Which None of the Actors Are Standing Still** The race for technological supremacy has only just begun and may change China in ways that its leadership does not expect, changing the

momentum of change, while unlocking new sources of unpredictability. China's leaders may aspire to control global innovation from a central location by enabling state-sponsored entities to lead outbound investment, but that investment can only become sustainable if the private sector follows in due course and eventually takes the lead. Technological competition with the West could set off intense competitive pressures in which lateral channels open within China to hubs of decision making outside of China.[11]

11. **Coalitional Stability and the Social Foundations of Communist Rule Shape China's Trajectory at the Risk of Institutional Sclerosis**
Underlying the probability of which scenario will prevail is the one factor that has contributed to the stability of authoritarian government in China's past. The CCP continues to recruit administrative talent from a broad pool to deliberately dilute the independent influence of privately acquired wealth. This is designed to protect the monopoly of the political leadership, much as the meritocratic admission to the mandarinate helped ensure loyalty to the emperor. Since the CCP took power, it has not appointed a single member of the business elite to the Politburo. Thus, the CCP has devised a system of mechanisms that encourage access to the global economy for enterprises while making company managers dependent upon the highest levels of government decision making, thus reducing the potential political influence of independent economic agents. Reform that grants wealth holders the tools to compromise the coalitional stability of communist rule is not welcome. Will this model be compatible with the regime's goals of achieving preeminence in global innovation, or will it cause the demise of private initiative, and the nurturing of black-market supply chains? It was through a particular network structure, and the formula for coalitional stability that it encouraged, that Europe was able to adapt disruptive new technologies to foster inward development and outward expansion. Will China's particular framework for coalitional stability, one that excludes individual bearers of wealth from political leadership, prove to be as conducive in the promotion and exploitation of innovation?

12. **Systemic Corruption in China Results in the Regime's Demise** There is a danger in basing stability on a coalitional structure that consolidates political and economic control and impairs civil society: it invites elites

linked to the state to engage in subterfuge, and this has been a major contributor to the demise of regimes in the past.

Many other scenarios can be imagined, and while China and the United States wrestle over the rules of trade, there is a larger question. Will either East or West have sufficient leverage to exercise top-down control over the decentralized forces of global economic competition? Going global may transform China into a hub within a larger system, and a giant hub at that, but one that is not centrally positioned to control all others. The complexity of the global economy far exceeds the capability of any top controlling mechanism. It is illusory to premise confidence on belief in control that is dispensed from a central place, whether it is the Politburo Standing Committee, the US Congress, the US presidency, or the European Council.

In formulating strategy for the future, policymakers of China and the West share a fundamental cognitive limitation. Both make sense of global economic opportunities and challenges through the lens of history, in reference to their own store of institutional and cultural experiences formed over extended periods. The structure of the global political economy is changing, becoming more densely connected, and neither is cognitively equipped to adequately understand how this will impact their coevolution as economic partners or their prospects for internal stability. Let's see the challenges they face.

NOTES

1. Overseas direct investment as a national strategy was initiated on September 18, 1997, when the 15th Party Congress Report announced the intention "to encourage outbound investment when comparative advantage permits, so as to better utilize two markets and two resources at home and abroad." The concept of "stepping overseas," or "going abroad," which denotes outbound investment, was introduced in the 10th Five-Year Plan for National Economic and Social Development in 2001, the year China joined the WTO.

2. Between 2007 and 2011, China's share of world economic growth (24.3 percent) already exceeded that of the US (7.2 percent).

3. Non-ruling parties include: the Revolutionary Committee of the Chinese Kuomintang, founded in 1948; the China Democratic League, founded in 1941; the China National Democratic Construction Association, founded in 1945; the China Association for Promoting Democracy, founded in 1945; the Chinese Peasants' and Workers' Democratic Party, founded in 1930; the China Zhi Gong Party, founded in 1925; the Jiusan Society, founded in 1945; and the Taiwan Democratic Self-Government League, founded in 1947. These parties are housed by the Chinese People's Political Consultative Conference, which the constitution subordinates to the CCP leadership. Important civil society organizations include: the All-China Federation of Trade Unions, the largest trade union in the world with 302 million members in 1,713,000 primary trade union organizations; the Communist Youth League of China; the All-China Women's Federation; the All-China Federation of Industry and Commerce; the All-China Federation of Taiwan Compatriots; the All-China Federation of Returned Overseas Chinese; the China Science and Technology Association; and the Communist Youth League of China, also known as the Young Communist League of China.

4. The Party School conducts training of party members at various levels. Training sessions can be anywhere from two weeks to twelve months (www.ccps.gov.cn).

5. In China's 2,914 colleges and universities, with some 20 million students, curriculums are being created to inculcate Xi Jinping Thought.

6. Fan explores the rise of an authentic Confucianism "with a moral and political thought style substantially different from that of the West" (2011, 1). He contrasts this to Western-influenced neo-Confucianism, studied in Taiwan or by Chinese in the West, which he criticizes for wrongly trying to come to terms with the hegemony of Western moral presumptions about the role of the individual in society. Pines (2012) traces Chinese conceptions of political order to their historic roots in the pre-imperial age, when, after a lengthy period of internal turmoil, thinkers sought ways establish peace and stability. Zhao (2015) discusses the origins of Confucian ideas about commerce in the polity – which date to the Qin dynasty – and about harmonious relations with neighboring cultures. The point of reference for the development of Chinese national identity was other *cultures* on its periphery, he argues, not other states. Thus it came to matter less who was at the helm of the state so long as its

fundamental cultural values were respected. This differed from the West, where national identity was eventually fused with the existence of the nation state.

7. This concern may also have been driven by the risks of volatile ecological conditions. The steppes that housed and fed the nomadic tribes were vulnerable to small variations in rainfall, reducing the herds needed to sustain the population.

8. This was an extension of the National Poverty Alleviation Plan of 1994–2010. Before the 1994 plan, the government relied on transfer payments to local government.

9. The official United States and EU views converged in 2016 when the EU joined the United States in not granting China market economy status. "Europeans hope that a China with open markets and a firm rule of law will be more likely to respect human rights and allow democratic freedoms." Europeans also believe that a more open, democratic, and law-abiding China will be a better partner in building the kind of multilateral global order that most Europeans want (Barysch, Grant, and Leonard 2005, 1).

10. Lighthizer said: "The sheer scale of their coordinated efforts to develop their economy, to subsidize, to create national champions, to force technology transfer, and to distort markets, in China and throughout the world, is a threat to the world trading system that is unprecedented."

11. The need for collaboration in science and technology can be an incentive to observe international rules, and could foster more responsible and transparent practices in China.

# 9  Global Networks over Time

with Kevin Comer, Jack Goldstone, and David Masad

## 9.1  NETWORK STRUCTURE IN INTERNATIONAL RELATIONS

Just as it is possible to analyze China's increasing wealth and role on the world stage using annualized GDP growth rates, import totals, outward direct investment, and the rise of private enterprise, we can use metrics to quantify the relationships between states in the international system, and to track their dynamics over time. By treating states as nodes within networks, and conducting quantitative analyses of these network structures, it is possible to detect changing patterns of interstate relations. This can enable deeper insights into the political, economic, and ideological links between nations, and open conventional balance-of-power analyses to new sets of criteria.

In this chapter we consider three critical networks, representing military, political, and economic power, and we apply three measures of network structure – density, diameter, and centrality – over the course of several decades to highlight the dynamics of interstate relations in each. The analysis provides new findings on the dynamics among nations in the Cold War and post-Cold War years. It explores how ever more widely linked and densely constructed networks are transforming international relations, creating new linkages and flows of influence among states.

Until recently, relations among states in the international system were understood through a classical narrative of treaties, conflicts, ideologies, and interests of various state actors. Complex interdependencies certainly exist in that narrative, but they exist mostly at the center, among the dominant actors, not in the system's periphery. Today it is widely accepted that a timeline of diplomatic and military events in a world of organized state violence is an inadequate description of the dynamics among nations. Advances in the understanding of networks that add considerable nuance to that dominant-actor bias have appeared in studies by Anne-Marie Slaughter (2017), Zeev Maoz (2011), Lars-Erik Cederman (1997), Emilie Hafner-Burton, Miles Kahler, and Alexander Montgomery (2009), and Strange (1996), among others.

The importance of networks in the study of power and international relations is championed by Slaughter in *The Chessboard and the Web* (2017). Slaughter argues that the increasing density and complexity of interactions between states and substate actors will necessitate the United States adopting new grand strategies of connection to maintain the security of its citizens' interests. Although this chapter confirms Slaughter's account of the increasing density of the network, and provides quantitative analysis to support her argument, we argue that it is because of this density and interconnectedness that the concept of a grand strategy, which simply uses connection to enhance power, is inadequate. Understanding the changing structures of global networks, wherein the ability of any single actor to influence linkages within the system has been greatly reduced, is vital to understanding the limitations of any grand strategy employed.

A binary view of human history as a continuous duality of hierarchy and networks depicts a false dichotomy. All human- and nature-made networks are constructed "hierarchically," although the degree of centralization can vary. This chapter explores quantitatively the degree of hierarchy in the structures of three specific networks both during and after the Cold War. We show that their properties today differ significantly from those they exhibited during the Cold War, with local players having expanded regional roles. Moreover, we show that the degree of hierarchy differs across the different networks, and varies over time. Thus, benchmarking the bipolarity of the Cold War as a stable equilibrium that suddenly changed after 1990 is misleading. The use of network metrics to analyze changes in international relations since World War II reveals the nuances of more varied patterns that can rapidly permeate and transform the macro system.

## Globalization and the Lessons of Complexity

Advances in network science enable us to depict regime stability and system transitions with increasing precision. Stable systems typically undergo change more quickly at lower levels than at the top; the faster transmission cycles at those lower levels can replenish the higher levels with novelty and information about options, and enable reform for better management at the system level. Resilience arises from the ability of hierarchical systems to accommodate rapid changes at the lower levels without destabilizing the overall topology. In Chapters 4–6, we saw how the historical vitality of the West derived from the recurrence of great revolutions, each of which built upon earlier accomplishments, creating something new and different yet retaining the context of a shared European tradition. Intermittent episodes of renewal didn't fundamentally alter the defining properties of the network of intermarried royal houses, and its durability enabled economic and legal change to occur within a common European context.

But once the higher-order structures grow unstable, the impacts are inevitably systemic, in the same way that climate change may destroy entire forest systems while individual forest fires simply cause those forests to renew. When assessing stability in the global system, we thus need to pay attention to whether changes in lower-level networks are contained by a stable hierarchical structure at higher levels. When we look for sources of stability in current international relations, we observe a rapid transition away from Cold War and even post-Cold War patterns. Higher- and lower-level networks no longer behave "hierarchically," but as increasingly entwined, self-organizing, and ever-shifting resource flows and alliances, without a consistent hierarchical structure. We will be looking at some of these lateral network linkages in the pages that follow.

The rise of new patterns and processes at various network levels has implications for global stability. As discussed in Chapter 2, at some threshold, network densification itself can propagate shocks, making the entire system more fragile. When stable hierarchical conditions no longer exist to cushion system-level stability from lower-level disorders, instability can originate anywhere in the system and spread rapidly. And since 2001, higher-order stability has been dissipating, while lower-level networks are transforming rapidly. In the new global topology, the reduced influence of centralized control levers enables regimes such as North Korea, Saudi Arabia, and Turkey to step out of dependent relationships and flex their muscles in pursuit of greater regional influence. The autonomous region of Catalonia, the unrecognized Moldova breakaway section Transnistria, the Kurds, the Palestinian Authority, Hezbollah, and al Qaeda are all nodes that exert a growing influence, and some may become states. Nonstate and substate actors can become intertwined and their boundaries blurred, as with Hezbollah and Syria.

## Hierarchy in Global Networks over Time

We often think of the Cold War international order as a clash of hierarchical systems: the two superpowers wielded influence over regional powers that in turn exercised their own influence over still lower actors, in much the same way that a military command structure or a large corporation might operate. But the term *hierarchy* has implications that are somewhat misleading when applied to the international system before or after that era. Even during the Cold War, the system of international relations did not work according to a clearly delineated conception of hierarchy.

During the Cold War, various networks of countries were "structured" as communities, or blocs. The community clustered around the NATO bloc, including key non-NATO allies such as Australia, exhibited a high degree of lateral connectivity with many bilateral relationships. In the Soviet sphere, the countries interacted less with one another and more with the USSR directly. Nevertheless, within these two high-order networks, multiple actors competed within their own power bases, according to their own interests – and the networks of cooperation and competition between these actors played critical roles in determining how the blocs as a whole behaved. For example, Turkey, Saudi Arabia, Egypt, and Israel were all beneficiaries of US protection from the USSR, but they pursued their own interests and rivalries within the Middle East. Like the NATO bloc, the Soviet bloc was not entirely hierarchical, especially if we consider China's role as a weaker but somewhat independent partner in that socialist community.

Within the Western sphere, there were multiple hubs, and even though the United States was the central (i.e., most important) hub, the network had the resilience of a multihub, scale-free system. Years later, the larger Western community has continued to find cohesion around issues of environment and trade, despite the variance of views within it and the fact that the Soviet bloc's behavior was more in line with our familiar notion of a hierarchy, with the USSR at the "top" of a pyramidal structure and other states "below" it.

Even during the Cold War, the two networks were not neatly delineated. Although the two hegemons would have preferred to be the exclusive providers (or withholders) of armaments, diplomatic protection, and trade and manufacture – these resources were critical to maintaining hierarchy – there were many overlapping ties. Countries could still trade and partner with countries from either faction, even if most of their trade was within the same network (the nonaligned movement did not command sufficient resources to break away entirely). For example, US grain shipments went to the USSR. Most behavior, however, formally correlated across each network, which is to say that a community detection algorithm finding two Western bloc countries in the arms trade network would be likely to find them in the UN co-voting network, as well.

Over time, countries built many subsidiary linkages among themselves, and as these linkages acquired more "traffic," they did not have to pass through one of the major hubs. Thus a country might be in one community in the arms trade network (e.g., the community of countries that buy arms from France), in another community in the UN co-voting network (the Islamic world community), and in still another in global trade (a China-centric network of trade partners). Yet as countries build more links across different communities, instability from one sector can now spread more readily across the entire system. Consider how drought and war in Syria, via subsequent migration flows to Europe, combined with anxieties raised by jihadist terror attacks from Paris to Pakistan, helped shift the outcome of voting on Britain's membership in the European Union – all through a greater density of ties, abetted by global communications and social media.

What does it mean when a centrally determined strategy proves to be inadequate to deal with, much less contain, the dynamics of interactive risk that can arise from any scale, and spread and magnify through a complex interactive environment? And what does this mean for geopolitical stability?

## The Center Does Not Hold

We can trace the disintegration of hegemonic stability to changes in the higher-order structures that have characterized the evolving system of international relations. The disintegration is an unintended consequence of Cold War polices designed by the West to isolate and overtake the Soviet Union by linking war-torn Europe, along with its former colonies (in South and East Asia and the Middle East), into a global system of trade. System dynamics changed faster than expected as the diffusion of diplomatic, military, and economic power among the "lower-level" partners increased rapidly. In winning the Cold War, the West traded a set of known risks for a set of unknown ones.

The erosion of hegemonic stability has become a major concern in international relations (Waltz 2008). Political analyst Moisés Naím at the Carnegie Endowment for International Peace writes about the "end of power" as a general phenomenon that penetrates to the boardroom and the classroom (2013), and Slaughter (2012) argues that international power is transitioning from states to networks of sub-state actors. Yet no network of substate actors is replacing a *hierarchy* of states. The connections of states to one another, e.g., through arms trades or UN voting, are themselves showing network properties that preclude the guarantee of power to a central position (Easley and Kleinberg 2010).

As with the potential outcomes for power shifts between the United States and China, discussed in Chapter 8, a global shift in the balance of power can also result in a wide range of potentially stable outcomes, but this shift can also weaken the stability of the overall system. When the most powerful attractors start to lose primacy, their weakness invites competition from challengers. And as more members gain an equal footing, each has a greater incentive to seek the best outcome for itself, even at the expense of others and of system stability.

This process of power dissipation and deconcentration has led global thinkers in the West to seek options that would guarantee the preservation of liberal internationalist values. Slaughter (2012, 2017), for example, has proposed maximizing *network centrality* as the latest grand strategy through which the United States can maintain its leadership role, acting as the "supernode" in those networks most important to advancing its interests and security.[1] It is important to note here that Slaughter is conflating node centrality with network centralization. In fact, centrality is the measure of a point, i.e., the node's position and boundaries, in social network analysis and graph theory; while centralization is the mathematical depiction of a network's location within the greater system, based on node centrality, among other measures. Centralization is a measure of system-level cohesion or integration. The centrality of a node, be it a state or nonstate entity, within a network can be quantified, e.g., by how many links separate it from any other node, as in Watts's (2003) six degrees of separation, or by how many links pass through it, as connections are increasingly made between nodes across the network. When Slaughter advocates "network centrality," she is promoting "supernode centrality within a network."[2]

However, maintaining centrality is not sufficient to ensure power within the international system (Newman 2003). It is not only a country's position within the network that determines power; the overall *structure of the larger global network* itself matters as well. If the global network structure is hierarchical, with a hegemon at the "top," then the centrality of a supernode may indeed be a source of power. This has been the US position since the end of World War II. However, if the network is decentralized, or "flat," and the most central actor's centrality is not much higher than, or almost identical to, the next most central actor, then the central position is far less meaningful. In fact, it is impossible to restore centrality to a particular node within a network that has become decentralized. Global influence is now more evenly distributed among the United States, the EU, and China than in the Cold War period. As the network structure changes, the strategy must change as well.

As we look at the global networks of diplomatic influence, weapons sales, trade and manufacturing, and finance that have contributed to the stability of the liberal internationalist regime since World War II and throughout the Cold War, we can better understand how power is tied to the underlying *structures* of these networks, and why power cannot be understood as an attribute of any single state within the network. We need to understand power as an attribute of the *larger system*, being concentrated or diffused as the system's structure changes – and not only as a consequence of the rise of challengers from the periphery or the growing strength of informal shadow networks. The concept of actor centrality is an incomplete measure of power within the system, and an incomplete framework for building global order. The degree of system centralization is paramount.

## 9.2 END-OF-POWER MEASURES IN THE INTERNATIONAL NETWORK STRUCTURE

The global network is made up of sets of nodes (states) connected to one another by links, such as trade, military aid, or diplomatic cooperation. Because the states belong to a larger, ever-changing, and evolving system, their linkages change and evolve as well. Understanding the differing effects of network structure on behavioral outcomes helps to clarify how the shifting role of power shapes the system's direction.

Hierarchy is a familiar concept, consisting of a pyramidal structure with a few states at the "top" and other states "below" them, as with the Soviet bloc. Resources, information, and power flow up through this particular network topology to the dominant states, which in turn distribute them back downward, along with instructions and coordination. The states at the top of the hierarchy gain power from their central position within these flows. We can also think of a hierarchy as a lateral network topology in which the states at the top of the network hierarchy are "central," while those at the bottom constitute a much larger "periphery." This corresponds to a far greater extent to the network structure of the West.

A state gains power and influence if one or more other states depend on it for access to any of these flows. A state may gain power, for example, from its *betweenness*, meaning that it is an essential conduit of communication and coordination between stronger and weaker states. Thus Turkey gains disproportionate power in the global system from its *betweenness centrality*: refugees to Europe from Syria and points east must flow through Turkey; military supplies from Europe and the United States for their operations in the Middle East must as well, as do natural gas and oil from Russia and Iraq.

If the global network structure resembles that of a hierarchy, the most central states will obtain significant power from their ability to control the flows within the network. But as the network loses its centralization and multiple alternative flows develop, the relative centrality of its nodes will confer less power and exclusivity than if the network itself had maintained a centralized structure. Indeed, this appears to be the case in many of today's global networks. For example, non-Western economies are exceeding the West in the consumption of global energy flows, and this impels developing nations into new strategic and economic alliances that tend to bypass the West.[3] As states amass additional links of their own, exporting to more countries or importing from new sources, their dependence on the central node weakens. They can remain connected to one another, and may even disconnect from and bypass the center. At this point, centrality ceases to be essential to possessing power. It is from this perspective that we consider several networks, each of them key to maintaining hierarchy, to determine if the United States can realistically aspire to stabilize the entire network by virtue of its long-established centrality.

We can find evidence for the "end of power" in the changing structures of the three networks we consider in the next section: those that co-vote in the UN; those that deal in major arms transfers; and overall international trade and financial markets. For each we have built a time series of network structure, assembled annually, and computed structural metrics for each network/year (Figures 9.1–9.3) using three different measures.

The first structural metric we use is centrality, which has been a topic in several chapters and which can be measured in different ways. More than thirty different measures of centrality have been introduced in the literature on social networks. Each has a unique relationship to some social force. To consider the influences of major actors in the international system, the two quantitative measures most commonly used are *closeness centrality* (the average distance between a node and all other nodes) and *betweenness centrality*. Closeness centrality is the inverse of the average path distance of a node to all other nodes, and indicates how close or far a node is to all other nodes. Betweenness centrality, again, measures how frequently a node falls along the shortest paths of other node pairs and suggests the potential role of a node in bridging other nodes.

While closeness and betweenness centrality are useful metrics for understanding a node's position in a hierarchy over time, these measures are less helpful for understanding the dynamics of the overall hierarchical structure. For this, we use another measure,

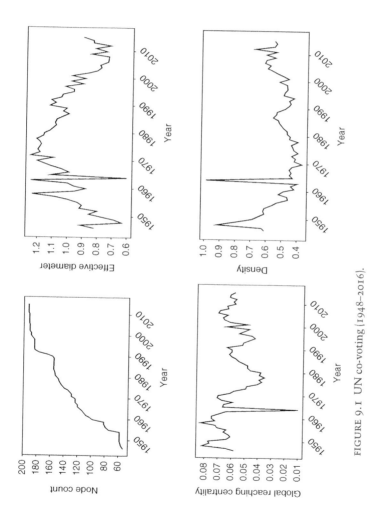

FIGURE 9.1 UN co-voting (1948–2016).

new to this chapter, known as *global reaching centrality* (GRC), which is a metric of a *network's* hierarchy and centralization (Mones, Vicsek, and Vicsek 2012).[4] GRC has to do with the number of nodes that a node can reach beyond its direct connections in a network. That is why it is suitable for measuring the influence of a country in the global network. If this metric is high for a network, it indicates a single highly connected node; a low value demonstrates a relative parity across the nodes with regard to number of connections (i.e., there are multiple regional hubs, rather than a single centralized node).

The second structural metric we use is a measure of *effective diameter*, which indicates how connected or disconnected the nodes of the network are. If the diameter measure is low, then most nodes can draw a path to any other node with only one or two edges, or at most one intermediate node – the sign of a well-connected network. If the diameter is greater, there are more intermediate nodes in the connecting paths between nodes, thus indicating a less well-connected network.

The final metric we use is *graph density*, which demonstrates the importance of the well-connected nodes. As a network gains density, most nodes will be connected to most other nodes, and because they are all well connected, none is particularly unique or important. However, as density decreases, most nodes will relinquish connectivity and remain connected to just a few others, leaving those that are still well connected to many nodes central to the graph and in a more important position. Unlike the discussion of royalty networks in Chapter 4, where we examined the distribution of influence among various actors in a single, timeless network, the analysis of this chapter is on the changing dynamics and structure (centralization) of specific networks (arms trade, UN votes, and international trade) over specific periods. And while examining eigenvector centrality and degree distribution helped to describe the network dynamics of royal houses, these measures are of limited use here, which is why we emphasize the GRC metric.

These metrics are all inversely proportional to the number of nodes in the graph: as the node count increases, *ceteris paribus*, all other metrics are expected to decrease. In addition to the node count of the network, the network metrics are calculated as follows: graph density = (# of edges) / (# of possible edges); effective diameter = the maximum length of shortest path between 90 percent of node-pairs (Leskovec, Kleinberg, and Faloutsos 2005); and GRC is computed following Mones, Vicsek, and Vicsek (2012). They are graphed and discussed in the next sections.

## Network 1: Diplomatic Influence and Cooperation

Hierarchical trends in the international diplomatic system during the Cold War are readily observable in UN voting patterns (Voeten 2004). The United States and the Soviet Union exercised power over their respective networks of allies, which in turn found security under the nuclear umbrella of one great power or the other.

Even at its peak, the United States lacked sufficient economic and logistical resources to impose its norms on the world through the use of overwhelming force. And the loss of its relative economic power after 1965, amid the recovery of the war-torn European economies, made that goal even more elusive. US leadership came to depend increasingly on economic soft power but was further eroded by its alliances with dictatorial governments in Iran, the Philippines, and Vietnam, and with purveyors of medieval social norms such as Saudi Arabia. After the fall of the Thiệu government and the US retreat from South Vietnam, perceptions of American misgovernment, misman-agement, and abuse of power at home undermined its credentials to lead others abroad. Gaps developed between the United States and its allies, and within the Western alliance, the diplomatic system became increasingly decentralized.

Only after the collapse of the Soviet Union in 1991 did the international diplomatic system begin to circle back around, with the United States, as the sole remaining superpower, asserting a grand strategy of "order building." The fall of the Berlin Wall two years earlier had restored US legitimacy and allowed its leaders to attribute the decline of the Soviet Union to the latter's undemocratic governance. Yet in 2003 the decade-long rise in co-voting and cooperation in the UN began to recede, and, in the years since, and despite the absence of another power to take its place, the United States, formerly at the center of a stable bloc of nations, has seen its diplomatic power diluted. The international diplomatic network is once more growing decentralized. Greater global connectivity now enables states to form new ad hoc coalitions and alliances that can change as often as the headlines. The age of stable political communities is over. The new form of geopolitics that is taking shape will gradually replace the old, leaving uncertain what effective global coordination will look like. Looking toward the future we would want to see, for example, if there is an uptick in China-centric vote patterns.

We have recreated UN co-voting networks using the records of all UN General Assembly votes by each member, from 1946 through 2016. An edge has been added between two countries if they voted identically for at least one resolution; the edge weight represents the proportion of the identical votes, i.e., the number of identical votes divided by total number of resolutions in that year. All unanimous votes have been removed, and vote coding is reduced to agreement "yes" or "no" ("no" being coded for votes of abstain, or absent, or no).

As shown in Figure 9.1, the metrics of co-voting records in UN voting show a trend through the early Cold War of decreasing graph density (the growing importance of a few major nodes), culminating in a nadir in the early 1970s, before continuing to rise intermittently to the present day. This corresponds to a similar, if inverse, trajectory of increasing effective diameter (the connectedness of the nodes), resulting in an apex around the early 1970s and decreasing toward the present day. A lower-density, high-diameter graph in UN voting indicates a lack of consensus across resolutions, where countries are not voting in similar fashion.

Conversely, a high-density, low-diameter graph in this context would indicate resolutions passing nearly unanimously, and most if not all of the voting members agreeing on resolutions, and therefore linked with one another in the graph. This has increasingly been the pattern among nations' voting records from the 1970s to the present, with a slight reversal after 2011. In 1964–1965, there was a spike in unity in voting records, due to the formation of the Non-Aligned Movement and then the G77 as UN voting blocs. GRC does not vary widely across the time period examined, with the exception of the spike in 1964–1965, indicating a lack of change in the relationship between central states (US, USSR/Russian Federation) and their clients on the peripheries of the major voting blocs.

The dynamics shown in Figure 9.1 differ remarkably from the dynamics generally discussed in narrative stories of the Cold War and post-Cold War era, with regard to international political coalitions. Since the early 1970s, shared voting across states has steadily increased. This indicates a steady decline in the polarization and hierarchy of diplomatic relations since the height of the Cold War, a trend that was only briefly reversed during the post-Cold War period from 1989 to 1995, but then resumed.

## Network 2: Arms Trade and Transfers

The arms trade is another salient example of the role of network structure in determining power relations. While the United States remained the world's largest government-to-government arms exporter in 2015, this ranking bestows far less hegemonic power than in the past.

Military weapons sales between governments typically indicate a preference in political ties, rendering data on arms trade, such as those collected by the Stockholm International Peace Research Institute (SIPRI), useful for assessing the strength of those ties (SIPRI 2017).[5] While individual trades may occur for economic reasons, they are unlikely to take place between rivals. A major arms-export state may gain leverage over another state through offers to provide or withhold arms from that state, or its rivals.

After World War II, the United States exercised global control over weapons manufacture. It was able to do so because its industrial base dominated the global production of technologically advanced manufacturing, and it could deny weapons to subordinate allies such as Iran without fear that they would turn to other providers. However, arms diffusion is closely tied to industrial diffusion, and as manufacturing capacity disperses, the number of arms exporters also increases. More countries are exporting arms, and they are exporting to more countries. During the Cold War, allies of both the United States and USSR wanted compatible weapon systems to enable interoperability during a major war with the other bloc. As the risk of large-scale coalition war diminishes, so does the importance of having compatible equipment.

Similarly, when more countries prosper from trade, they can purchase more expensive weapons systems. If there were few suppliers, alliance considerations would outweigh a desire for profit. However, as more suppliers enter the market, countries lose the power to completely deny arms to other countries, so the importance of power position to the arms trade diminishes and the importance of revenue increases. The trade of weapons of all kinds thrives in open markets, and the United States no longer exercises control over the exchange of critical weapons systems, except at the very high end. Fungibility in the supply network markets drives US sales, not a desire for centrality – pursuing centrality in the arms trade doesn't add to relational power. The indiscriminate selling for the sake of maintaining centrality means that the United States is actually willing to forgo power while potentially arming enemies and alienating friends.

Figure 9.2 depicts military cooperation by recreating arms trade networks, using the database published by SIPRI for the period 1950–2016. The dataset includes only major conventional weapons and components (i.e., it excludes small-arms transfers). The networks are directed, with an edge representing a major arms transfer from a national source or an armed organization to a receiving party. The edge weight represents normalized-to-trend indicator values. Arms

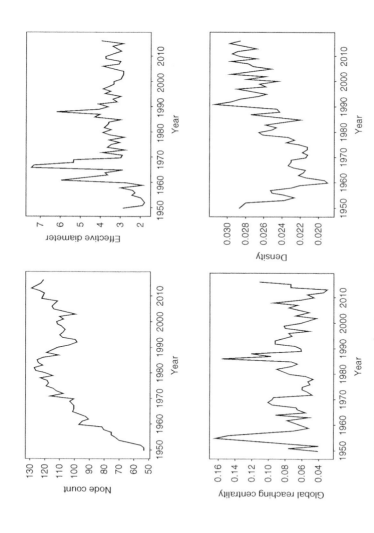

FIGURE 9.2 Arms transfers (1950–2016).

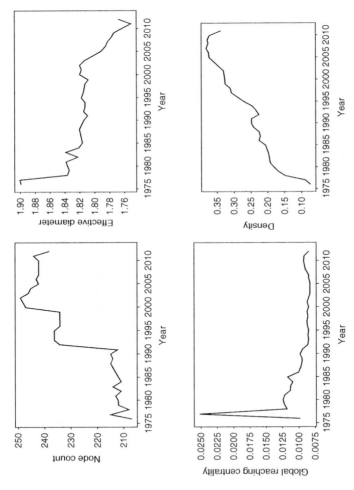

FIGURE 9.3 International trade networks (1976–2016).

transfers in the dataset labeled as Unknown Country or Unknown Rebel Group are removed when constructing networks.

As shown in Figure 9.2, the period corresponding to the Cold War in the arms trade network is marked by low density and moderately high centrality, signifying the overwhelming importance of the leaders of the two ideological blocs (United States, Soviet Union) to the global arms trade network. For the period following the end of the Cold War, the graph density increases, and centrality decreases, indicating a much more diffuse arms trade network not reliant on trade from a superpower. For the second decade of the twenty-first century, while density remains high, centrality has also increased substantially. Unlike the high centrality during the Cold War era, which has low graph density due to most countries only interacting with their ideologically corresponding superpower, this period of high centrality and relatively high density indicates countries linked to multiple partners, and the emergence of multiple hubs of trade. This points to new local hegemonies, either geographic or ideological, for arms and sponsorship in conflict.

Unlike the analysis for the UN voting records, the records of arms trades seem to fit closer to the standard narrative of international relations: that the end of the Cold War prompted a change in the network structure. However, as of 2013, the network seems to have acquired a new structure of multiple hegemonies, distinct from both the Cold War and the post-Cold War eras.

### Network 3: Manufacturing and Global Trade

Globalization increases the number of countries trading with one another, making the system's network of trade and manufacturing more interdependent and interconnected, and at the same time, more decentralized. This increase in density is a consistent trend, and every year manufacturing networks become further decentralized. As more countries produce and trade with one another, the less essential any one country becomes to the network as a whole. The ability of a key manufacturer to exclude others from obtaining its products diminishes, as does the ability of states to embargo other states. Diffusion of industrial capability has reduced the ability of any one state to withdraw vital supplies or to close its markets when it chooses.

The globalization of production, stemming from a deregulation process begun under the Carter administration in the 1970s, has had the unexpected consequence of reducing the coercive power of the United States while creating economic capabilities in emerging countries. One can see evidence of the diffusion of economic power, and its shift away from control by the governments of the old industrial nations, in the steady transfer of manufacturing capability abroad. The north-to-south share of global trade has been shrinking since the 1960s. Many Western corporations now obtain a large percentage of their profits from overseas manufacture and sales.

The globalization of production via direct foreign investment, formation of foreign affiliates, licensing, relocation, joint ventures, and franchising all contribute to the well-documented trend of knowledge diffusion. Manufacturers that rely on a worldwide network of distributers, suppliers, and customers don't necessarily align their vital corporate interests with the national interests of their countries, which ultimately diffuses state power. Becoming a central hub of consumption will not reverse this trend. A large consumer nation acquires centrality only by virtue of giving up control over access to its markets. In other words, what it gains via a wide range of global supply chains, it loses in its ability to control who sells in its local markets.

Economic links no longer imply political or ideological partnerships. This new pattern precludes certain diplomatic options and will cause the political and economic components of foreign policy to be more detached from each other than during the Cold War era. This more pragmatic turn may produce an international system based primarily on interests, rather than on rules or principles. It also raises a question that cannot yet be answered: As economic interdependence increases, will military hegemony become more elusive?

We have recreated the trade networks using the UN Comtrade Database 1976–2012. The dataset includes exports of all goods. As shown in Figure 9.3, the UN Comtrade metrics show a nearly monotonic increase in density, and a stepped but strong decrease in diameter through the period 1976–2012. (The large steps in the falling effective diameter reflect the expansion of the General Agreement on Tariffs and Trade in the mid-1970s and the accession of China to the WTO in 2001.) This demonstrates that links through trade between countries have increased every year since the data have been collected. More countries are trading with each other, rather than trading through third parties. Similarly, the slow decrease in network centrality across the graph demonstrates the corresponding narrative of the decrease of centralization. As countries make trade deals with each other and increase their own capability for production, the importance of any single country for trade diminishes.

However, since 2010, there has been a sharp downturn in graph density, and the largest uptick in diameter since the 1980s. These changes reflect the impact of the global recession in 2007–2009 on trading patterns, showing that the reduction in density and reach of trade links caused by the recession had, as of 2012, not yet been reversed. But despite the rise of economic nationalism, with the resumption of growth we expect the upward trend in graph density to resume. The connection of one kind of globalization to other kinds, e.g., cultural, social, climate/ecological, will also determine which groups succeed relative to others.

## A Fourth Factor: Global Financial Networks and Market Reconcentration

Financial networks are the most centralized global networks. Financial market capability is governance-intensive, making it difficult to replicate or transfer to overseas markets. Social institutions are less mobile than physical infrastructure, and, as a result, sophisticated financial markets, which require these social institutions to remain stable and profitable, exist in only a handful of countries that can guarantee them. Within this concentration of financial assets in a few centers resides a familiar paradox: highly centralized financial markets do not bestow structural power.

A surprisingly weak correlation exists between financial market centrality and structural power. In fact, where governments use financial policy as a foreign relations tool, they risk reducing the attractiveness of their financial markets. The emerging powers China, India, Brazil, and Russia don't adequately restrict state discretion over the use of funds in the domestic financial system. The weakness of the firewalls between banks and politicians prevents their state-dominated banking systems from occupying central positions within the global system (Prasad 2014). No matter how much their relative share of global GDP grows, without institutional guarantees of rules over discretion, uncertainty will drive financial activity to other centers.

Meanwhile, the United Kingdom and the United States have gained positions of increased centrality by maintaining strong firewalls to reduce political discretion, reducing the risk of governmental confiscation by taxes or seizure (Oatley et al. 2013). Nevertheless, centrality in the finance network is similar to centrality in the arms trade; it doesn't discriminate and allows the same access to foes and friends alike.

Of the older global institutions – including the UN Security Council, the World Bank, the WTO, and NATO – the IMF is doing the best job of living up to expectations. This is because the networks of finance, more than those of trade or diplomacy, are still highly centralized and rotate around a few hubs. They also behave according to principles that are commonly understood, and are the same for all economies. But the IMF has a limited mandate, and what works in finance is unlikely to be an operative norm for general global stability.

Moreover, the recent birth of several China-led rivals to the IMF and World Bank – the BRICS-funded New Development Bank, the Asian Infrastructure Investment Bank, the South–South Cooperation Fund, and the China Silk Road Fund – has led to a further decentralization of global lending for emerging economies (Elgin-Cossart and Hart 2015). If these new institutions grow and operate effectively, the result will further diversify networks of global finance, in parallel with the evolution of networks of arms purchases and global trade.

## 9.3 NETWORK PROPERTIES AND POWER IN INTERNATIONAL RELATIONS

Slaughter (2012) is correct to suggest that, in a highly interconnected world, nonstate and substate networks have an important and growing role to play. In a world of vastly extended networked interdependence, with rising density and declining diameter, the network structure will not provide the "relevant choke points, switches, and sources of influence" (Slaughter 2012, 46) to the incumbent powers.

The most significant consequence of this change in network topology is the transition from a traditional hierarchy to a decentralized structure, and this alters the logic of relations among all powers, large and small, in ways we are only beginning to comprehend (Leskovec, Kleinberg, and Faloutsos 2005). As long as the patterns of global diplomatic, military, and trade networks remain non-hierarchical, centrality alone will not bestow structural power. Even where US centrality has been best maintained, as in the financial markets and the global arms trade, its real power has not endured. Other actors can bypass it while competitors offer alternative global communities. The system no longer privileges a hegemon with the power to exclude others from access to essential resources.

A critical point here is that the jump in network density is driving hegemony, as a property of the system, toward decline. This means that institutional order cannot depend on the power of a few major actors maintaining higher-order structures. A second point is that stability depends on a set of rules that treat all actors similarly and create resilience for dense, varied, lower-level relationships. However, the risk remains that cooperation will break down and the likelihood of resorting to force to achieve an intended outcome might actually increase, since the necessary level of collective effort will not materialize.

To design stable global institutions that can increase future global cooperation, policymakers must first understand the basic forces that underlie networks and the strategic behaviors that different structures induce. To fully comprehend the loss of hegemony in the system of international relations requires a recognition that highly independent global networks are vulnerable to failure at all scales, not only at the top.[6]

Whether they originate in the West, or in China or Russia, hegemonic efforts to redesign the world and drive global progress miss an important insight: globalization – and the dense interconnectivity and heightened competition it fosters – inherently weakens hierarchical control structures while fostering an environment of many powerful forces jostling for influence. The ambitions and strategic designs of various agents matter, but the patterns of self-organizing regularities of the wider ecology matter even more.

This is a lesson that comes straight from the life sciences, including ecology and biological evolution: in an environment of amplified interactions and responses, agents must constantly adjust their behaviors according to new sets of rules and the expected reactions of other agents. They construct niches to ensure their survival, and as the rules change, and the niches multiply, the stability of the larger network will be altered.

The optimism after the fall of the Berlin Wall made it possible for those at the top of the global value chain to believe in the power of top-down directional evolution. They expected their hierarchical power to increase when their major adversary, the communist bloc, collapsed. Yet they didn't anticipate that the growing density and shrinking diameter of network relations brought by globalization would continue largely unchecked. Neglecting the network structure of the system as a whole, and the limits it places on hierarchical advantage, is a parochial concept that no longer holds, and it has led to policy failures in Iraq,

Afghanistan, Somalia, Sudan, and elsewhere in the Middle East and Africa.

## 9.4 A TANGLED WEB IN THE GLOBAL ECONOMY

Complexity has become the central problem in international relations. The links among nations, and among subgroups within nations, are increasing at an escalating rate. The diffusion of global norms is no longer top down. The web of interactions has become so tangled that it hampers efforts at directional evolutionary stewardship by dominant players that seek to repel unfavorable traits or variations. Today the global drivers of institutional and cultural selection may exert pull from any point in the system; and the institutions for governance present themselves in different ways in different environments. It hardly matters what the topic is; at this stage of globalization, the coevolutionary drivers of policy diffusion are not even necessarily positioned at the "top" of the system. The fastest-evolving parts of the world are the middle-income zones in which the selection of norms and rules arise from interactions with peers. Much of this appears to be nondirectional, but it may have an effect on what traits persist and are subsequently adapted globally.

The prominence of developing nations in the hyperconnectivity of globalization cannot be reconciled with the presumption that a reversion to hegemony is inevitable. Globalization itself is not new; the flows of capital, goods, and services that cross national boundaries in 2019 (as a percentage of national product) don't significantly exceed the period before 1914. But the direction of the flow has changed. Before the twenty-first century, the current was hierarchically determined by the dominant position of the societies of the global north. Because the movement of goods, services, and ideas is no longer essentially from the periphery to the center, the struggle to occupy a central, or top, position will not by itself determine how globalization evolves.

Today's globalization differs from that of previous periods in the explosive speed and extent of south–south interconnectivity that does not pass through major hubs in the more economically advanced quadrant of the global economy. This difference has major political economy ramifications because it disables the hierarchical ordering of the larger system and challenges its rules. Diffusion also makes it harder for the dominant players to channel political conflict into manageable goals, which contributes to an impression that the system's hegemonic structures are not delivering – and this, too, increases the motivation of dissatisfied parties to challenge its foundations.

An increase in interactions may have many advantages, but too much connectivity can exacerbate the vulnerability of systems (Brummitt, D'Souza, and Leicht 2012). Unwanted connectivity can spread unchecked and produce surprising combinations. One of these surprises is a resurgence of antiglobalist nationalism, spurred by the globalization of economic links and international migration, which is taking root even in the very heartland of international liberalism, the United States and the United Kingdom.

The absence of hierarchical structures to maintain order, combined with the rapid spread and densification of global network ties, leaves populations feeling vulnerable to uncontrolled external influences. Without a consensus on responsible global governance, individuals and state actors will be drawn to nationalism, factionalism, and realpolitik as methods of conflict resolution. Welcome to what political scientist Charles Kupchan deems "no one's world," a habitat for factions and populations self-organized according to their own rules of complexity, without a viable and credible set of global institutions capable of responding to the hyper-risks of a hyperconnected world (2012).

## 9.5   A POST-HEGEMONIC TRANSITION UNFOLDS

This chapter has applied network metrics to examine the interactions of states, testing conventional understandings of recent shifts in global relations. By some measures, such as UN voting records, there is a trend toward greater homogeneity and greater consensus. In others, such as the arms trade, new structures are emerging. But most important, in all networks there is a decreasing level of hierarchy, and a decrease in the network power associated with a central position. In this environment it would be a mistake to overly focus on the risk coming from any one source no matter how preponderate it may seem.

The interdependence among many of globalization's components increases the risk that change anywhere in the system – Afghanistan, Israel, Myanmar, North Korea, Syria, Turkey, or Yemen – can trigger an event whose consequences magnify as they spread. The drama experienced in a single generation, beginning with the fall of the Berlin Wall in 1989 and continuing through the explosive spread of the Internet and social media, the cataclysm unleashed by the 2001 attacks on the New York World Trade Center towers, the global financial meltdown of 2007, the suddenness of the Arab Spring in 2010, the surge of refugees and their political impacts – all these lead to the inescapable conclusion that failure in one network can ripple through an entire ecology and propel the emergence of unexpected properties with the power to transform social relationships in an entire system (Helbing 2013).

Such systemic risks will not have optimal solutions in a complex, densely networked world in which the various agents trade and communicate among themselves according to their own self-interests. Their dense connections enable the momentum to propel the structure and dynamics of global political economy into multiple interdependencies, which makes the interconnectedness of the threats the greatest dilemma for global strategy.

This is the great transition in global political economy we are watching unfold.

NOTES

1. Slaughter (2017, 161–82) explains that in an interconnected world in which a government is but one of the players, it needs a network-oriented strategy offering power within networks and power over them, enabling its bearer to enjoy the advantage of multiple strategies of connection.

2. In his influential essay in *Social Networks*, mathematical sociologist Linton Freeman writes that "for the study of social networks we need measures of graph centralization based on differences in point centralities." (1978/1979, 227). Noting Freeman's work in social network analysis and network centralization, the British sociologist John Scott explains: "Related to the measurement of point centrality is the idea of the overall 'centralization' of a graph, and these two ideas have sometimes been confused by the use of the same term to describe them both. ... Confusion is most likely to be avoided if the term 'centrality' is restricted to the idea of point centrality, while the term 'centralization' is used to refer to particular properties of the graph structure as a whole. Centralization, therefore, refers not to the relative prominence of points, but to the overall cohesion or integration of the graph" (2000, 102).

3. In 2010, non-OECD countries consumed 54 percent of world energy and their oil demand surpassed that of Western nations. That consumption is projected to reach 65 percent by 2040, growing at a 2.2 percent annual rate (EIA 2013)

4. In Mones, Vicsek, and Vicsek (2012) hierarchy is an essential feature of many natural and human-made networks, and they help to provide a measure quantifying it.

5. For more reports, see Congressional Research Service reports on conventional weapons at https://fas.org/sgp/crs/weapons.

6. We can speculate about this increased vulnerability by asking whether the Syrian crisis would have been preventable if the structure of global power were different. For example, if the USSR had remained intact, would it have exercised sufficient control over Syria's status as a Cold War-era client state to suppress the Arab Spring uprising from the start, rather than see it escalate into a full-blown civil war involving regional and international powers? Would the Soviets have helped provide better governance in Syria, which would have mitigated the effects of the drought that decimated the countryside from 2006 through 2010? Would they have taken more decisive action to control the refugee flow? While we aren't able to test this hypothesis explicitly, we can suggest a plausible scenario: in a more hierarchically structured bimodal global environment like that of the Cold War, the Syrian crisis would not have unfolded into a full-fledged global crisis. If the hegemonic network structures of the Cold War had remained intact, it might have been

a crisis of one side or the other, and this might have led to measures to contain its spread. Yet the Cold War methods of attaining stability by propping up unpopular leaders do not solve the core problems of weak domestic governance, and will not end the cycle of violence in regions such as the Middle East.

# 10 A Future of Diminishing Returns or Massive Transformation?

## 10.1 DEATH BY DIMINISHING RETURNS IS NOT WITHOUT PRECEDENT

Considering the trends of key global networks, the prospect of a major transition in the years ahead is not implausible. One prediction frequently circulated is a slow death through diminishing returns, a linear process with continuous variables. In a world accustomed to austerity and shrinking budgets, it is easy to imagine a system-wide collapse that results from the piling on of social expenditures that ultimately deplete all revenues.

US anthropologist Joseph Tainter has offered a hypothesis for understanding the threshold of system failure (1988). A society is a problem-solving organization, he writes, that responds to challenges with diversification and specialization. But as its economy becomes more complex, the marginal costs of added complexity will at some point exceed the marginal benefits of specialization. Once it crosses that threshold, there is a "diminishing return to complexity," that is, the costs to sustain the levels of complexity already attained will rise more rapidly than any gains in productivity.

Among Tainter's numerous examples is the collapse of the Western Roman Empire, which initially met adversity by increasing complexity through conquest but eventually ran out of financing to support it (2006). The tax collectors couldn't gather enough to keep up with the demands of a string of challenges – barbarian invasions, crop failures, the spread of Christianity and its conflict with existing Roman customs and beliefs – whose solutions required still more complexity, impoverishing both governments and populations, and resulting in civil wars and invasions. "The strategy of the later Roman Empire," he explains,

> was to respond to a near-fatal challenge in the third century by increasing the size, complexity, power, and costliness of the primary problem-solving system – the government and its army. The higher costs were undertaken not to expand the empire or to acquire new wealth, but to maintain the status quo. The benefit/cost ratio of imperial government declined. In the end the Western Roman Empire could no longer afford the problem of its own existence. (Tainter 2006, 97)

Can this type of collapse, caused by diminishing returns, happen in a modern capitalist society? There is already evidence that "declining marginal returns affect some of the most important complex organizations upon which today's capitalist societies are based" (Bonaiuti 2014). And Tainter cites health care as one area in which declining marginal returns are readily observable, noting that "from 1930 to 1982, the productivity of the American health system in improving life expectancy fell by about 60 percent" (2006, 95). Throughout the twentieth century, major advances in public health had massive impacts on quality of life. As proper sanitation systems became universal, as new vaccines were discovered, and as antibiotics were invented, life expectancy in the developed countries soared and mortality rates plummeted. In the United States, change of similar magnitude would be unlikely today, when half of all males and 63 percent of all females now live to the age of 80. As Tainter notes, "the inexpensive diseases and ailments were conquered first" (2006, 95), and medicine is becoming more expensive to develop. As of 2014, health care made up 17 percent of US GDP, up from 13 percent in 2000, but with no real improvement in life expectancy or child mortality to match. Another example of declining marginal returns in medicine is that billions are spent on medical research in the United States every year for every drug that is approved, yet penicillin was discovered by accident and developed at a cost of around US$20,000.

Global demand for natural resources is accelerating, depleting known supplies while spreading negative environmental impacts. In what amounts to a textbook example of declining marginal returns, each dollar spent on new resources provides less and less return. The United Nations Environment Programme reports that "since 2000, metal prices have risen 176 percent, rubber prices by 350 percent, energy prices by an average of 260 percent, and food prices by more than 100 percent" (2014, 23). Greentech may be driving growth and new jobs and growing faster than most other sectors of the economy, but its contribution to global GDP is not increasing as quickly as the costs of global environmental degradation.

The idea that innovation and new technology have stopped driving growth and that productivity in innovation has declined finds support in Robert Gordon's *The Rise and Fall of American Growth* (2016). In the past, major technological improvements, such as the steam engine, the assembly line, and electricity, drove economic growth, and Gordon predicts that the last of those innovations has come and gone. The inventions of the foreseeable future may not be revolutionary enough to restart US economic growth. Again, diminishing returns is the culprit; each new breakthrough requires an ever-increasing amount of specialized knowledge. Every advancement must build on previous stores of information and therefore takes more effort, time, and money to achieve a smaller effect. This perspective of diminishing returns amid decelerating innovation is also central to Thomas Homer-Dixon's book *The Upside of Down: Catastrophe, Creativity, and the Renewal of Civilization*, on the dangers of imminent societal collapse (2006). He extends Tainter's perspectives, presenting many examples in which the marginal costs rise and the marginal benefits drop in complex societies that have to expend more effort and money to meet emerging risks (219–23). He also warns that the developed world's ability to grow at a pace to meet new challenges may be approaching a threshold beyond which large-scale investments do not yield large-scale returns.

Indeed, both Tainter and Homer-Dixon show us that governments already find themselves unable to enact policies that offer viable protection against the vicissitudes of the global economy. Both raise valid and urgent concerns about whether science and technology will produce dramatic changes in solving major problems over the next twenty-five years. They base their concerns on the insufficient pace of technological transformation of the previous twenty-five years. Indeed, the kind of catastrophe they describe, death by diminishing marginal returns, can happen; any set of individual variables that make up the global economy can experience diminishing returns. However, descriptions of diminishing returns confine themselves to a single variable or a set of variables, and do not tell us how the whole system is changing or offer insight about what can happen to the overall structure of the network. As Chapter 2 informed us, understanding individual nodes in a network is different from being able to describe changes to the overall network structure.

In theoretical models, Sergey Buldyrev et al. (2010) show that interdependent systems can be more fragile than any single network in isolation; for example, the way that a failure in cybersecurity or physical infrastructure will proliferate depends on the nexus of financial and political coordination, making its failure a problem of complexity. Similarly, interdependent networks can fragment abruptly as a result of small disruptions (Vespignani 2010, 984). Complex systems exhibit thresholds whose vulnerabilities from the interactions of self-organizing processes create new patterns of connectivity that make themselves known suddenly. The result is a phase transition – that point during the network development of a complex system when, at some critical value, a new network property suddenly appears. The transition can be abrupt, as with an infection that mushrooms into a pandemic.

When networks are densely coupled, they are prone to explosive connectivity in which an initial localized failure in one network can spill over to another. Cascading events are observable in traffic, in consumer behavior, in voting, in economic meltdowns, and in less tangible cultural behaviors, such as trust and cooperation. Policy failures can flare up in the form of a pandemic, a refugee surge, a civil war (Goldstone et al. 2014). The effects of such local events can magnify if not addressed quickly and decisively. As increasingly greater resources are consumed, one transition can lead to another, and the scale of interventions will not keep up with the pace of change. The behavioral rules motivating the agents modify as those agents adapt to their changing landscapes, and at some point the erstwhile rules of social coordination lose their grip.

With these observations in mind, we must ask if the next great transition will be a crisis of diminishing returns, or a massive transformation of the system of international relations and the global economy nested within it.

Phase transition dynamics are apparent in the unprecedented density of interconnections in global networks of diplomacy, technology, entertainment, social media, trade, energy, and armaments; and this presents the possibility that a small shock may trigger a massive transformation across the entire system. These dynamics are observable in network topology. In densely interconnected networks, such as tightly coupled infrastructures, when systems become highly interconnected, globally dynamic processes of self-organization can occur.

## 10.2   WHERE WILL NEW RULES OF GLOBAL GOVERNANCE ORIGINATE?

From the perspective of rising levels of interconnected risk, it is reasonable to ask if policymakers in both China and the West are acting responsibly when each projects confidence that it has already achieved the achievable, and that other nations just need to follow its example. Belying the hubris of the incumbent powers, the global power diffusion will mean that both East and West will face the same challenge of navigating with no captain at the helm and in an environment in which there exists no optimal model of regime stability.

History offers a lens to help identify the foundations of resilience, as well as failures to accommodate transition processes. Western resilience emerged organically through the local interactions of agents accommodating themselves to self-organizing dynamics within the system. The system's safeguard was an ability to grow in scale by adding new nodes to its network structure.

The West's legal system is an ancient and key mechanism that contributes adaptiveness to its network structure. Consider the legacy of the Roman Imperium: even more than Rome's roads, bridges, and aqueducts, the spirit of its laws lives on today with the freedom to represent many societal interests, not only those of political leaders who might like to employ the legal framework to their own advantage. Instead, lawmaking reflects a broader range of interests and expertise that allow it to be more adaptive to market and social conditions, and this adaptiveness of the law enhances the capacity of society to update its responses to unforeseen challenges. In China, lawmaking and enforcement reflect, above all else, the political interests of the CCP and its overriding interest in its own survival, albeit the survival of an organization that enjoys a significant degree of trust and credibility because it is known to recruit inclusively and promote on the basis of merit.

## 10.3 AN AGE OF UNCERTAINTY CALLS FOR REVISED EXPECTATIONS

The great historical transitions in this book were structural percolations followed by changing patterns of social organization. The changes occurring globally today raise many questions about what new patterns will eventually emerge from the current percolation.

Since the late 1960s, the West's share of world GDP has declined. The shift first appeared in two oil crises in the 1970s, when the Organization of the Petroleum Exporting Countries (OPEC) became a powerful body representing developing-country producers. This proved to be an important juncture in the drop in the West's relative share of global GDP. The Green Revolution, which brought progress to agriculture, was another contributing factor in the revival of the economies of the global periphery. Beginning in the 1990s, the economic growth rates of developing economies started to exceed those of the West. This trend has continued since 2000, when the economies of the rest (the combined lower- and middle-income countries) grew five times faster than the West's. Their combined GDP increased by 100 percent, that of the West by only 20 percent.[1] Their consumption of global energy flows already exceeds the West's and will rapidly increase, impelling them into new strategic and economic alliances with one another, alliances that tend to bypass the developed world.[2] This constitutes a change in patterns of global connectivity – the underlying grid is being rewired, and the magnitude of this change falls into the category of a structural percolation.

The factors behind the accelerated pace of economic convergence of the rest toward developed-country levels are likely to continue driving the behavioral and ideological transition of a globalizing world economy. During the period leading up to the 1980s, socially mobile populations around the world that sought better lives for themselves and their children had every reason to look to the West for guidance. This is much less true today. As the West's share of world manufacturing and technology transfer continues to fall, its share of global GDP diminishes, its share of world population declines, and hopes dim for a certain form of stabilization based upon Western principles.

The West is no longer blindly imitated by others, even among its developing-nation allies. A world searching for new principles of world order now has many places to look, and that search reduces the scope for diplomacy to a narrower set of issues. A failure to agree on general principles of governance is leading countries to separate their political and economic interests in international relations. China, Saudi Arabia, Russia, and Turkey are all examples of globalizing economies that are not seeking to align ideologically with the West and that have developed direct ties with each other.

Another reason for the eclipse of the West's leadership is the growing share of global growth of the former socialist economies.[3] Since regaining the share of the world economic growth that they had held before the Soviet Union's breakdown, few of the former republics – only the westernmost states of Latvia, Lithuania, and Estonia – have made significant steps toward embracing the values of the Western nations of political freedom, tolerance, and reliance on civil society as drivers of social organization.

Income growth and the economic modernization of the rest have yet to produce a political convergence with Western norms and Western forms of domestic governance. As the West engages with other legal cultures in the formation of an emerging world law, the quality that sets the Western legal tradition apart – its political and judicial institutions whose longtime legitimacy resides in binding those who govern to the same laws as other citizens, and the tradition of political restraint that this binding confers – rarely has transferred effectively to regions where the cultural antecedents are absent. It is no longer possible to deny that China's experiences can provide lessons about alternative pathways to economic renewal. Rivalry among cultural values introduces a healthy dose of competition, and China's spectacular performance in raising its living standards has shown another way to provide the life priorities for individuals trying to escape from poverty and illiteracy. Inevitably, this divergence in social values will be projected onto struggles over shaping the policies of global institutions, the governance of those institutions, and perceptions of their legitimacy. However, there is no reason to believe that nations in need of reform will find it easier to adapt to China's integrated, top-down system of public administration than the West's bottom-up system.

Yet while the gap between high- and medium-income countries has been shrinking, the separation between the middle- and low-income countries is increasing. Exponential population growth without exponential GDP growth will also be a source of endemic unrest that could derail and reverse growth rates overall. Both China and the

West see the magnitude of this threat and have devised very different policies to address it. The West insists on the importance of the rule of law, civil society, the private sector, and inclusive voting. China is in closer physical proximity to the countries that currently lack strong links to the global economy and where the struggle between traditionalism and globalization are most intense. Its approach to closing the widening gap at the bottom is to focus on building infrastructure to attract global investment.

The number of people internally displaced at the start of 2018 was estimated at an all-time high, 68.5 million (Skretteberg 2018). The effects have been felt and the backlash is already severe; witness the riots and electoral shifts in various corners of the world. Yet the surges in outward-bound migration are only just beginning to make themselves felt in host countries. Where there are individuals with little to lose from a violent restructuring of the order at home, the attraction of global movements that promise radical change will grow. Whoever can control and direct these forces for radical change will gain considerable influence over global policymaking for some time to come (Greenhill 2010). Whether China or the West will be best equipped to handle these unfamiliar threats will have a great bearing on their relative global influence and their ability to shape the trajectory of the world economy.

Even if you live in an advanced country, you can be sure of just one thing – that the network structure in which the next era of global capitalism evolves will be radically different from the environment in which it first triumphed. There will be new forms of market competition, but also new measures of self-preservation by incumbent capital – new forms of insulation of incumbent businesses via political redistribution and protectionism. At some point, the redistribution and protective regulation may end up extremely costly for national governments to deliver. If stable markets do not emerge from the pattern of inconsistent and erratic adjustments, the politics of advanced economies will eventually succumb to the acrimony of political polarization. Social fragmentation within countries will escalate, and schisms between countries will multiply. As trade linkages among nations grow, spikes in uncertainty will synchronize.[4] It is in the context of these general social and economic trends that the heightened risks of global interconnectivity must be understood. Both the higher-order structure and the content of information that flows within the network are changing, and our expectations and strategies will have to change accordingly.

At any point, a small initial failure can precipitate a structural breakdown.

## NOTES

1. For comparison of the relative dynamics of the GDP of the West and the rest, see Bolt and van Zanden (2013); World Bank (2016); and Grinin and Korotayev (2015).

2. The US Energy Information Administration (EIA) estimates that "delivered residential energy in the non-OECD region, which accounted for 46 percent of the world's total delivered residential energy consumption in 2010, grows to 51 percent of the world's total in 2020 and 61 percent in 2040, as a result of generally faster economic and population growth than in the OECD" (EIA 2013, 116). In 2015, China's share of world primary energy consumption (23 percent) surpassed that of the US (17 percent). At current rates of expansion, the growth of oil demand of non-OECD countries is projected to exceed that of Western nations by significant margins (EIA 2017).

3. The "rest" includes the third world and the second world, i.e., the former USSR and former Communist countries of Eastern Europe. By the mid-2000s, the former second world returned to its pre-crisis levels of output. Because of the inclusion in the "rest" of the second world, which experienced a catastrophic decline in the early 1990s, the successful reduction of the gap in developing countries generally went unnoticed (Grinin and Korotayev 2015, 101). If the second world is excluded, Grinin and Korotayev report a considerable increase of the third world's share of global GDP.

4. This is consistent with the finding that "uncertainty spikes tend to be more synchronized within advanced economies and between economies with tighter trade and financial linkages" (Ahir, Bloom, and Furceri 2018).

# 11 Network Structure and Economic Change: East vs. West

What is a polity and what is an economy? What is Europe and what is China? Both are vast webs of information transmission, zones of social activity whose members all experience the fundamental effects of communication, directly or indirectly, with one another. How connections emerged within these systems, and what characteristics their enduring ties share, are elemental questions of social evolution. How the nodes are linked has vast implications for how the web functions, yet while these networks are the products of human action and purpose, their forms and intent are without specific author.

Network structure is a prerequisite to the creation of a common culture that enables nations to form a shared identity and purpose. If households are isolated, they cannot form groups. Network structure removes the impediments to communication beyond immediate kin, clans, or tribes, allowing interactions to become scalable. And it is the design of the network structure that determines how information flows among diverse constituents.[1]

For a community to grow, it must acquire the social capacity – the mechanisms and institutions – to enable information diffusion. Yet information diffusion is rarely direct; it involves building connections from peripheral to more centrally located nodes, enabling these to become hubs. A successful system, one that is cost efficient, requires "bridge nodes" that connect the distant nodes and reduce path lengths across the system. We have examined the bridge nodes historically made up of monarchies, emperors, aristocratic alliances, and dynasties. But forming linkages is costly, and as the network becomes larger, the social cost of sustaining connectivity increases. Subordinating personal ties to institutional ties of governance, law, and law enforcement offers the best way to unify the polity; but building formal institutions across society can be both prohibitively expensive and technically unmanageable.

There are also trade-offs between efficiency of flow and its penetration among the different constituents of a given polity. If the structure (topology) has only a few hubs, this can constrain pathways of communication; redundancy among many connectors makes it easier for local clusters to cooperate, but more difficult for system administrators to control content. System administrators in different network environments will have different preferences and different capacities to influence the flow of information. But no social organization, from a family firm to a multinational state, can escape the dilemma of having to balance limits on communication with conserving resources.[2] Inequality arises from the trade-offs concerning how the costs are to be distributed, who gets to be part of a well-resourced hub, and who is relegated to the periphery (Flannery and Marcus 2014).

## 11.1   FLOW AND STRUCTURE: COMMUNICATION AND CONNECTION

In network design, an overarching generalization holds, regardless of time, place, or cultural predisposition: connection is a matter of structure, but communication is a question of flow. Structure and flow contribute interdependently to the evolution of social organization with feedbacks in both directions. Structures shape the flow of information, which in turn leads to behavioral changes that produce pressures for further structural transformations.

In Part II, we observed how the content of flow – the ideas, the beliefs, the norms, even the choice of technology – across the network will differ, depending on whether the bridging nodes are an aristocracy selected by blood ties or a bureaucracy selected by competitive examination. Will the historical differences in the functionality and inclusiveness of the network structures of European origin and those of Chinese descent persist and cause inescapable conflict? Will the co-evolve into new and unforeseen amalgamations?

The great cultural systems are beginning to impinge on one another in a shared global environment. The rise of China, whose economic structure differs from the economies that have dominated global capitalism, sets up a struggle to reshape the global economy. In Chapters 7–10, we saw that differences in network topology that alter the balance between internal order and local adaptability will also influence geopolitical balances, conflict, and opportunities for innovation globally. Competition in ideas, in goods and services, and in technology will all influence who is connected to whom and how.

## 11.2 NETWORK RESILIENCE AND REVOLUTION IN THE WEST

The ability of Europe's royal elites to both foment and survive large disruptions resided in their small-world connectivity. Small-world network connectivity is more robust to perturbations than more centralized network architectures. This property of resilience is critical because the path to the industrialization of Europe included highly disruptive episodes of cultural and intellectual change.

The mystery of Europe's industrialization, in Mokyr's words, resides in how new techniques result from "technological breakthroughs that constitute discontinuous leaps in the information set" (1990b, 351). The challenge is to understand how innovation can become so contagious that it makes leaps from time to time. The social network analysis in this book points to two overlooked contributors. First, the network of royal households encouraged a fundamentally disruptive process that invited technological rivalry in a way that put their own authority increasingly at risk. The sovereigns, the legal institutions, and the judges, who might have seen their power eclipsed by the spread of radical technologies, survived to harness the forces unleashed by technology. Second, European industrialization was the end product of several complementary but disruptive cultural transformations, including the Reformation, the Scientific Revolution, and the Enlightenment. As a phenomenon, it was neither exclusively material nor cultural. It was a new way of perceiving the world, as well as a new way to organize production and harness energy.

Information, more than production systems, can proliferate by leaps since physical infrastructure does not constrain it. In this regard, industrialization was a pan-European cultural dynamic that resembled the Renaissance, the Reformation, and the Enlightenment. Each of these transformations occurred when a breakthrough in a single population triggered multiple larger adaptations, creating a Europe-wide era of change, expanding sociotechnical capability across the continent. Berman explains that continuity, despite successive transformation, is the West's essential quality. Industrialization is indispensable in its own right, but it is also part of a larger process of successive cultural transformations in which there "were new forms of nationhood, new forms of government, new economic institutions, new class relations, new concepts of history, new concepts of truth ... whose repercussions were felt throughout Europe" (Berman 2003, 1). What these episodes had in common was that they were transitions in the information sets that spread laterally across European society and were shared across various levels of society. Leaps in industrial technology that started in the late eighteenth century led to new forms of social organization and then to World War I, in which monarchy as a governing institution was among the casualties.

11.3   NETWORK STRUCTURE AND STABILITY IN EUROPE AND CHINA

To gain a better sense of how large, system-level transitions might unfold in the future, we have reviewed several of the transitions of the past millennia during which major transformations of both institutions and behavior occurred. We have sought to uncover general principles underlying various historical patterns of regime transition and decay, and to identify the rules of complex self-organized order that govern how large systems evolve and why they vary. Many examples are provided of small differences in network structure that affect not only the degrees of naturally arising self-organizing behaviors, but also how and when a given stable state becomes unstable, and what qualitatively different state might result. Among the principal findings are that two dynamical, large-scale phenomena endow China and Europe with different institutional possibility frontiers. Europe's network topology had evolutionary advantages in two areas that China's lacked.

## 1. Innovation and Adaptability

Differences in network structure cause different thresholds for the diffusion of innovations and receptivity to transformative change. In the European pattern, the distributed connectivity of the hubs provided multiple pathways through which information could flow from local units through the whole system and back. There was a capacity for ideas and inventions to spread across the continent without encountering cut-points. Innovations propagated because the various highly connected hubs offered a selection of alternative pathways. This degree of freedom for the diffusion of information was a collective property that the Chinese system did not possess. Its own hub-and-spoke political organization left more of the routing activity in the hands of system administrators and provided them with filtering mechanisms to reduce the spread of undesirable behaviors and beliefs, and to interrupt the spread of potentially disruptive technologies. This, however, limited the extent of self-organizing complex behavior in which individuals could engage and produce innovations that transformed society.

## 2. Resistance to Collapse

The Chinese system was less robust against random failures. If the central hub was removed, the administrative system could collapse. In contrast, the network of interconnected European monarchies could endure cycles of abrupt and massive shifts in local social organization. The web of interconnectivity that it formed enabled frequent leaps in social capacity over long periods and without regime collapse, spurred by sociological or technological changes at lower levels of organization. It would take the deletion of a large number of the principal hubs for the system of interconnected European monarchies to collapse. Differences in the resilience of the higher-order structure produced differences in the risk tolerance of regime administrators.

In sum, network topology influences historical development via its influence on stability, adaptiveness, and diffusion, i.e., the receptivity to innovation of social organization. The Great Divergence was a suite of many disruptive innovations in all aspects of society that spanned 1,000 years and reshaped the European identity. It was possible as well because the Western system is more resilient to episodes of turbulence, and this is reflected in different attitudes toward political and social risk of system administrators, a difference that makes the global conflict between tyranny and liberty a contest between different systems of network organization.

## Resilience in the European Network Architecture

In premodern Europe and China there were hubs – the interconnected royal families in Europe, and in China a hierarchical bureaucratic system with a central node on the top – that linked any two points in the system and allowed information and behaviors to spread rapidly beyond their points of origin. The hubs enabled influence to travel more widely than it would in a network whose ties are merely local and in which connectivity was personal. But again, there were important differences between the flows of information that were determined by the different network topologies.

In the Europe of kings and queens small-world connectivities deprived administrators of cut-points that could otherwise curtail potentially disruptive and transformative behaviors and prevent these from cascading across physical and cultural distances. The highly skewed clustering of connectivity among a small number of principal nodes, i.e., the network of interconnecting monarchies and aristocracies, arose in an organic process, resembling a nature-made system, with a number of large hubs scattered geographically, culturally, and economically. Redundancy accumulated because individual agents could not be prevented from linking in a self-interested manner. The network's receptivity to cascading information flows was quite unusual; if the continent had not experienced waves of self-organized, bottom-up cultural transformation, there would have been no takeoff into sustained growth. Its system-wide political continuity, provided by its higher-order network of monarchies, remained intact until after World War I, and the stability this provided enabled Europe's productive capacity to eventually exceed that of China's, despite the latter's 2,000 years of imperial rule.

The relationships between the hubs in Europe, as measured by degree distribution and centrality over time, were rarely constant; distributions shifted, sometimes dramatically, but without altering the overall robustness of the system. For example, the sixteenth-century Protestant Reformation transformed some of the royal houses and created a new cluster of Protestant monarchies, but it did so without compromising the overall hierarchical source of system order. Catholic and Protestant royal houses rarely intermarried, yet they continued to forge political and military alliances that preserved the balance of power among the decentralized system of interconnected hubs. And the drastic polarization of Europe caused by the Reformation still didn't prevent the monarchies from collaborating when their survival as a class was at stake. Thus there was continuity within a changing cultural and geopolitical landscape.

In premodern Europe, change processes that arose in one region of the network became highly contagious. Diffusion occurred in a random fashion, with new information spreading far and wide through "infection" of only a tiny fraction of the large network (Yang, Tang, and Gross 2015). Adding more nodes did not significantly increase the average path length of each node to any other. These small-world properties have endowed Europe's network structure with an advantage for the synchronization of large-scale change processes that has continued through to the present.

But in any network, cascades are never synchronized to the extent that variety is eliminated and alternative pathways forever shuttered. A particular diffusion process, no matter how powerful, attenuates at some point and will not eliminate all distinctively local variants, ensuring the preservation of heterogeneous properties within the larger system.

No matter how sweeping the impact of change, conversion to the majority view is never total: uniformity is only relative, never complete. Some groups remain that can resist the majority and remain outside the sweep of contagion, leaving behind the seeds from which future waves of deviation can originate. Isolation or independence in one period can be a source of new patterns that arise to dominate the next. Such patterns of regional autonomy do exist in Chinese history; for example, Hebei province (which surrounds most of the modern-day Beijing municipality) was politically and culturally isolated during the Tang dynasty (618–907) yet came to have a large influence over the reforms introduced by the Song dynasty (960–1279). But once it was absorbed, its impact on innovation diminished. The contribution of Hong Kong's limited autonomy to modern China's economic take-off is strikingly similar.

The European system's small-world clustering continues to play a key role in holding the network together because it brings the otherwise highly dispersed nodes closer together. Even when key components malfunction, the global information-carrying ability of the network remains intact. There is no center to attack since the nodes lack homogenous degree distributions and most have few connections, while a few (the hubs) have many. Should even several of the major hubs suffer deletion, the remaining highly connected hubs will still be able to synchronize, preserving system-level stability. A large number of the major hubs (institutional centers of power) must be eliminated to destroy the macro-network stability.

## Network Stability with Chinese Characteristics

China's imperial dynasties bequeathed political, social, and ideological foundations for national unity, including a mix of broadly held political ideals, institutions, and unified communication and commercial networks, that endured largely intact for two millennia. Yet behind that legacy of cultural unity resides a source of enduring structural weakness. China's network structure allows for the addition of a greater number of edges (links) to existing hubs, but the formation of new hubs that could channel traffic to and from the center is hampered. While the result is stability, it comes with a loss in flexibility. There is a greater tendency toward system-wide breakdown when stresses arise that remove the central, most connected hub. Its removal drastically alters the network's topology and decreases the ability of the remaining hubs to communicate with one another. Should clusters of nodes see their links to the system disappear or be cut off from the main cluster, network fragmentation could occur. Thus, a highly centralized connectivity distribution can affect survivability and be exploited by those seeking to damage the system. Linkages in the Chinese system were subjected to greater centralized scrutiny, and the Confucian ideology suppressed the formation of formal linkages that served individual interests over those of the emperor; due to an enfeebled civil society, subterfuge and bribery by officials were difficult to monitor, creating an internally generated weakness.

Will the centralized, star-like topology that constitutes China's governance system still make it vulnerable? Is there a risk of repeating the pattern of the imperial system, which could cause the collapse of modern China into isolated clusters? Understanding these historical precedents can add perspective to questions of current interest in global political economy. Since the end of the Qing dynasty, the populations of mainland China have again experienced the devastating impacts of instability and regime weakness on economic growth and human welfare. For Chairman Mao and his comrades, the classical Chinese dynastic system was a topic of continuous study. He is reputed to have repeatedly read *The Dream of Red Mansions*, the classic eighteenth-century text of Cao Xueqin, which reveals the inevitability of decay and self-destruction lurking beneath the stylish pleasure gardens of the erudite and sophisticated. Being similarly steeped in knowledge of the rise and decay of dynasties predisposes China's leaders to take insulating measures, such as censoring the Internet, checking academic course content, and requiring enterprise owners to join the party and be guided by its mission. There continues to be an inclination to hinder the acquisition of power and prestige from sources that are independent of the regime. But such insulating strategies create vulnerabilities that are hard to monitor since state officials also operate within the norms of the larger society.

Chinese society is highly connected via personal ties and interpersonal connections. *Guanxi*, as this is known, is a defining element of business and culture, and permeates every level of Chinese society. Although not officially authorized, it is "the central form by which normative behavioral codes are maintained" (Gold, Guthrie, and Wank 2002, 20) and has been recognized in early Confucian thought about relations in society. Today, the party leadership occupies the hubs that dominate system-wide connectivity, but clientelism, a form of *guanxi*, infuses the bureaucracy at all levels and penetrates its vertical ties with civil society. Official thinking since Mao has decried *guanxi*, recognizing that neither modern society nor a modern economy can be built on a foundation of interpersonal relationships, and that dependence on personal relationships – whether based on *guanxi*, clan, lineage, or friendship – will prevent the formation of strong firms and effective civil organizations.

Taking a short-term view, a weak civil society is something that state officials might welcome. Without strong civic associations, even *guanxi* cannot contest the concentration of authority in the institutions of the state. Yet if we consider the long-term horizon of state/society relations, the persistence of *guanxi* will eventually erode central power structures. Both the "state," i.e., the governing bodies, and civil society are open systems, and what occurs in one sphere has repercussions for the other, affecting the legitimacy of both. For example, when managers in state organizations find that "pulling strings" is a low-cost way to get things done, it belies their claims of impartiality and reveals a lack of structural capacity to stop the use of connections in the wider society, an impediment to effective governance that no Chinese regime has been able to overcome. It undermines any appeal the state might make to formally stand for public or communal values. The nation's continuous, practically permanent crusade to eliminate official corruption is handicapped by the absence of civic organizations that can act with neutrality as watchdogs. By suppressing civil society, the party makes discovering the subterfuges of local officials more difficult.

Fear of emerging chaos is memorialized in the narrative by which the CCP justifies its grip on power. However, such fear could lead to self-defeating efforts. The measures China is taking to ensure unity and system preservation today may cause major fractures later. Avoidance of reform risks a possible upsurge of accumulating tensions. Bolstering system stability by strengthening centralized control mechanisms may undermine system resilience, reproducing the very weaknesses its designers seek to avoid and causing a massive disruption in the future (Dobson et al. 2007). The cycles of repression could escalate, and censorship become so extensive that the regime ceases to be trusted, and no one feels safe. Small doses of disorder may be the best way to reduce pressures that can lead to massive disruption, but Chinese officials have few such valves to release the buildup of such pressure.

## 11.4 NETWORK ANALYSIS OF GLOBAL SYSTEMS IN ECONOMIC HISTORY

A central theme throughout this study is that without some institutionalized form of highly skewed, small-world connectivity, we would have remained in the sparsely connected, chaotic, and timeless world of our prehistoric ancestors, governed by parochial and particularistic norms and secretive rituals. What such a "large-world" system would actually look like is unimaginable today. Modern network science shows us that information diffusion in complex social organization is realized by small-world mechanisms of communication that reduce the path lengths between the system's nodes via the placement of a few highly connected bridge nodes.

Small-world connectivity reduces violent power transitions and secures stability for the society, yet it is costly to establish (requiring resources, time, effort and money) and comes with highly imperfect compromises of basic human needs and equity. In the historical regimes of both China and the West, those who occupied the position of bridge node, e.g., chiefs and sovereigns, were unconstrained by direct accountability mechanisms with the people they ruled over; they could bestow titles and privileges to their offspring and followers. Today in much of the world, this would be unacceptable. In modern political systems, even after the abolition of hereditary offices, small-world connectivity still can cause authority to be unresponsive and inefficient and contain costly barriers of entry – but networks of mutual encouragement can form, creating the possibility of innovation and contestation and the potential for long-term planning that enables great historical transformations to occur.

We arrive at this final insight. The world's citizens now have two influential versions of highly skewed small-world connectivity, both of which increase information diffusion but rest upon fundamentally different civic values and are sustained by seemingly incompatible governance norms. Both require trade-offs of values and sacrifices of resources. China's institutional framework is premised upon the implicit equality of all citizens before an all-powerful state that all citizens will obey. The other model emphasizes civic protections and personal achievement but tolerates differences and disaccord among constituents. The choice of integration or separation of East and West before us is ultimately about how truth is to be derived – whether it will be delivered administratively from the top down or from the self-organizing dynamics of agents whose autonomy is assured and protected, as they try to change their options even as they adapt their beliefs to their environment. The five great economic transitions have much to tell us about whether those options are random or predetermined.

Network structure is an essential determinant of long-term historical change, with implications for the balance between stability and adaptability that reach well beyond our present day – yet it is a design without a designer. It is the mystery that confirms Hayek's economic notions of "organized complexity," and that lies behind Napoleon's march into Russia, and the propensity toward administrative corruption that explain the cycles of decay and renewal that permeate China's history. It is what now brings East and West alike to uncertain crossroads in globalization. It follows some recognizable and well-documented "rules," chief among them that as connectivity grows denser, whether between royal houses or trade partners, it unlocks new sources of unpredictability for the structure of the system. The great transformations in world history illustrate these rules of self-organization, and sorting them into a unified narrative serves a dual purpose: to demonstrate why large-scale economic change should resume its central place in economic analysis, and how it can serve as the basis of a new paradigm of human progress.

## NOTES

1. Communication can occur through the polity, through cultural and religious symbolism, and through the market. The market provides prices for which there is no exact analogue in the polity, and can grow beyond the boundaries of the polity; but this doesn't make it independent of the other networks that hold the polity together.
2. The energy, or resource, demands of connectivity across cultural and physical distances is significant. Mechanisms for communicating and ensuring the performance of the many collective tasks, such as defense, ideological consistency, and disaster management, are all resource-intensive and require organizational specialization throughout the polity.

# References

Acemoğlu, Daron, and James A. Robinson. 2006. *Economic Origins of Dictatorship and Democracy*. Cambridge University Press.

Achlioptas, Dimitris, Raissa M. D'Souza, and Joel Spencer. 2009. "Explosive Percolation in Random Networks." *Science* 323 (5920): 1453–55.

Ahir, Hites, Nicholas Bloom, and Davide Furceri. 2018. "The World Uncertainty Index." Working Paper. www.policyuncertainty.com/media/WUI_mime o_10_29.pdf.

Anderson, Philip Warren. 1972. "More Is Different." *Science* 177 (4047): 393–96.

Andrade, Tonio. 2016. *The Gunpowder Age: China, Military Innovation, and the Rise of the West in the World History*. Princeton University Press.

Angelucci, Charles, Simone Meraglia, and Nico Voigtländer. 2017. "The Medieval Roots of Inclusive Institutions: From the Norman Conquest of England to the Great Reform Act." Working Paper No. 23606. Cambridge, MA: National Bureau of Economic Research.

Aoki, Masahiko. 2001. *Toward a Comparative Institutional Analysis*. MIT Press.

Arthur, Brian. 1989. "Competing Technologies, Increasing Returns, and Lock-In by Historical Events." *Economic Journal* 99 (394): 116–31.

——— 2009. *The Nature of Technology: What It Is and How It Evolves*. New York: Penguin Books.

——— 2014. *Complexity and the Economy*. Oxford University Press.

Axelrod, Robert. 1997. "The Dissemination of Culture: A Model with Local Convergence and Global Polarization." *Journal of Conflict Resolution* 41 (2): 203–26.

Axtell, Robert. 2014. "Beyond the Nash Program: Aggregate Steady-States without Agent-Level Equilibria." Working Paper. Institute for New Economic Thinking, University of Oxford.

——— 2019. "Dynamics of Firms: Data, Theories and Agent-Based Models." Working Manuscript. George Mason University.

Bai, Chong-En, Chang-Tai Hsieh, and Zheng (Michael) Song. 2014. "Crony Capitalism with Chinese Characteristics." New Perspectives on Macroeconomics, Trade, and Development Conference, June 2–3, 2014, Cowles Foundation for Research in Economics, Yale University, New Haven,

CT and 2014 Annual Meeting of the Society for Economic Dynamics, 2014 Meeting Papers 1145, June 26–28, 2014, Toronto, Canada.

Bak, Per, Chao Tang, and Kurt Wiesenfeld. 1987. "Self-Organized Criticality: An Explanation of the 1/f Noise." *Physical Review Letters* 59 (4): 381–84.

Bandy, Matthew. 2004. "Fissioning, Scalar Stress, and Social Evolution in Early Village Societies." *American Anthropologist* 106 (2): 322–33.

Barabási, Albert-László. 2003. *Linked: How Everything Is Connected to Everything Else and What It Means for Business, Science, and Everyday Life.* New York: Penguin Group.

Barabási, Albert-László, and Réka Albert. 1999. "Emergence of Scaling in Random Networks." *Science* 286 (5439): 509–12.

Barboza, David. 2009. "Contradictions in China, and the Rise of a Billionaire Family." *New York Times,* January 1. www.nytimes.com/2009/01/02/busi ness/worldbusiness/02yuan.html.

Barysch, Katinka, Charles Grant, and Mark Leonard. 2005. "Embracing the Dragon: The EU's Partnership with China." Center for European Reform.

Bavel, Bas Van. 2016. *The Invisible Hand? How Market Economies Have Emerged and Declined since AD 500.* Oxford University Press.

Beinhocker, Eric D. 2006. *Origin of Wealth: Evolution, Complexity, and the Radical Remaking of Economics.* Harvard University Press.

Berman, Harold. 1983. *Law and Revolution,* Vol. 1: *The Formation of the Western Legal Tradition.* Harvard University Press.

2003. *Law and Revolution,* Vol. 2: *The Impact of the Protestant Reformations on the Western Legal Tradition.* Harvard University Press.

Bhullar, Bhart-Anjan S., Zachary S. Morris, Elizabeth M. Sefton, Atalay Tok, Masayoshi Tokita, Bumjin Namkoong, Jasmin Camacho, David A. Burnham, and Arhat Abzhanov. 2015. "A Molecular Mechanism for the Origin of a Key Evolutionary Innovation, the Birdbeak and Palate, Revealed by an Integrative Approach to Major Transitions Invertebrate History." *Evolution* 69 (7): 1665–77.

Bloch, Marc. 1961. *Feudal Society: The Growth of Ties of Dependence and Social Classes and Political Organization.* Translated by L. A. Manyon. University of Chicago Press.

1973. *Royal Touch: Sacred Monarchy and Scrofula in England and France.* Translated by J. E. Anderson. McGill-Queen's University Press.

Bolt, Jutta, and Jan Luiten van Zanden. 2013. "The First Update of the Maddison Project: Re-estimating Growth before 1820." Maddison Project Working paper no. 4. www.ggdc.net/maddison/maddison-project/abstract.htm?id=4.

Bonaiuti, Mauro. 2014. *The Great Transition.* New York: Routledge.

Bracton, Henry de. 1968. *On the Laws and Customs of England*. Translated by Samuel E. Thorne. Cambridge: Belknap Press. First published c.1235.

Bramoullé, Yann, Andrea Galeotti, and Brian Rogers. 2016. *The Oxford Handbook of the Economics of Networks*. Oxford University Press.

Brandt, Loren, Debin Ma, and Thomas Rawski. 2014. "From Divergence to Convergence: Reevaluating the History behind China's Economic Boom." *Journal of Economic Literature* 52 (1): 45–123.

Brenner, Neil, Bob Jessop, Martin Jones, and Gordon Macleod (Eds.). 2003. *State/Space: A Reader*. New York: Wiley-Blackwell.

Broido, Anna, and Aaron Clauset. 2019. "Scale-Free Networks Are Rare." *Nature Communications* 10 (1017): 1–14.

Brummitt, Charles D., Raissa M. D'Souza, and E. A. Leicht. 2012. "Suppressing Cascades of Load in Interdependent Networks." *Proceedings of the National Academy of Sciences of the United States of America* 109 (12): E680–89. www.pnas.org/content/109/12/E680.

Buldyrev, Sergey V., Roni Parshani, Gerald H. Paul, Eugene Stanley, and Shlomo Havlin. 2010. "Catastrophic Cascade of Failures in Interdependent Networks." *Nature* 464: 1025–28.

Burt, Ronald S. 1992. *Structural Holes: The Social Structure of Competition*. Harvard University Press.

Campos, Jose Edgardo, and Hilton L. Root. 1996. *The Key to the Asian Miracle: Making Shared Growth Credible*. Washington, DC: Brookings Institution Press.

Cannadine, David. 1999. *The Decline and Fall of the British Aristocracy*. New York: Random House.

Cederman, Lars-Erik. 1997. *Emergent Actors in World Politics: How States and Nations Develop and Dissolve*. Princeton University Press.

Chandler, David. 2014. *Resilience: The Governance of Complexity*. New York: Routledge.

Chen, Wei, and R. M. D'Souza. 2011. "Explosive Percolation with Multiple Giant Components." *Physical Review Letters* 106 (11): 115701–04.

Chen, Wei, Z. Zheng, and R. M. D'Souza. 2012. "Deriving an Underlying Mechanism for Discontinuous Percolation." *Europhysics Letters* 100 (6): 66006.

Chen, Yudan. 2016. "Two Roads to a World Community: Comparing Stoic and Confucian Cosmopolitanism." *Chinese Political Science Review* 1 (2): 322–35.

Chen Yun. 1988. *Selected Works of Chen Yun, 1926–1949*. Beijing: Foreign Languages Press.

Cheung, Steven N. S. 1982. "Will China Go 'Capitalist'?: An Economic Analysis of Property Rights and Institutional Change." Hobart Paper 94. London: Institute of Economic Affairs.

China Daily. 2018. "Xi Delivers Speech at 40th-Anniversary Conference of Reform and Opening-Up." December 18. www.chinadaily.com.cn/a/201812/18/WS5 c1854a7a3107d4c3a001612_1.html.

Chung, Jae Ho. 2016. "The Rise of China and East Asia: A New Regional Order on the Horizon?" *Chinese Political Science Review* 1: 47–59.

Coase, Ronald, and Ning Wang. 2012. *How China Became Capitalist*. New York: Palgrave.

Crouzet, F. 1967. "England and France in the Eighteenth Century: A Comparative Analysis of Two Economic Growths." In *The Causes of the Industrial Revolution in England*, edited by Ronald Max Hartwell. 139–74. London: Taylor and Francis.

CSIS. 2017. "US Trade Policy Priorities: Robert Lighthizer, United States Trade Representative." Speech. Washington, DC: Center for Strategic and International Studies. www.csis.org/events/us-trade-policy-priorities-robert-lighthizer-united-states-trade-representative.

Das, Mitali, and Papa N'Diaye. 2013. "Chronicle of a Decline Foretold: Has China Reached the Lewis Turning Point?" Working paper no. 13/26. Washington, DC: International Monetary Fund.

Davidson, Neil. 2012. *How Revolutionary Were the Bourgeois Revolutions?* Chicago: Haymarket Books.

Deng Xiaoping. 1993. "Key Points on Talks given in Wuchang, Shenzhen." In *Deng Xiaoping Wenxuan*. 370–83. Beijing: People's Press.

Diamond, Jared. 2005. *Guns, Germs, and Steel: The Fates of Human Societies*. New York: Norton.

Dittmar, Jeremiah. 2011. "Information Technology and Economic Change: The Impact of the Printing Press." *Quarterly Journal of Economics* 126 (3): 1133–72.

Dobson, I., B. A. Carreras, V. E. Lynch, and D. E. Newman. 2007. "Complex Systems Analysis of Series of Blackouts: Cascading Failure, Critical Points, and Self-Organization." *Chaos* 17 (2): 026103.

Duby, Georges. 1974. *The Early Growth of the European Economy: Warriors and Peasants from the Seventh to the Twelfth Century*. Cornell University Press.

Dunbar, Robin I. M., and Richard Sosis. 2018. "Optimizing Human Community Sizes." *Evolution and Human Behavior* 39: 106–11.

Easley, David, and Jon Kleinberg. 2010. *Networks, Crowds, and Markets: Reasoning about a Highly Connected World*. Cambridge University Press.

EIA. 2013. "International Energy Outlook 2013: With Projections to 2040." DOE/ EIA-0484. Washington DC: US Energy Information Administration.

2017. "Beyond China and India, Energy Consumption in Non-OECD Asia Continues to Grow." *Today in Energy.* www.eia.gov/todayinenergy/detail .php?id=32972.

Eisenstein, Elizabeth. 1979. *The Printing Press As an Agent of Change: Communications and Cultural Transformations in Early Modern Europe,* Vol. 1. Cambridge University Press.

Elgin-Cossart, Molly, and Melanie Hart. 2015. "China's New International Financing Institutions: Challenges and Opportunities for Sustainable Investment Standards." Washington DC: Center for American Progress.

Elias, Norbert. 1983. *The Court Society.* Oxford University Press.

Elliott, Matthew, Benjamin Golub, and Matthew Jackson. 2014. "Financial Networks and Contagion." *American Economic Review* 104 (10): 3115–53.

Epstein, Joshua, and Robert Axtell. 1996. *Growing Artificial Societies: Social Science from the Bottom Up.* Washington, DC: Brookings Institution Press.

Fairbank, John King. 1948. *United States and China.* Harvard University Press.

Fan, Ruiping. 2011. "Introduction: The Rise of Authentic Confucianism." In *The Renaissance of Confucianism in Contemporary China,* edited by Ruiping Fan. 1–17. Dordrecht: Springer.

Finer, S. E. 1997. *The History of Government from the Earliest Times.* 3 vols. Oxford University Press.

Flannery, Kent, and Joyce Marcus. 2014. *The Creation of Inequality: How Our Prehistoric Ancestors Set the Stage for Monarchy, Slavery, and Empire.* Harvard University Press.

Foley, Duncan. 1994. "A Statistical Equilibrium Theory of Markets." *Journal of Economic Theory* 62 (2): 321–45.

Freedom House. 2018. "Freedom in the World 2018: Democracy in Crisis." Freedom House. Washington, DC. https://freedomhouse.org/report/freedom-world/freedom-world-2018.

Freeman, Linton. 1977. "A Set of Measures of Centrality Based on Betweenness." *Sociometry* 40 (1): 35–41.

1978/1979. "Centrality in Social Networks Conceptual Clarification." *Social Networks* 1: 215–39.

Fried, Johannes. 2016. *Charlemagne.* Harvard University Press.

Fukuyama, Francis. 2011. *The Origins of Political Order: From Prehuman Times to the French Revolution.* New York: Farrar, Straus and Giroux.

2014. "At the 'End of History' Still Stands Democracy. Twenty-Five Years after Tiananmen Square and the Berlin Wall's Fall, Liberal Democracy Still

Has No Real Competitors." *Wall Street Journal*, June 6. http://online.wsj.com /articles/at-the-end-of-history-still-stands-democracy–1402080661.

Fung, Yu-Lan. 1948. *A Short History of Chinese Philosophy*, edited by Derk Bodde. New York: Macmillan & Co.

Gang, Deng. 1997. *Chinese Maritime Activities and Socioeconomic Consequences, c. 2100 BC–1900 AD*. New York: Greenwood Publishing Group.

Gavrilets, Sergey. 2004. *Fitness Landscapes and the Origin of Species*. Princeton University Press.

Geels, Frank. 2004. "From Sectoral Systems of Innovation to Socio-technical Systems: Insights about Dynamics and Change from Sociology and Institutional Theory." *Research Policy* 33 (6–7): 897–920.

Gernet, Jacques. 1996. *A History of Chinese Civilization*. Cambridge University Press.

Gold, Thomas, Doug Guthrie, and David Wank (Eds.). 2002. *Social Connections in China: Institutions, Culture, and the Changing Nature of "Guanxi."* Cambridge University Press.

Goldstone, Jack A., Hilton Root, and Monty G. Marshall. 2014. "The Impact of Global Demographic Change on the International Security Environment." In *Managing Conflict in a World Adrift*, edited by Chester A. Crocker, Fen Osler Hampson, and Pamela Aall. 241–54. Washington, DC: US Institute of Peace Press and Center for International Governance Innovation.

Gordon, Robert. 2016. *The Rise and Fall of American Growth: The US Standard of Living since the Civil War*. Princeton University Press.

Greenhill, Kelly M. 2010. *Weapons of Mass Migration: Forced Displacement, Coercion, and Foreign Policy*. Cornell University Press.

Greif, Avner, and Christopher Kingston. 2011. "Institutions: Rules or Equilibria?" In *Political Economy of Institutions, Democracy and Voting*, edited by Norman Schofield and Gonzalo Caballero. 13–43. New York: Springer.

Greif, Avner, and Guido Tabellini. 2010. "Cultural and Institutional Bifurcation: China and Europe Compared." *American Economic Review* 100: 135–40.

Grinin, Leonid, and Andrey Korotayev. 2015. *Great Divergence and Great Convergence: A Global Perspective*. Switzerland: Springer International.

Hafner-Burton, Emilie M., Miles Kahler, and Alexander H. Montgomery. 2009. "Network Analysis for International Relations." *International Organization* 63 (3): 559–92.

Hall, Peter A., and David Soskice (Eds.). 2001. *Varieties of Capitalism: The Institutional Foundations of Comparative Advantage*. Oxford University Press.

Hartwell, Robert. 1966. "Markets, Technology, and the Structure of Enterprise in the Development of the Eleventh-Century Chinese Iron and Steel Industry." *Journal of Economic History* 26 (1): 29–58.

1967. "A Cycle of Economic Change in Imperial China: Coal and Iron in Northeast China, 750–1350." *Journal of Economic and Social History of the Orient* 10: 103–59.

1982. "Demographic, Political, and Social Transformations of China, 750–1550." *Harvard Journal of Asiatic Studies* 42 (2): 365–442.

Hausmann, Ricardo, César A. Hidalgo, Sebastián Bustos, Michele Coscia, Sarah Chung, Juan Jimenez, Alexander Simoes, and Muhammed Ali Yildirim. 2011. *The Atlas of Economic Complexity: Mapping Paths to Prosperity.* MIT Press.

Havrylyshyn, Oleh, Xiaofan Meng, and Marian L. Tupy. 2016. "25 Years of Reforms in Ex-Communist Countries: Fast and Extensive Reforms Led to Higher Growth and More Political Freedom." *Policy Analysis* 795. Washington, DC: Cato Institute.

Hayek, Friedrich. 1944. *The Road to Serfdom.* University of Chicago Press.

1973. *Law, Legislation and Liberty*, Vol. 1: *Rules and Order*. University of Chicago Press.

1976. *Law, Legislation and Liberty*, Vol. 2: *The Mirage of Social Justice*. University of Chicago Press.

1979. *Law, Legislation and Liberty*, Vol. 3: *The Political Order of a Free People*. University of Chicago Press.

Helbing, Dirk. 2013. "Globally Networked Risks and How to Respond." *Nature* 497: 51–59.

Hexter, J. H. 1961. *Reappraisals in History: New Views on History and Society in Early Modern Europe.* New York: Harper Torchbooks.

Hilton, Rodney. 1985. *Class Conflict and the Crisis of Feudalism: Essays in Medieval Social History.* London: Bloomsbury Academic.

Hindriks, Frank, and Francesco Guala. 2015. "Institutions, Rules, and Equilibria: A Unified Theory." *Journal of Institutional Economics* 11 (3): 459–80.

Hodgson, Geoffrey M., and Thorbjørn Knudsen. 2010. *Darwin's Conjecture: The Search for General Principles of Social and Economic Evolution.* Chicago University Press.

Hofstede, Geert, and Michael Harris Bond. 1988. "The Confucius Connection: From Cultural Roots to Economic Growth." *Organizational Dynamics* 16 (4): 5–21.

Holland, John. 1995. *Hidden Order: How Adaptation Builds Complexity.* New York: Basic Books.

1998. *Emergence: From Chaos to Order.* Oxford University Press.

Holling, Crawford Stanley. 1973. "Resilience and Stability of Ecological Systems." *Annual Review of Ecology and Systematics* 4: 1–23.

Holling, C. S., and L. Gunderson. 2002. *Panarchy: Understanding Transformations in Human and Natural Systems*. Washington, DC: Island Press.

Holling, C. S., D. W. Schindler, B. W. Walker, and J. Roughgarden. 1995. "Biodiversity in the Functioning of Ecosystems: An Ecological Synthesis." In *Biodiversity Loss: Economic and Ecological Issues*, edited by C. S. Holling and B. O. Jansson, C. Perrings, K. G. Maler, and C. Folke. 44–83. Cambridge University Press.

Homer-Dixon, Thomas. 2006. *The Upside of Down: Catastrophe, Creativity, and the Renewal of Civilization*. Washington, DC: Island Press.

Jackson, Matthew. 2010. *Social and Economic Networks*. Princeton University Press.

———. 2014. "Networks in the Understanding of Economic Behaviors." *Journal of Economic Perspectives* 28 (4): 3–22.

Jensen, Henrik. 1998. *Self-Organized Criticality: Emergent Complex Behavior in Physical and Biological Systems*. Cambridge University Press.

Jiang Zemin. 2002. "Build a Well-Off Society in an All-Round Way and Create a New Situation in Building Socialism with Chinese Characteristics." Report delivered at the 16th National Congress of the Communist Party of China, November 8. www.chinadaily.com.cn/china/2007-07/10/content_6142007 .htm.

Johnson, Jeffery. 2013. *Hypernetworks in the Science of Complex Systems*. Imperial College Press.

Johnson, Jeffrey, Andrzej Nowak, Paul Ormerod, Bridget Rosewell, and Yi-Cheng Zhang (Eds.). 2017. *Non-equilibrium Social Science and Policy: Introduction and Essays on New and Changing Paradigms in Socio-Economic Thinking*. New York: Springer International Publishing.

Jones, Eric. 1981. *The European Miracle: Environments, Economies and Geopolitics in the History of Europe and Asia*. Cambridge University Press.

Jupille, Joseph, Walter Mattli, and Duncan Snidal. 2013. *Institutional Choice and Global Commerce*. Cambridge University Press.

Kauffman, Stuart A. 1993. *The Origins of Order: Self-Organization and Selection in Evolution*. Oxford University Press.

———. 1995. *At Home in the Universe: The Search for the Laws of Self-Organization and Complexity*. Oxford University Press.

Kelly, J. M. 1992. *A Short History of Western Legal Theory*. Oxford University Press.

Kissinger, Henry. 2014. *World Order*. New York: Penguin Press.

Kupchan, Charles A. 2012. *No One's World: The West, the Rising Rest, and the Coming Global Turn*. Oxford University Press.

Kuran, Timur. 1997. *Private Truths, Public Lies: The Social Consequences of Preference Falsification*. Harvard University Press.

Kydland, F., and E. C. Prescott. 1977. "Rules Rather than Discretion: The Inconsistency of Optimal Plans." *Journal of Political Economy* 85 (3): 473–92.

Landes, David. 2006. "Why Europe and the West? Why Not China?" *Journal of Economic Perspectives* 20 (2): 3–22.

Lardy, Nicholas R. 2019. *The State Strikes Back: The End of Economic Reform in China?* Washington, DC: Peterson Institute for International Economics.

Lee, Deokjae, Young Sul Cho, and Byungnam Kahng. 2016. "Diverse Types of Percolation Transitions." *Journal of Statistical Mechanics* (December 124002). Special Issue on Statphys 26.

Leskovec, Jure, Jon Kleinberg, and Christos Faloutsos. 2005. "Graphs over Time: Densification Laws, Shrinking Diameters and Possible Explanations." Association of Computing Machinery, Special Interest Group on Knowledge, Discovery, and Data Mining (SIGKDD)." *Proceedings of the Eleventh ACM SIGKDD*, 177–87. Chicago. www.cs.cornell.edu/home/kleinber/kdd05-time.pdf.

Levin, Simon. 1992. "The Problem of Pattern and Scale." *Ecology* 73 (6): 1943–67.

Lewis, W. Arthur. 1954. "Economic Development with Unlimited Supplies of Labour." *The Manchester School* 22 (2): 139–91.

Li, David, and Francis Lui. 2004. "Why Do Governments Dump State Enterprises?: Evidence from China." In *Governance, Regulation, and Privatization in the Asia-Pacific Region*, edited by Takatoshi Ito and Anne Krueger. 211–30. University of Chicago Press.

Lin, Justin Yifu. 1995. "The Needham Puzzle: Why the Industrial Revolution Did Not Originate in China." *Economic Development and Cultural Change* 43 (2): 269–92.

2009. *Economic Development and Transition Thought, Strategy, and Viability*. Cambridge University Press.

Linstedt, Dan. 2010. "Data Vault Modeling." DanLinstedt.Com.

Liu, P. L. Alan. 1983. "The Politics of Corruption in the People's Republic of China." *American Political Science Association* 77 (3): 602–23.

Lu, Mingjun. 2016. "The Bene-Ideal: China's Cosmopolitan Vision of World Order." *Chinese Political Science Review* 1 (2): 336–52.

Maddison, Angus. 2001. *The World Economy: A Millennial Perspective*. Paris: Organization for Economic Cooperation and Development.

Mann, Susan. 1987. *Local Merchants and the Chinese Bureaucracy, 1750–1950*. Stanford University Press.

Mao Tse-Tung. 1965. "On Practice." In *Selected Works of Mao Tse-Tung*, Vol. 1. 295–309. Beijing: Foreign Languages Press.

Maoz, Zeev. 2011. *Networks of Nations: The Evolution, Structure, and Impact of International Networks, 1816–2001*. Cambridge University Press.

Marongiu, Antonio. 1968. *Medieval Parliaments: A Comparative Study*. London: Eyre and Spottiswoode.

Marx, Karl, and Friedrich Engels. 1992. "Division of Labour and Mechanical Workshop. Tool and Machinery." In *Collected Works*, Vol. 33, *Marx: 1861–1863. A Contribution to the Critique of Political Economy Notebooks I–vi*. New York: International Publishers.

Mathias, Nisha, and Venkatesh Gopal. 2001. "Small-Worlds: How and Why." *Physical Review E* 63 (2). https://doi.org/10.1103/PhysRevE.63.021117.

Mayer, Arno. 1981. *The Persistence of the Old Regime*. New York: Pantheon Books.

McNamara, Jo Ann. 1994. "The Herrenfrage: The Restructuring of the Gender System, 1050–1150." In *Medieval Masculinities: Regarding Men in the Middle Ages*, edited by Clare A. Lees, Thelma Fenster, and Jo Ann McNamara. 3–30. University of Minnesota Press.

Mike, Karoly. 2017. "The Intellectual Orders of a Market Economy." *Journal of Institutional Economics* 13 (4): 899–915.

Ministry of Commerce. 2017. "Statistical Bulletin of China's Outward Foreign Direct Investment." People's Republic of China.

Mokyr, Joel. 1990a. *The Lever of Riches: Technological Creativity and Economic Progress*. Oxford University Press.

1990b. "Punctuated Equilibria and Technological Progress." *American Economic Review, Papers and Proceedings* 80 (2): 350–54.

2017. *A Culture of Growth: The Origins of the Modern Economy*. Princeton University Press.

Mones E., L. Vicsek, and T. Vicsek. 2012 "Hierarchy Measure for Complex Networks." *PLoS ONE* 7(3): e33799. https://doi.org/10.1371/journal.pone.0033799.

Morgenthau, Hans. 1962. "A Political Theory of Foreign Aid." *American Political Science Review* 56 (2): 301–9.

Morris, Ian. 2010. *Why the West Rules – For Now: The Patterns of History, and What They Reveal about the Future*. New York: Farrar, Straus and Giroux.

Myerson, Roger. 2008. "The Autocrat's Credibility Problem and Foundations of the Constitutional State." *American Political Science Review* 102 (1): 125–39.

Naím, Moisés. 2013. *The End of Power: From Boardrooms to Battlefields and Churches to States, Why Being in Charge Isn't What It Used to Be.* New York: Perseus Books.

National Association of Realtors. 2017. "2017 Profile of International Activity in the US Residential Real Estate." Washington, DC.

Needham, Joseph. 1956. *Science and Civilization in China*, Vol. 1. Cambridge University Press.

1969. *The Grand Titration: Science and Society in East and West.* Toronto: Allen & Unwin.

Newman, Mark E. J. 2003. "The Structure and Function of Complex Networks." *SIAM Review* 45 (2): 167–256.

Newman, Mark, Albert-László Barabási, and Duncan Watts. 2006. *The Structure and Dynamics of Networks.* Princeton University Press.

North, Douglass. 1968. "Sources of Productivity Change in Ocean Shipping." *Journal of Political Economy* 76 (5): 953–70.

1990. *Institutions, Institutional Change and Economic Performance.* Cambridge University Press.

1991. "Institutions." *Journal of Economic Perspectives* 5 (1): 97–112.

North, Douglass, John Joseph Wallis, and Barry R. Weingast. 2009. *Violence and Social Order: A Conceptual Framework for Interpreting Recorded Human History.* Cambridge University Press.

Oatley, Thomas, Kindred Winecoff, Andrew Pennock, and Sarah Bauerle Danzman. 2013. "The Political Economy of Global Finance: A Network Model." *Perspectives on Politics* 11 (1): 133–53.

Odling-Smee, John F., Kevin N. Laland, and Marcus W. Feldman. 2003. *Niche Construction: The Neglected Process in Evolution.* Monograph in Population Biology 37. Princeton University Press.

Ormerod, Paul. 2012. *Positive Linking: How Networks and Incentives Can Revolutionise the World.* London: Faber and Faber.

OTMP. 2018. "How China's Economic Aggression Threatens the Technologies and Intellectual Property of the United States and the World." Washington DC: Office of Trade and Manufacturing Policy. www.whitehouse.gov/wp-content/uploads/2018/06/FINAL-China-Technology-Report-6.18.18-PDF.pdf.

Padgett, John, and Walter Powell. 2012. *The Emergence of Organizations and Markets.* Princeton University Press.

Parker, Geoffrey. 1996. *The Military Revolution: Military Innovation and the Rise of the West 1500–1800.* Cambridge University Press.

2008. *The Cambridge Illustrated History of Warfare.* Cambridge University Press.

Pejovich, Svetozar. 1999. "The Effects of the Interaction of Formal and Informal Institutions on Social Stability and Economic Development." *Journal of Markets and Morality* 2 (2): 164–81.

People's Daily. 2000. "Haier History." www.peopledaily.com.cn/GB/channel3/23/20000802/169351.html.

Pierson, Paul. 2000. "Increasing Returns, Path Dependence, and the Study of Politics." *American Political Science Review* 94 (2): 251–67.

———. 2004. *Politics in Time: History, Institutions, and Social Analysis.* Princeton University Press.

Pines, Yuri. 2012. *The Everlasting Empire: The Political Culture of Ancient China and Its Imperial Legacy.* Princeton University Press.

Polanyi, Michael. 1958. *Personal Knowledge: Towards a Post-critical Philosophy.* London: Routledge.

Pollard, Sidney. 1973. "Industrialization and the European Economy." *Economic History Review* 26 (4): 636–48.

Prasad, Eswar S. 2014. *The Dollar Trap: How the US Dollar Tightened Its Grip on Global Finance.* Princeton University Press.

Preiser-Kapeller, Johannes. 2015. "Calculating the Middle Ages? The Project 'Complexities and Networks in the Medieval Mediterranean and Near East.'" *Medieval Worlds* 1 (2): 100–27.

Pritchett, Lant. 1977. "Divergence, Big Time." *Journal of Economic Perspectives* 11 (3): 3–17.

Purzycki, Benjamin Grant, Coren Apicella, Quentin D. Atkinson, Emma Cohen, Rita Ann McNamara, Aiyana K. Willard, Dmitris Xygalatas, Ara Norenzayan, and Joseph Henrich. 2016. "Moralistic Gods, Supernatural Punishment and the Expansion of Human Sociality." *Nature* 530 (7590): 327–30.

Qian, Yingyi, and Barry Weingast. 1997. "Federalism as a Commitment to Preserving Market Incentives." *Journal of Economic Perspectives* 11 (4): 83–92.

Qing, Jiang. 2012. *A Confucian Constitutional Order: How China's Ancient Past Can Shape Its Political Future.* Translated by Edmund Ruden. Edited by Daniel Bell and Ruiping Fan. Princeton University Press.

Reeves, Colin R. 2005. "Fitness Landscapes." In *Search Methodologies: Introductory Tutorials in Optimization and Decision Support Techniques,* edited by Edmund Burke and Graham Kendall. 681–705. New York: Springer.

Reischauer, E. O., and J. K. Fairbank. 1958. *East Asia: The Great Tradition.* Boston: Houghton Mifflin.

Richerson, Peter J., and Robert Boyd. 2005. *Not by Genes Alone: How Culture Transformed Human Evolution.* University of Chicago Press.

Richter, Hendrik, and Andries Engelbrecht, eds. 2014. *Recent Advances in the Theory* and *Application of Fitness Landscapes*. New York: Springer.

Roderich, Ptak. 1993. "China and the Trade in Cloves, circa 960–1435." *Journal of the American Oriental Society* 113 (1): 1–13.

1998. "From Quanzhou to the Sulu Zone and Beyond: Questions Related to the Early Fourteenth Century." *Journal of Southeast Asian Studies* 29 (2): 269–94.

Root, Hilton L. 2005. *Capital and Collusion: The Political Logic of Global Economic Development*. Princeton University Press.

2013. *Dynamics among Nations: The Evolution of Legitimacy and Development in Modern States*. MIT Press.

2018. "Keynes, Hayek, and the Roots of Complexity Theory in Economics." *Policy and Complex Systems* 4 (1): 155–72.

Rosenberg, Nathan, and Luther Earle Birdzell. 1986. *How the West Grew Rich: The Economic Transformation of the Industrial World*. New York: Basic Books.

Ryan, Magnus. 2014. "Roman Law in Medieval Political Thought." In *The Cambridge Companion to Roman Law*, edited by David Johnston. 423–51. Cambridge University Press.

Schot, Johan, and Frank W. Geels. 2008."Strategic Niche Management and Sustainable Innovation Journeys: Theory, Findings, Research Agenda, and Policy." *Technology Analysis & Strategic Management* 20 (5): 537–54.

Schumpeter, Joseph A. 1951. *Imperialism and Social Classes*. Edited by Paul M. Sweezy. New York: Augustus M. Kelley.

Scott, John. 2000. *Social Network Analysis*. London: Sage Publications.

Sharma, Vivek Swaroop. 2015. "Kinship, Property, and Authority: European Territorial Consolidation Reconsidered." *Politics & Society* 43 (2): 151–80.

Shepsle, Kenneth A. 1979. "Institutional Arrangements and Equilibrium in Multidimensional Voting Models." *American Journal of Political Science* 23: 23–57.

2006. "Old Questions and New Answers about Institutions: The Riker Objection Revisited." In *The Oxford Handbook of Political Economy*, edited by Donald A. Wittman and Barry R. Weingast. 1031–49. Oxford University Press.

Sibani, Paolo, and Henrik Jeldtoft Jensen. 2013. *Stochastic Dynamics of Complex Systems: From Glasses to Evolution*. Series on Complexity Science. Imperial College Press.

Simon, Herbert A. 1962. "The Architecture of Complexity." *Proceedings of the American Philosophical Society* 106 (6): 467–82.

2000. "Can There Be a Science of Complex Systems?" In *Proceedings from the International Conference on Complex Systems on Unifying Themes in*

*Complex Systems,* edited by Yaneer Bar-Yam. 3–14. Cambridge, MA. Perseus Books.

SIPRI. 2017. "Increase in Arms Transfers Driven by Demand in the Middle East and Asia, Says SIPRI." Stockholm International Peace Research Institute. https://sipri.org/media/press-release/2017/increase-arms-transfers-driven-demand-middle-east-and-asia-says-sipri.

Skretteberg, Richard. 2018. "2019 Will Be Another Year of Crisis." Norwegian Refugee Council. www.nrc.no/shorthand/fr/2019-will-be-another-year-of-crises/index.html.

Slaughter, Anne-Marie. 2012. "A Grand Strategy of Network Centrality." In *America's Path: Grand Strategy for the Next Administration,* edited by Richard Fontaine and Kristin Lord. 43–56. Washington, DC: Center for New American Security.

——— 2017. *The Chessboard and the Web: Strategies of Connection in a Networked World.* Yale University Press.

Smith, Eric, and Duncan Foley. 2008. "Classical Thermodynamics and Economic General Equilibrium Theory." *Journal of Economic Dynamics and Control* 32 (1): 7–65.

Southern, Richard William. 1953. *The Making of the Middle Ages.* Yale University Press.

Stein, Peter. 1999. *Roman Law in European History.* Cambridge University Press.

Strange, Susan. 1996. *The Retreat of the State: The Diffusion of Power in the World Economy.* Cambridge University Press.

Strogatz, Steven H. 2003. *Sync: The Emerging Science of Spontaneous Order.* New York: Hyperion.

Svensson, Erik, and Ryan Calsbeek. 2012. *The Adaptive Landscape in Evolutionary Biology.* Edited by Erik Svensson and Ryan Calsbeek. Oxford University Press.

Tackett, Nicolas. 2014. *The Destruction of the Medieval Chinese Aristocracy.* Harvard University Press.

Tian, Qing. 2017. *Rural Sustainability: A Complex Systems Approach to Policy Analysis.* Switzerland: Springer International Publishing.

Tainter, Joseph. 1988. *The Collapse of Complex Societies.* Cambridge University Press.

——— 2006. "Social Complexity and Sustainability." *Ecological Complexity* 3: 91–103.

Taylor, Nathaniel L. 2005. "Inheritance of Power in the House of Guifred the Hairy: Contemporary Perspectives on the Formation of a Dynasty." In *The Experience of Power in Medieval Europe, 950–1350,* edited by Robert III Berkhofer, Alan Cooper, and Adam J. Kosto. 129–51. Burlington: Ashgate.

Tocqueville, Alexis de. 1955. *The Old Regime and the French Revolution*. New York: Anchor. First published 1856.

Travers, Jeffrey, and Stanley Milgram. 1969. "An Experimental Study of the Small World Problem." *Sociometry* 32 (4): 425–43.

Trebilcock, Clive. 1981. *The Industrialization of the Continental Powers 1780 –1914*. Boston: Addison Wesley Longman.

Truman, Harry S. 1949. Truman's Inaugural Address. Harry S Truman Presidential Library and Museum. www.trumanlibrary.org/whistlestop/50yr_archive/ina gural20jan1949.htm.

Turchin, Peter. 2008. "Arise 'Cliodynamics.'" *Nature* 454: 34–35.

United Nations Environment Programme. 2014. "Decoupling 2: Technologies, Opportunities and Policy Options." A report of the Working Group on Decoupling to the International Resource Panel, by E. U. von Weizsäcker, J. de Larderel, K. Hargroves, C. Hudson, M. Smith, M. Rodrigues.

USCC. 2016. "Report to Congress of the US–China Economic and Security Review Commission: Executive Summary and Recommendations." Washington DC: US–China Economic and Security Review Commission. www.uscc.gov/sites/de fault/files/annual_reports/2016Annual Report to Congress.pdf.

USTR. 2018. "Finding of the Investigation into China's Acts, Policies, and Practices Related to Technology Transfer, Intellectual Property, and Innovation Under Section 301 of the Trade Act of 1974." Washington DC: Office of the US Trade Representative. http://datatopics.worldbank.org/world-development-indicators.

Van de Walle, Nicolas. 2001. *African Economies and the Politics of Permanent Crisis, 1979–1999*. Cambridge University Press.

Vega-Redondo, Fernando. 2007. *Complex Social Networks*. Cambridge University Press.

Vespignani, Alessandro. 2010. "Complex Networks: The Fragility of Interdependency." *Nature* 464: 984–85.

Voeten, Erik. 2004. "Resisting the Lonely Superpower: Responses of States in the United Nations to US Dominance." *Journal of Politics* 66 (3): 729–54.

Von Glahn, Richard. 2016. *The Economic History of China: From Antiquity to the Nineteenth Century*. Cambridge University Press.

Wallerstein, Immanuel. 2004. "The Rise of State-System: Sovereign Nation-States, Colonies and the Interstate System." In *World-Systems Analysis*, by Immanuel Wallerstein. 42–59. Duke University Press.

Waltz, Kenneth. 2008. *Realism and International Politics*. New York: Routledge.

Wang, Xiangqin, Zhong Yanhao, and Shen Yi (Eds.). 1997. *Zhongguo minzu gongshangye fazhan shi* (The History of Chinese National Commerce and Industry). Shijiazhuang: Hebei Renmin chubanshe.

Watts, Duncan. 2003. *Six Degrees: The Science of a Connected Age*. New York: W. W. Norton.

———. 2004. "The 'New' Science of Networks." *Annual Review of Sociology* 30: 243–70.

Watts, Duncan J., and Steven H. Strogatz. 1998. "Collective Dynamics of 'Small-World' Networks." *Nature* 393: 440–42.

Weber, Max. 1927. *General Economic History*. London: Allen & Unwin.

Wilson, Woodrow. 1917. Wilson's War Message to Congress. United States: 65th Congress, 1st Session. Washington DC: US Senate.

World Bank. 2016. "World Development Indicators 2016." Washington, DC. https://openknowledge.worldbank.org/bitstream/handle/10986/23969/9781464806834.pdf.

Wu, Mark. 2016. "The 'China, Inc.' Challenge to Global Trade Governance." *Harvard International Law Journal* 57 (2): 261–323.

Wu, Weiyi, and Hong Fan. 2016. "The Rise And Fall of the 'Up to the Mountains and Down to the Countryside' Movement: A Historical Review." *Rozenberg Quarterly*. Amsterdam. http://rozenbergquarterly.com.

Xi Jinping. 2017. "Full Text of Xi Jinping's Report at 19th CPC National Congress." *China Daily*, October 18. www.chinadaily.com.cn.

Xu, Yi, Bas van Leeuwen, and Jan Luiten van Zanden. 2018. "Urbanization in China, ca. 1100–1900." *Frontiers of Economics in China* 13 (3): 322–68.

Yang, Hui, Ming Tang, and Thilo Gross. 2015. "Large Epidemic Thresholds Emerge in Heterogeneous Networks of Heterogeneous Nodes." *Nature, Scientific Reports* 5 (13122): 1–12.

Zanden, Jan Luiten van, Eltjo Buringh, and Erik Maarten Bosker. 2012. "The Rise and Decline of European Parliaments, 1188–1789." *Economic History Review* 65 (3): 835–61.

Zhao, Dingxin. 2015. *The Confucian-Legalist State: A New Theory of Chinese History*. Oxford University Press.

Zoellick, Robert B. 2005. "Whither China: From Membership to Responsibility?" September 21. Remarks to National Committee on US–China Relations. https://192001-2009.state.gov/s/d/former/zoellick/rem/53682.htm.

# Index